Marriages, Births, Deaths and Removals
of
New Castle County, Delaware

1801–1850

F. Edward Wright

HERITAGE BOOKS
2021

HERITAGE BOOKS

AN IMPRINT OF HERITAGE BOOKS, INC.

Books, CDs, and more—Worldwide

For our listing of thousands of titles see our website
at
www.HeritageBooks.com

Published 2020 by
HERITAGE BOOKS, INC.
Publishing Division
5810 Ruatan Street
Berwyn Heights, Md. 20740

International Standard Book Number
Paperbound: 978-1-68034-506-3

CONTENTS

Introduction

This book contains church records, court records, marriage bonds and a few cemetery inscriptions for New Castle County for the period 1801-1850. Earlier church records of New Castle County were published in two volumes. Volume 1 covered the records of Immanuel Church, Welsh Tract Baptist Meeting, Marriages from Newark Monthly Meeting, Wilmington Monthly Meeting, Pencader Presbyterian Church, Asbury Methodist Episcopal Church, St. Peters' Catholic Church and Marriage Bonds of New Castle County. Volume 2 covered the records of Old Swedes Church.

The Quaker birth records during this period appear to be in uncharacteristic disorder. Perhaps this reflects the Hicksite and Orthodox split in 1827. I have identified the marriages as to the Hicksite or Orthodox. One peculiar entry is that of Jacob Balderston of the city of Baltimore, Maryland and Ruth Ann Dawson, of Easton Maryland who married in 1834 at the house of Thomas H. Dawson in Easton. This record was recorded with other Orthodox marriages of Wilmington Monthly Meeting, rather than with the records Third Haven Monthly Meeting in Easton, which was at this date entirely Hicksite.

Records of Immanuel Church (Episcopal) from 1714 to 1824 are contained in volume 1 of Early Church Records of New Castle County Delaware and are therefore not included in this volume.

We owe the discovery of the New Castle County marriage bonds to Gilbert Cope. He rescued these records from destruction at the county courthouse in the early 1900s. The notation, "mark" is presumed to mean the individual signed the bond with his mark.

The records of Holy Trinity were sometimes difficult to read because of the worn condition of the pages and poor handwriting. The researcher should keep this in mind and consider possible alternate spellings to those shown.

F. Edward Wright
Lewes, DE
2009

Abbreviations

b. - born
ch. - children
d. - died
dau. - daughter
m. - married
bapt. - baptized

Wilmington Monthly Meeting
Births and Deaths

1797 – 1850

Children of Joshua and Ann Johnson (d. 11/25/1804): Samuel Pennock, b.
5/24/1794; Sarah, b. 1/7/1797; William, b. 2/21/1799

Children of William and Elizabeth Robinson: Hanson, b. 2/27/1799, d. 2/13/1800;
Nicholas, b. 12/7/1800; Francis, b. 8/7/1802; William, b. 5/23/1804; Samuel
Hanson, b. 10/7/1806; Hanson, d. 2/13/1800; Nicholas, d. 6/28/1801;
Francis, d. 3/18/1805

John Ferriss (son of Zachariah Ferriss) and Lydia his wife, daughter of Jonathan
and Mary Zane of the city of Philadelphia were married the 10th of 10 month
1771. Lydia died aged 31-5-20 on 3/30/1782. John Ferriss and Ann Gilpin
daughter of Vincent and Abigail Gilpin were married 25th 9 month 1783.

Children of Joseph and Deborah Bringhurst. William, b. 9/25/1800; Mary D b.
7/4/1806; Joseph, b. 9/26/1807

Children of Joseph and Hester Grubb; Samuel Spackman, b. 2/2/1803; Edward, b.
11/23/1804; Hannah, b. 12/20/1806

Children of Samuel and Ruth Nichols: Lydia, b. 9/17/1786; Hannah, b. 3/8/1789;
Joseph, b. 6/21/1791; Margaret, b. 1/17/1793; Ruth, b. 10/15/1795;
Elizabeth, b. 9/29/1798. Joseph Nichols d. aged 10 mos. and a few days. Ruth
Nichols d. aged 11 mos. and 2 days.

John Richardson Latimer b. 10-12-1793; Mary Richardson Latimer b. 29/7/1796;
Henry Latimer b. 21/5/1799; James Latimer b. 26/1/1802.

Children of Thomas and Deborah Spackman: Samuel C. b. 9/2/1796; Joseph b.
19/12/1799; George b. 11/9/1801; Anna b. 18/9/1803.

Children of Cyrus and Abigail Newlin: Robert, b. 1/17/1778; Samuel, b.
2/25/1781; Isaac, b. 2/27/1783; Cyrus, b. 3/15/1785; Abigail, b. 10/29/1787.

Abigail Newlin, wife of Cyrus, d. 11/25/1787.

Cyrus Newlin and his second wife Sarah had issue: Cyrus, b. 2/26/1793; Mary, b.
11/1/1795; Thomas Shipley, b. 7/14/1799.

Children of Robert and Mary Newlin: Samuel b. 5/19/1802; Abigail b. 4/24/1804;
Cyrus b. 11/7/1806.

Samuel Newlin d. 11/3/1782

Cyrus Newlin, son of Cyrus and Sarah d. 9/4/1793

Children of Thomas and Margaret Stapler: Mary, b. 9/5/1780; Sarah, b.
9/23/1782; Esther, b. 1/14/1785; Stephen, b. 5/22/1787; John, b. 11/4/1789;
William A. b. 21st of 12 month 1792.

Children of Robert and Rachel Wilkinson; Mary, b. 7/28/1804; Rebecca, b.
1/13/1806.

"The account of births and burials heretofore kept in this book by direction of the
Monthly Meeting is discontinued, and the following, substituted in pursuance
of the conclusion of the yearly Meeting of 1806, and conveyed in the revised
discipline printed in that year from which the forms of Births and Burials are

taken."

Births

Mary Mendinhall, b. 10/31/1807, dau of Eli and Mary, Wilmington.

Thomas C Spackman, b. 11/3/1807, son of Thomas and Deborah, Wilmington.

Hannah Sheward Walker, b. 10/3/1806, dau of William and Jane, Wilmington.

Martha Poole, b. 12/29/1807, dau of William and Sarah, Brandywine.

Ann Wilkinson, b. 9/4/1807, dau of Robert and Rachel, Wilmington.

Robert Johnson, b. 11/30/1807, son of Jos. and Margaret, Stanton.

Eliza Wolleston, b. 12/28/1807, dau of Jeremiah and Mary, Stanton.

Ann Harlan, b. 8/11/1808, dau of Caleb and Edith, Stanton.

Amos Eastburn, b. 2/19/1808, son of David and Elizabeth, Stanton.

James Canby, b. 2/2/1808, son of James and Elizabeth, Brandywine.

Sarah Richardson, b. 2/4/1808, dau of Joseph and Ann.

Elizabeth White, b. 3/10/1808, dau of John and Mary.

Richard Richardson, b. 4/18/1808, son of Ashton and Mary.

Mary Hanson Robinson, b. 5/24/1808, dau of William and Elizabeth, Wilmington.

Elizabeth Pusey Seal, b. 6/19/1808, dau of William and Rachel, Wilmington.

Anne Jefferiss, b. 6/20/1808, dau of Isaac and Anne.

Rebecca Maule, b. 7/7/1808, dau of Jos. and Rebecca, Wilmington.

Sarah Alricks, b. 8/23/1808, dau of Jacob and Lydia, Wilmington.

Elenor Squibb, b. 9/24/1808, dau of Robert and Mary, Wilmington.

Elizabeth Stroud, b. 10/30/1808, dau of Samuel and Elizabeth, Wilmington.

Anna S Kearns, b. 2/29/1808, dau of Levi and Deborah, Stanton.

Ellis Sanders, b. 12/5/1808, son of Ellis and Hannah, Stanton.

Benjamin Ferris, b. 2/17/1809, son of Wm and Luranna, Stanton.

Amy Wolleston, b. 4/29/1809, dau of Jeremiah and Mary, Stanton.

Joseph Johnson, b. 9/23/1809, son of Joshua and Margaret, Stanton.

Joseph S Dixon, b. 2/12/1803, son of John and Mary, Wilmington.

Isaac Shipley Dixon, b. 3/12/1805, son of John and Mary, Wilmington.

Samuel Hadley Dixon, b. 5/9/1809, son of John and Mary, Wilmington.

Jno. Poultney Hanson, b. 3/20/1809, son of Thos. and Mary, Wilmington.

Isaac Walter Starr, b. 7/15/1805, son of Elisha and Ann, Wilmington.

Mary Ann Starr, b. 2/12/1807, dau of Elisha and Ann, Wilmington.

Ashbridge Starr, b. 12/7/1808, dau of Elisha and Ann, Wilmington.

Mary Norris Logan, b. 4/17/1809, dau of Albanus and Maria, Wilmington.

Edwin Dixon, b. 2/19/1809, son of Isaac and Margt., Wilmington.

Edward Bringhurst, b. 5/22/1809, son of Joseph and Deborah, Wilmington.

Thomas J Megear, b. 6/11/1809, son of Michael and Phebe, Wilmington.

Charles Gilpin, b. 11/17/1809, son of Edward and Lydia, Wilmington.

Josiah Bell Eas(t)burn, b. 1/13/1810, son of David and Elizabeth, Stanton.

Anna Poole, b. 2/7/1810, dau of William and Sarah, Wilmington.

Mary Stapler, b. 6/14/1810, dau of Stephen and Sarah, Stanton.
Rebecca Keerrans, b. 7/11/1810, dau of Levi and Deborah, Stanton.
Robert Richardson, b. 7/6/1810, son of Ashton and Mary, Wilmington.
Lydia Chambers, b. 10/13/1810, dau of Joseph and Deborah, Stanton.
Elizabeth Tatnall, b. 10/20/1810, dau of Edward and Margery, Brandywine.
Isaac Jeffries, b. 7/3/1810, son of Isaac and Anne, Wilmington.
Isaac Wollaston, b. 11/18/1810, son of Jeremiah and Mary, Stanton.
Francis Robinson, b. 11/20/1810, son of Wm and Elizabeth, Wilmington.
Thomzin Richardson, b. 11/26/1810, dau of Joseph and Anna, Wilmington.
Sarah Seal, b. 11/25/1810, dau of William and Rachel, Wilmington.
Edmund Canby, b. 2/3/1804, son of James and Elizabeth, Brandywine.
James Canby, b. 2/2/1808, son of James and Elizabeth, Brandywine.
Samuel Canby, b. 7/9/1811, son of James and Elizabeth, Brandywine.
Nathan Wilkinson, b. 2/21/1811, son of Robert and Rachel, Wilmington.
Saml Timothy Hanson, b. 2/8/1811, son of Thomas and Mary, Wilmington.
Mary Walker, b. 3/7/1811, dau of William and Jane, Wilmington.
Susanna Lambourn, b. 4/14/1811, dau of Eli and Rebecca, Wilmington.
James Stroud, b. 8/23/1811, son of Samuel and Elizabeth, Wilmington.
Mary Anna Dixon, b. 9/19/1811, dau of John and Mary.
Hannah Corbit Saunders, b. 10/2/1811, dau of John and Hannah, Wilmington.
Lewis Henry Saunders, b. 10/2/1811, son of John and Hannah, Wilmington.
Sarah Hastings Brian, b. 11/29/1811, dau of James and Mary, Wilmington.
Joseph Ferriss, b. 2/11/1811, son of John and Ann, Stanton.
Amy Chambers, b. 9/5/1811, dau of Joseph and Deborah, Stanton.
David Eas(t)burn Jr, b. 9/28/1811, son of David and Elizabeth, Stanton.
Thomas Lobb Meteer, b. 2/8/1811, son of Samuel and Martha, Stanton.
Edmond Caleb Bonsall, b. 12/9/1811, son of Isaac and Mary, Stanton.
Elizabeth Lewis Mason, b. 1/16/1812, dau of Barratt and Ann, Wilmington.
Henry Lea, b. 2/16/1812, son of Thomas and Sarah, Brandywine.
Edward Richardson, b. 7/6/1812, son of Joseph and Ann, Country.
Morton Poole, b. 7/10/1812, son of Wm and Sarah, Brandywine.
Elizabeth Richardson, b. 8/28/1812, dau of Ashton and Mary, Country.
Ziba Ferris Bringhurst, b. 9/19/1812, son of Joseph and Deborah, Wilmington.
Edward Hillis, b. 10/14/1812, son of Eli and Martha, Wilmington.
Susannah Robinson, b. 11/10/1812, dau of Wm and Elizabeth, Wilmington.
Joseph Tatnall, b. 11/27/1812, son of Edward and Margery, Brandywine.
Edith Harlan, b. 7/19/1812, dau of Caleb and Edith, Stanton.
Margaret Stapler, b. 9/11/1812, dau of Stephen and Sarah, Stanton.
Mary Ann Chambers, b. 11/19/1812, dau of Joseph and Deborah, Stanton.
Ann Ferris Mason, b. 2/3/1813, dau of Barrett and Ann, Wilmington.
Wm Savory Hanson, b. 2/3/1813, son of Thomas and Mary.
Sarah Ann Reynolds, b. 3/6/1813, dau of John and Ann, Wilmington.
William Sheward, b. 3/23/1813, son of Caleb and Mary, Wilmington.

Catherine R Canby, b. 5/11/1813, dau of James and Elizabeth, Brandywine.
Eli W Lamborn, b. 5/13/1813, son of Eli and Rebecca, Wilmington.
Joseph C Grubb, b. 7/6/1813, son of Joseph and Hester, Wilmington.
George P Hallowell, b. 7/19/1813, son of Wm and Mary, Wilmington.
George Lea, b. 12/3/1813, son of Thomas and Elizabeth E, Brandywine.
Sarah Fisher Stapler, b. 11/25/1813, dau of John and Ann, Wilmington.
Wm Gibbons Walker, b. 12/30/1813, son of William and Jane, Wilmington.
Elizabeth B Hillis, b. 12/15/1813, dau of Eli and Martha, Wilmington.
Thomas S Dixon, b. 12/25/1813, son of John and Mary, Wilmington.
Thomas Wollaston, b. 11/26/1813, son of Jeremiah and Mary, Stanton.
Elizabeth Eastburn, b. 3/3/1813, dau of David and Elizabeth, Stanton.
Ann Johnson, b. 6/30/1813, dau of Joshua and Margaret, Stanton.
Margaret Stapler Dawson, b. 10/30/1813, dau of Daniel and Sarah S, Stanton.
Margaret Stroud, b. 11/23/1813, dau of Caleb and Esther, Stanton.
Jno. Pennock Sanders, b. 4/24/1798, son of Amos and Grace, Stanton.
Caleb Sanders, b. 3/18/1799, son of Amos and Grace, Stanton.
Ann Sanders, b. 3/29/1803, dau of Amos and Grace, Stanton.
Ellis Sanders, b. 6/29/1804, son of Amos and Grace, Stanton.
Rachel Wilkinson, b. 2/2/1814, dau of Robert and Rachel, Wilmington.
Charles Gibbons, b. 3/30/1814, son of Wm and Rebecca, Wilmington.
Wm Barratt Mason, b. 5/23/1814, son of Barratt and Ann, Wilmington.
Martha Bartram Bonsall, b. 7/24/1814, dau of Isaac and Mary, Wilmington.
Sarah Tatnall, b. 9/10/1814, dau of Edward and Margery, Brandywine.
Joseph Richardson, b. 10/13/1814, son of Joseph and Ann, Country.
Wm Welton Warner, b. 11/12/1814, son of Wm and Esther Warner, Wilmington.
Caleb Harlan, b. 10/13/1814, son of John and Elizabeth, Stanton.
Charles Reynolds, b. 11/4/1801, John and Ann, Wilmington.
George Reynolds, b. 7/9/1803, son of John and Ann, Wilmington.
Eliza. Osborne Reynolds, b. 11/13/1805, dau of John and Ann, Wilmington.
Osborne Reynolds, b. 3/9/1808, son of John and Ann, Wilmington.
Lydia Reynolds, b. 12/6/1810, dau of John and Ann, Wilmington.
Sarah Ann Reynolds, b. 3/6/1813, dau of John and Ann, Wilmington.
Francis Henry Reynolds, b. 3/23/1815, son of John and Ann Reynolds,
     Wilmington.
Francis Canby, b. 1/8/1815, son of James and Elizabeth, Brandywine.
Edward Lea, b. 2/4/1815, son of Thomas and Elizabeth, Brandywine.
Hanson Robinson, b. 2/7/1815, son of Wm and Elizabeth, Wilmington.
Sarah Richardson, b. 2/15/1815, dau of John and Margaret, Wilmington.
Sarah Hollowell, b. 2/16/1815, dau of William and Mary, Wilmington.
Mary Richardson, b. 2/20/1815, dau of Ashton and Mary, Country.
Ann Poultney Hanson, b. 4/12/1815, dau of Thomas and Mary, Wilmington.
Jonathan Lamborn, b. 5/2/1815, son of Jonathan and Rachel, Wilmington.
Anna Ferris, b. 6/11/1815, dau of Benjamin and Frances, Brandywine.

Lydia Haines, b. 7/12/1815, dau of Malon and Elizabeth, Wilmington.
Lewis Gardner Mason, b. 9/16/1815, son of Barret and Ann, Wilmington.
Joseph Woodrow, b. 10/4/1815, son of Joseph and Deborah, Country.
Alfred Bonsall, b. 10/15/1815, son of Isaac and Mary, Wilmington.
Emma Dixon, b. 11/20/1815, dau of John and Mary, Wilmington.
Anna Maria Meteer, b. 3/18/1813, dau of Samuel and Martha, Stanton.
Martha Lobb Meteer, b. 9/20/1815, dau of Samuel and Martha, Stanton.
John Sanders, b. 1/22/1815, son of Benjamin and Elenor, Stanton.
Hannah Eastburn, b. 7/15/1815, dau of David and Elizabeth, Stanton.
Rebecca Stapler, b. 7/27/1815, dau of Stephen and Sarah, Stanton.
Joshua Wollaston, b. 8/5/1815, son of Jeremiah and Mary, Stanton.
Elisha Dawson, b. 5/15/1816, son of Daniel and Sarah, Stanton.
Sarah Grubb, b. 1/1/1816, dau of Joseph and Hester, Wilmington.
George Richardson, b. 1/29/1816, son of Joseph and Ann, Wilmington.
Sarah Ellen Gibbons, b. 2/7/1816, dau of William and Rebecca, Wilmington.
James Lea, b. 5/21/1816, son of Thomas and Elizabeth, Brandywine.
Sarah Betts, b. 5/26/1816, dau of Samuel and Grace, Wilmington.
James Brian Stapler, b. 6/2/1816, son of John and Ann, Wilmington.
William Webb, b. 6/27/1816, son of Benj. and Catherine, Wilmington.
Lindley Smyth, b. 7/28/1816, son of David and Anna C, Wilmington.
Anna Richardson, b. 8/11/1816, dau of John and Margaret, Wilmington.
Joseph Tatnall, b. 10/14/1816, son of Edw'd and Margery, Brandywine.
Rebecca Hollowell, b. 11/4/1816, dau of William and Mary, Wilmington.
James Lewis, b. 11/13/1816, son of Evan and Sydney Ann, Wilmington.
Elizabeth Robinson, b. 12/14/1816, dau of William and Elizabeth, Wilmington.
Mary R Mason, b. 12/16/1816, dau of Barret and Ann, Wilmington.
Mary T Seal, b. 12/17/1816, dau of William and Rachel, Wilmington.
Joseph Baker, b. 1/26/1817, son of Amassa and Sarah, Wilmington.
Mary Bonsal, b. 3/14/1817, dau of Isaac and Mary, Wilmington.
Benjamin Ferris, b. 4/2/1817, son of Benjamin and Fanny, Wilmington.
Sarah Richardson, b. 4/5/1817, dau of Ashton and Mary, Country.
Isaac Garrett Sheward, b. 6/14/1817, son of Caleb and Mary, Wilmington.
Sarah Lea, b. 10/16/1817, dau of Thomas and Eliza E, Brandywine.
Wm M Ferris, b. 10/21/1817, son of Ziba and Eliza, Wilmington.
Martha Stroud, b. 12/9/1817, dau of Caleb and Esther, Wilmington.
Isaac Lamb, b. 12/9/1817, son of Isaac and Rachel, Wilmington.
Edward Gibbons, b. 12/7/1817, son of Wm and Rebecca, Wilmington.
Thomas Hanson, b. 12/22/1817, son of Thomas and Mary, Wilmington.
John Tatum, b. 12/24/1817, son of David and Hepseba, Wilmington.
Ruth Eastburn, b. 1/19/1817, son of David and Elizabeth, Stanton.
Nathaniel F Kinsey, b. 8/22/1817, son of John and Elizabeth, Stanton.
Mary Sanders, b. 5/9/1817, dau of Benjamin and Elenor, Stanton.
Eliza. Starr Phillips, b. 8/14/1797, dau of Wm D and Phebe, near Stanton.

Sarah Phillips, b. 8/2/1799, dau of Wm D and Phebe, near Stanton.
Sidney Gregg Phillips, b. 8/11/1801, son of Wm D and Phebe, near Stanton.
Ann Phillips, b. 12/28/1803, dau of Wm D and Phebe, near Stanton.
Phebe Phillips, b. 12/30/1806, dau of Wm D and Phebe, near Stanton.
Robert Phillips, b. 11/28/1808, son of Wm D and Phebe, near Stanton.
Lydia Phillips, b. 5/6/1811, dau of Wm D and Phebe, near Stanton.
Mary Jane Phillips, b. 4/6/1813, dau of Wm D and Phebe, near Stanton.
Hannah Phillips, b. 5/25/1815, dau of Wm D and Phebe, near Stanton.
Newton Lamborn, b. 1/23/1818, son of Eli and Rebecca, Wilmington.
Richard Reynolds, b. 2/21/1818, son of John and Ann, Wilmington.
John J Webb, b. 3/22/1818, son of Ruben and Sarah, Wilmington.
Lewis Bonsall, b. 6/17/1818, son of Isaac and Mary, Wilmington.
Sarah Morris Smith, b. 7/3/1818, dau of David and Anna, Wilmington.
Wm P Richardson, b. 7/22/1818, son of John and Margaret, Country.
Mary Webb, b. 7/24/1818, dau of Benjamin and Catherine, Wilmington.
Edward Tatnall, b. 9/30/1818, son of Edward and Margery, Brandywine.
Eliza. Tatnall Baily, b. 10/3/1818, dau of Samuel and Hannah, Wilmington.
Charles C Mason, b. 12/10/1818, son of Barrett and Ann, Wilmington.
Sarah Wollaston, b. 7/15/1818, dau of Jeremiah and Mary, Stanton.
Samuel Eastburn, b. 10/30/1818, son of David and Elizabeth, Stanton.
Mary Peirce Hallowell, b. 1/3/1819, dau of William and Mary, Wilmington.
Mary Hanson Kirby, b. 1/18/1819, dau of Mark and Mary, Wilmington.
Martha Lea, b. 1/31/1819, dau of Thomas and Elizabeth Jr, Brandywine.
Elizabeth S Ferris, b. 2/6/1819, dau of Ziba and Elizabeth, Wilmington.
Edward Lewis, b. 2/28/1819, son of Evan and Sydney Ann, Wilmington.
Robert Canby, b. 4/7/1819, son of James and Elizabeth, Brandywine.
Nathan Baker, b. 5/7/1819, son of Amassa and Sarah, Wilmington.
Eliza. Cooper Tatum, b. 5/11/1819, dau of David and Hepseba, Wilmington.
Thomas Stapler, b. 5/19/1819, son of John and Ann, Wilmington.
Hannah Richardson, b. 5/23/1819, dau of Ashton and Mary, Wilmington.
Martha Ferris, b. 6/26/1819, dau of Benjamin and Fanny, Wilmington.
Edward Squibb, b. 7/5/1819, son of James and Catherine H, Wilmington.
Lewis Lamborn, b. 8/12/1819, son of Jonathan and Martha, Wilmington.
Dell Pennell Peters, b. 9/3/1819, dau of James and Mary Dell, Country.
Lydia Bettes, b. 9/13/1819, dau of Mahlon and Mary, Wilmington.
Thos. Stapler Dawson, b. 8/27/1819, son of Daniel and Sarah, Stanton.
Ann Sanders, b. 9/24/1819, dau of Benjamin and Elenor, Stanton.
Louis Gibbons, b. 11/7/1819, son of Wm and Rebecca, Wilmington.
Rebecca Jane Lamborn, b. 11/8/1819, dau of Eli and Rebecca, Wilmington.
Elizabeth Stroud, b. 11/9/1819, dau of Caleb and Esther, Wilmington.
Eleanor H Bonsall, b. 11/21/1819, dau of Isaac and Mary, Wilmington.
Jonathan Wetherald, b. 1/2/1820, son of Joseph and Mary, Wilmington.
George S Grubb, b. 1/9/1820, son of Joseph and Esther, Wilmington.

Elizabeth Webb, b. 3/18/1820, dau of Ruben and Sarah, Wilmington.
Elizabeth Richardson, b. 5/4/1820, dau of John and Margaret, Wilmington.
Sarah Eastburn, b. 7/24/1820, dau of David and Elizabeth, Stanton.
Sarah Kirk Betts, b. 7/27/1820, dau of Benjamin and Mary, Stanton.
Wm Barrett Mason, b. 9/3/1820, son of Barrett and Ann, Stanton.
Mary James Baily, b. 9/3/1820, dau of Samuel and Hannah, Stanton.
Lucy Smyth, b. 9/13/1820, dau of David and Anna, Wilmington.
Thomas Tatnall, b. 9/16/1820, son of Edward and Margery, Brandywine.
John P Hanson, b. 9/22/1820, son of Thomas and Mary, Wilmington.
Mary Ferris, b. 10/31/1820, dau of Ziba and Eliza, Wilmington.
Sarah Webb, b. 11/9/1820, dau of Benjamin and Catherine, Wilmington.
Rachel Lamborn, b. 1/21/1821, dau of Jonathan and Martha, Wilmington.
Wm Allen Stroud, b. 2/24/1821, son of Caleb and Esther, Wilmington.
Jacob Fussell Byrnes, b. 4/19/1821, son of Daniel and Esther, Wilmington.
David Ferris, b. 7/16/1821, son of Benjamin and Fanny, Wilmington.
Ann Richardson, b. 7/20/1821, dau of Ashton and Mary, Country.
Edward Kirby, b. 7/22/1821, son of Mark and Mary, Wilmington.
Margaret Gibbons, b. 7/24/1821, dau of Wm and Rebecca, Wilmington.
Thomas Lea, b. 8/22/1821, son of Thomas and Elizabeth, Brandywine.
Hannah Bunting Bonsall, b. 8/17/1821, dau of Isaac and Mary, Wilmington.
Elizabeth Grubb, b. 8/28/1821, dau of Joseph and Esther, Wilmington.
Elizabeth Sanders, b. 9/1/1821, dau of Benjamin and Elenor, Stanton.
Edward C Hewes, b. 9/4/1821, son of Aaron and Hannah, Wilmington.
Thomas Palmer, b. 9/17/1821, son of Moses and Sarah, Brandywine.
Hannah Pennell Peters, b. 9/21/1821, dau of James and Mary, Country.
Frances Bullock, b. 10/28/1821, dau of John and Rachel, Wilmington.
Enoch Lewis, b. 12/1/1821, son of Evan and Sidney Ann, Wilmington.
Mary Rodmond Richardson, b. 12/31/1821, dau of John and Margaret, Country.
Martha Haworth Wetherald, b. 1/31/1822, dau of Joseph and Mary, Wilmington.
Samuel Kinsey, b. 2/24/1822, son of Jno. and Margaret, Stanton.
William Tatnall, b. 3/11/1822, son of Edw'd and Margery, Brandywine.
Wm Canby, b. 4/11/1822, son of James and Elizabeth, Brandywine.
Esther Warner, b. 4/28/1822, dau of William and Esther, Country.
Lydia Tatum, b. 5/23/1822, dau of David and Hepzebah, Wilmington.
Edward Betts, b. 6/4/1822, son of Benjamin and Mary W, Wilmington.
Joshua Wollaston, b. 6/23/1822, son of Samuel and Elizabeth, Wilmington.
Maria Ann Eastburn, b. 7/25/1822, dau of Samuel and Huldah, Stanton.
Sarah Squibb, b. 8/25/1822, dau of Jms. R and Catherine, Stanton.
Ann P. Cranston, b. 9/4/1822, dau of William and Mary, Stanton.
Margaret Eastbourn, b. 9/24/1822, dau of David and Elizabeth, Stanton.
Sarah Ann Baily, b. 9/25/1822, dau of Saml. and Hannah James Baily, Stanton.
John Wardell Stapler, b. 10/21/1822, son of John and Ann, Wilmington.
Gulielma Hillis, b. 11/14/1822, dau of Saml. and Margaret, Wilmington.

Mary Lea, b. 11/23/1822, dau of Thos. Jr and Elizabeth E, Brandywine.

Eliza Webb, b. 11/25/1822, dau of Benjamin and Catherine, Wilmington.

Wm Ferris, b. 12/14/1822, son of Benjamin and Fanny, Wilmington.

Emily Betts, b. 1/10/1823, dau of Mahlon and Mary, Wilmington.

Wm Canby Smyth, b. 2/11/1823, son of David and Anna, Wilmington.

Emily Quimby, b. 3/7/1823, dau of John and _____, Stanton.

Abigail Brier, b. 2/15/1823, dau of Mark and Sarah, Brandywine.

Eliza. Tatnall Latimer, b. 4/17/1823, dau of Henry and Sarah Ann, Country.

Rebecca Gibbons, b. 7/2/1823, dau of Wm and Rebecca, Wilmington.

Lydia R Canby, b. 7/29/1823, dau of Chas and Ann, Wilmington.

Rachel R Webb, b. 8/26/1823, dau of James and Lydia R, Wilmington.

Rebecca S Lamborn, b. 6/15/1823, dau of Jona. and Martha, Wilmington.

Eliza. R Hanson, b. 11/19/1823, dau of Thomas and Mary, Baltimore.

Vincent Philip Bonsall, b. 12/20/1823, son of Isaac and Mary, Wilmington.

Franklin C Wilson, b. 1/29/1824, son of William and Aseneth.

John Richardson, b. 2/2/1824 son of John and Margaret, Country.

Ann Tatnall, b. 2/9/1824, daughter of Edward and Margery, Brandywine.

Edward Ferris b. 2/22/1824 son of Ziba and Eliza., Wilmington.

Mary Anna Smyth, b. 8/14/1824, daughter of David and Anna Wilmington.

Mary Walton Bonsall b. 2/18/1824, daughter of Abraham and Elizabeth, Wilmington.

Ann S. Hutton, b. b. 5/4/1824, daughter Joshua and Ann, Wilmington.

Elizabeth Kinsey, b. 9/16/1824, daughter of Jno. and Margaret, Stanton.

Catharine Ann Canby, b. 8/19/1824 daughter of Charles and Ann, Wilmington.

Lucy Richardson, b. 10/3/1824, daughter of Ashton and Mary, Country.

William R. Bullock, b. 10/4/1824, son of John and Rachel, Wilmington.

Henry Garret, b. 11/24/1824, son of Thomas and Mary, Wilmington.

Caleb J. Bonsall, b. 10/22/1824, son of Thomas and Susan P, Wilmington.

Sarah Breaer, b. 1/13/1825, daughter of Mark and Sarah, Brandywine.

Wm. S. Hilles, b. 1/28/1825, son Saml. and Margaret, Wilmington.

Edward Webb, b. 2/14/1825, son of Benj. and Catharine, Wilmington.

John J. Lewis, b. 4/27/1825, son of Enoch and Lydia, Wilmington.

Eliza. Ann Gibbons, b. 5/7/1825, daughter of William and Rebecca, Wilmington.

Edward Betts, b. 5/17/1825, son of Mahlon and Mary, Wilmington.

Owen Beverly Gause, b. 6/22/1825, son of Jesse and Martha, Country.

Mary Brian Stapler, b. 9/15/1825, daughter of John and Ann, Wilmington.

William P. Swayne, b. 9/24/1825, son of Huson and Susanna, Wilmington.

Mary Wetherald, b. 12/14/1825, daughter of Joseph and Mary.

Joseph P. Richardson, b. 12/16/1825, son of Jno. and Margaret, Country.

Edward Ferris, b. 12/20/1825, son of Benjamin and Fanny, Wilmington.

John L. Bonsal, b. 1/9/1826, son of Isaac and Mary, Wilmington.

Henry Lamborn b. 1/10/1826, son of Jona. and Martha, Wilmington.

Charles Bullock, b. 2/25/1826, son of John and Rachel, Wilmington.

Phoebe Ferris b. 3/15/1826, daughter of Ziba and Eliza, Wilmington.
William R.Canby, b. 4/1/1826, son of Charles and Ann, Wilmington.
Sarah Rowland, b. 4/19/1826, daughter of Joseph and Ann, Wilmington.
Anna R. Latimer, b. 4/20/1826, daughter of Henry and Sally Ann, near
    Wilmington.
Margaret Tatnall, b. 4/29/1826, daughter of Edwd, and Margery, Brandywine.
    Elizabeth Kinsey, b. 6/15/1826, daughter of John and Margaret, Wilmington.
    Skidmore Wilson, b. 6/4/1825, son of William and Aseneth, Wilmington.
Sarah Wilson, b. 6/4/1825, daughter of William and Aseneth, Wilmington.
Hiett Hutton, b. 1/7/1827, son of Joshua and Ann, Wilmington.
Elizabeth Breaer b. 1/17/1827, daughter of Mark and Sarah, Wilmington.
Henry Lewis, b. 2/1/1827, son of Enoch and Lydia, Wilmington.
Elizabeth Wilson, b. 3/8/1827, daughter of William and Aseneth, Wilmington.
William Henry Hewes, b. 4/19/1827, son of Aaron and Hannah, Wilmington.
Margaret Garrett, b. 6/13/1827, daughter of Thomas and Mary, Wilmington.
Henry Richardson b. 6/15/1827, son of John and Margaret, near Wilmington.
Mary R. Tatnall, b. 7/17/1827, daughter of Edwd. and Margery, Brandywine.
Rodmond Gibbons, b. 8/1/1827, son of William and Rebecca, Wilmington.
Saml. Canby Clement, b. 8/1/1827, son of Richard and Frances, Wilmington.
William Betts b. 8/3/1827, son of Mahlon and Mary, Wilmington.
Anna Webb b. 8/6/1827, daughter of Benjamin and Catharine, Wilmington.
David T. Buzby, b. 11/25/1827, son of Saml. and Maria, Wilmington.
Clement Biddle Smyth, b. 12/29/1827, son of David and Anna C. Wilmington.
Margaret Dixon b. 2/6/1828, daughter of Isaac and Margaret, Wilmington.
Susannah H. Wetherald b. 2/27/1828, daughter of Joseph and Mary, Wilmington.
Henry Latimer, 8/17/1828, son of Henry and Sally Ann, near Wilmington.
Ziba Ferris, b. 9/18/1828, son of Ziba and Eliza., Wilmington.
Caleb Pusey Kinsey, b. 1/10/1823, son of John and Margaret, Stanton.
William Sanders, b. 10/20/1823, son of Benjamin and Elenor, Stanton.
Rebecca C. Bailey, b. 5/12/1824, daughter of Saml, and Hannah, Stanton.
Ann Sanders, b. 2/4/1826, daughter of Benjamin and Elenor, Stanton.
Ann Latimer Bailey, b. 7/2/1826, daughter of Samuel and Hannah, Stanton.
Mary H. Squibb, b. 8/26/1826, daughter of James and Catharine, Stanton.
Joshua Johnson, b. 11/27/1826, son of Samuel P. and Mary Ann, Stanton.
James A. Bonsall, b. 2/3/1828, son of Abm. and Eliza., Stanton.
Esther Sanders, b. 2/9/1828, daughter of Benjamin and Elenor, Stanton.
Robert Squibb, b. 10/7/1828, son of James and Catharine, Stanton
John W. Rinsey, b. 10/25/1828, son of John and Margaret, Stanton.
Martha Smith Bailey, b. 11/30/1828, daughter of Saml. and Hannah, Stanton.
Mary Cranston Johnson, b. 1/8/1829, daughter of Samuel P. and Mary Ann,
    Staunton.
Elizabeth M. Paxson, b. 4/18/1825, daughter of Joseph and Phebe, Stanton.
Alfred J. Paxson, b. 6/15/1826, son of Joseph and Phebe, Stanton.

Sarah W. Paxson, b. 2/7/1828, daughter of Joseph and Phebe, Stanton.
Hannah P. Hutton b. 2/22/1829, daughter of Joshua and Ann, Wilmington.
Napoleon Bancroft, b. 3/20/1829, son of Jno. and Susanna, Wilmington.
Mary B. Rumford, b. 6/8/1829, daughter of William and Sarah, Wilmington.
William L. Marshall, b. 6/13/1829, son of William and Margaret, Wilmington.
Francis Gibbons, b. 7/15/1829, son of William and Rebecca.
Thomas Betts b. 9/2/1829, son of Mahlon and Mary, Wilmington.
Emily Webb, b. 2/23/1830, daughter of Benjamin and Catharine, Wilmington.
Joseph Galloway Rowland, b. 5/24/1830, son of Jos. G. and Ann B, Wilmington.
Margaret Bancroft b. 10/14/1830, daughter of Jno. and Susanna, Wilmington.
Jonas Pusey, b. 11/15/1830, son of Jonas and Hannah, Wilmington.
Eli Garrett, 12/2/1830, son of Thomas and Rachel, Wilmington.
Hannah C. Cranston, b. 2/16/1830, daughter of William and Mary, Staunton.
Margaret Ann Kinsey, b. 9/10/1830, daughter of John and Margaret, Staunton.
   Elizabeth C. Johnson, b. 3/25/1831, daughter of Samuel and Mary Ann,
   Staunton.
Caroline Gibbons, b. 4/17/1831, daughter of Wm. and Rebecca, Wilmington.
Frances Ferris, b. 4/26/1831, daughter of Ziba and Elizabeth, Wilmington.
Ellen Bonsall Squibb, b. 4/29/1831, Jas. and Catharine, Wilmington.
Samuel S. Grubb, b. 5/24/1831, son of Edward and Elizabeth, Wilmington.
Samuel Hayhurst, b. 5/27/1831, son of Thomas and Martha, Wilmington.
Wm W. Rumford, b. 6/2/1831, son of Wm S. and Sarah S, Wilmington
Joseph Wetherald, b. 7/2/1831, son of Joseph and Mary, Wilmington
Eliza. S. Mendinhall, b. 9/8/1831, dau. of Jesse and Sarah R., Wilmington
Mary Baynes, b. 9/9/1831, dau. of James and Martha, Wilmington.
Susanna Jane Marshall, b. 11/4/1831, dau. of Wm and Margaret, Wilmington
Elizabeth P. Breaer, b. 12/28/1831, dau. of Mark and Sarah, Wilmington.
Hannah E. Bonsall, 11/20/1831, dau. of Abram and Elizabeth, Wilmington
Rebecca M. Sanders, b. 7/23/1830, dau. of Benjamin and Eleanor, Staunton.
Wm Warner Hoopes, b. 5/2/1831, son of Ezra and Ann, Wilmington
Joshua Betts, b. 2/18/1832, son of Mahlon and Mary, Wilmington.
Henry Buzby, b. 9/23/1832, son of Samuel and Maria, Wilmington
Margaretta Hayhurst, b. 1/13/1833, dau. of Thomas and Martha, Wilmington
William S. Grubb, b. 2/10/1833, son of Edward and Elizabeth P., Wilmington
Percival Roscoe Smith, b. 5/21/1833, son of Samuel and Sarah, Wilmington.
Jno. Beezon Baynes, b. 8/25/1833, son of James and Martha, Wilmington.
Jos. Wetherald Baynes, b. 9/15/1833, son of Thomas and Sarah, Wilmington
Lydia T. Wilson, b. 10/3/1833, dau. of Wm and Aseneth, Wilmington
Isaac Rumford, b. 10/14/1833, son of Wm S. and Sarah S., Wilmington.
Simon Sherlock Cranston, b. 9/27/1833, son of Wm and Mary, Staunton
Edwd. Mendinhall, b. 2/27/1834, son of Jesse and Sarah R., Wilmington.
Anna Wetherald, b. 4/14/1834, dau. of Joseph and Mary, Wilmington.
Thomas M. Ferris, b. 4/17/1834, son. of Ziba and Eliza M., Wilmington.

Emilie Gibbons, b. 6/12/1834, dau. of Henry and Martha, Wilmington
George Burge Baynes, b. 11/22/1834, son of James and Martha, Wilmington.
Joseph W. Bancroft, b. 1/28/1834, son of John and Susan, Wilmington
Sarah T. Johnson, b. 12/13/1834, dau. of Wm and Sarah, Staunton.
Sarah Ann Webb, b. 12/11/1834, dau. of James and Lydia P., Wilmington
Saml. Dillwyn Smith, b. 5/27/1835, son of Saml. and Sarah, Wilmington.
Wm Poole Bancroft, b. 7/12/1835, son of Joseph and Sarah, Wilmington.
Wm P. Baynes, b. 8/17/1835, son of Thomas and Sarah, Wilmington.
Alfred Betts, b. 10/1/1835, son of Mahlon and Mary, Wilmington.
Martha B. Hayhurst, b. 10/8/1835, dau. of Thomas and Martha, Wilmington.
Rebekah Rumford, b. 2/24/1836, dau. of Wm S. and Sarah S., Wilminmgton.
John B. Bancroft, b. 3/3/1836, son of John and Susan, Wilmington.
Edward (?) Poole, b. 4/4/1836, son of Wm S. and Lydia, Wilmington.
Rebecca D. Gibbons, b. 6/20/1836, dau. of Henry and Martha, Wilmington.
Anna F. Grubb, b. 8/5/1836, dau. of Edward and Elizabeth P., Wilmington
Fanny Baynes, b. 5/31/1837, dau. of James and Martha, Wilmington.
Mary M. Poole, b. 6/23/1837, dau. of Wm S. and Lydia, Wilmington.
Jno. Haworth Baynes, b. 8/21/1837, son of Thomas and Sarah, Wilmington.
Henry Mendinhall, b. 8/26/1837, son of Jesse and Sarah, Wilmington.
Ella C. Buzby, b. 2/21/1837, dau. of Saml. and Maria, Wilmington.
Anna P. Johnson, b. 1834, dau. of Saml. P. and Mary Ann Staunton
Sarah Ellen Johnson, b. 10/10/1837, dau. of Saml. P. and Mary Ann, Staunton
Rebecca D. Gibbons, b. 5/5/1838, dau. of Henry and Martha, Wilmington.
Francis Ellwood Rumford, b. 6/5/1838, son of William S. and Sarah, Wilmington.
Susan Bancroft, b. 5/23/1838, dau. of John and Susan, Wilmington.
Sarah Cornelia Smith, b. 7/18/1838, dau. of Saml. and Sarah, Wilmington.
Mary W. Betts, b. 7/29/1838, dau. of Mahlon and Mary, Wilmington.
Sarah C. Baynes, b. 7/4/1838, dau. of James and Martha, Wilmington.
Mary R. Webb, b. 10/12/1838, dau. of James and Lydia P., Wilmington.
Anna P. Wollaston, b. 9/27/1838, dau. of Saml. and Philena, Wilmington.
Mary Wetherald Baynes, b. 7/1/1839, dau. of Thomas and Sarah, Wilmington.
Sarah Poole, b. 11/18/1839, dau. of Wm S. and Lydia, Wilmington.
Samuel Bancroft, b. 1/21/181840, son of Joseph and Sarah, near Wilmington.
Chas. Alfred Garrett, b. 5/24/1840, son of Ellwood and Catharine, Wilmington.
Henry Gibbons Jr., b. 9/24/1840, son of Henry and Martha, Wilmington.
Mary W. Wollaston, b. 9/24/1840, dau. of Saml. and Philena, Wilmington.
Francis Ferris, b. 11/5/1840, son of Ziba and Elizabeth, Wilmington.
Bencil Kendall, b. 5/11/1840, son of Jesse and Maria, Wilmington.
Saml. Marshall Johnson, b. 11/9/1840, son of Saml. P. and Mary Ann, Stanton.
John Lawton, b. 5/20/1840, son of Abraham and Sarah, Stanton.
Saml. Rodmond Smith, b. 4/20/1841, son of Albert W. and Eliz. W., Wilmington.
J. Francis Buzby, b. 5/9/1841, son of Saml. and Maria T., Wilmington.
Mary S. Mendinhall, b. 5/22/1841, dau. of Jesse and Sarah, Wilmington.

Wm W. Baynes, b. 7/27/1841, son of Thomas and Sarah, Wilmington.

Wm Poole Gibbons, b. 9/26/1842, son of Henry and Martha P., Wilmington.

Mary Hewes, b. 10/26/1842, du. of Edward C. and Sarah G. nr. Wilmington.

Mary Poole, b. 10/31/1842, dau. of Wm S. and Lydia M., Wilmington.

Ann S. Richardson, b. 9/27/1843, dau. of Saml. and Susanna, nr. Wilmington

Linton Smith, b. 8/-/1843, son of Albert W. and Eliz W., Wilmington.

Margaret R. Warner, b. 10/7/1844, dau. of Charles and Mary R., Wilmington.

Francis W. Cranston, b. 10/21/1844, son of Benj. and Hannah W., Stanton.

John R. Bringhurst, b. 1/8/1845, son of Jos and Anna R., Wilmington.

Edward Grubb, b. 2/19/1845, son of Geo. and Mary T., near Wilmington.

Alexis Smith, b. 3/23/1845, Wilmington.

Wm G. Mendinhall, b. 6/22/1845, son of Jesse and Sarah, Wilmington.

Emlen Hewes, b. 12/4/1845, son of Edward and Sarah, Wilmington.

Elizabeth W., Garrett, b. 12/5/1845, dau. of Ellwood and Catharine, Wilmington.

Eliza. R. Richardson, b. 9/18/1845, dau. of Saml. and Susanna, near Wilmington.

Chas. Wilson Betts, b. 9/2/1845, son of John and Phebe, near Wilmington.

Lucretia Mott Philips, b. 8/14/1842, dau. of Calvin and Jane J., near Wilmington.

Saml. Johnson Philips, b. 4/25/1844, son of Calvin and Jane J., near Wilmington.

Alexis Smith, b. 3/23/1845, son of Albert W. and Elizabeth, Wilmington.

Wm G. Mendenhall, b. 6/22/1845, son of Jesse and Sarah R., Wilmington.

Charles Wilson, b. 9/2/1845, son of John and Phebe Maria, Wilmington.

Eliza. R. Richardson, b. 9/18/1845, dau. of Saml. and Susanna, Wilmington.

Emlen Hewes, b. 12/4/1845, son of Edward C. and Sarah S., Wilmington.

Eliza. W. Garrett, b. 12/5/1845, dau. of Ellwood and Catharine, Wilmington.

Alfred Heald, b. 3/6/1846, son of Joshua T. & Hannah, Wilmington.

Hester R. Grubb, b. 5/15/1846, dau. of Geo. S. and Mary T., near Wilmington.

Mary A. Richardson, b. 2/15/1847, dau. of Saml. and Susanna, near Wilmington.

Mary S. Garrett, b. 2/28/1847, dau. of Henry and Catharine A., near Wilmington.

Sarah H. Price, b. 7/7/1847, dau. of Isaiah and Lydia, Wilmington.

Wm Henry Woodrow, b. 8/11/1847, son of Stephen and Rebecca, near
    Wilmington

Charles Hewes, b. 9/8/1847, son of Edward C. and Sarah S., Wilmington.

Alfred Dupont Warner, b. 9/10/1847, son of Charles and Mary R., Wilmington.

Margaret R. Bringhurst, b. 11/13/1847, dau. of Joseph and Anna R., Wilmington.

Mary P. Heald, b. 3/3/1848, dau. of Joshua T. and Hannah P., Wilmington.

Warren Garrett, b. 3/6/1848, son of Ellwood and Catharine W., Wilmington.

Edwd. H. Hampton, b. 6/13/1848, son of Edward H. and Anna W., Wilmington.

Walter H. Smith, b. 9/24/1848, son of Albert W. and Elizabeth, Wilmington.

Wm. B. Cranston, b. 9/27/1848, son of Benj. and Hannah W., Stanton.

Mary B. Smyth, b. 6/23/1848, dau. of Wm. C. and Emily, Wilmington.

Jane Richardson, 1/21/1849, dau. of Saml. and Susanna, near Wilmington.

Chas. Canby Garrett, b. 8/4/1849, son of Henry and Catharine Ann, Wilmington.

Mark Kirby, b. 9/1/1849, son of Joseph C., Wilmington.

Rachel S. Hill, b. 9/2/1849, dau. of John and Amy S., Wilmington.
Joseph Ernist, b. 1/29/1850.
Edith Florence Buzby, b. 3/23/1850, dau. of David T. and Mary, Wilmington.
Emily H. Garrett, b. 2/12/1850, dau. of Ellwood and Catharine W., Wilmington.
Andrew M. Bye, b. 9/24/1850, son of David T. and Mary, Wilmington.

WILMINGTON MONTHLY MEETING
Marriage certificates

John Dixon of Wilmington, son of Isaac Dixon of same place and Amy his wife
and Mary Shipley of borough afsd., dau. of Joseph Shipley of same place and
Mary his wife, m. at Wilmington Meeting 4-15-1802.
Joseph Grubb of Wilmington, son of John Grubb of Brandywine Hundred and
Hannah his wife and Hester Spackman, dau. of George Spackman late of
borough afsd. dec'd., and Thomacin his wife, m. at Wilmington Meeting
4-22-1802.
Warner Rasin, son of Abraham and Rosamond Rasin, dec'd., of Kent Co., MD,
and Margaret Wilkinson, widow of Wilmington, m. at Wilmington Meeting
11-11-1802.
John Erwin, son of Samuel and Naomi Erwin of Upper Penn's Neck, Salem Co.,
NJ, and Elizabeth Platt, dau. of John and Alice Platt of New Castle Hundred,
m. at Wilmington Meeting 11-18-1802.
Jonathan Evans of Upper Darby Twp., Delaware Co., PA, son of Jonathan Evans
and his dec'd. wife Sarah of same place and Elizabeth Pedrick of
Wilmington, dau. of Hugh and Elizabeth Pedrick late of Alloway's Creek
Twp., Salem Co., NJ, dec'd., m. at Wilmington Meeting 2-17-1803.
Robert Wilkinson of Wilmington, son of Joseph Wilkinson and Mary his wife,
both dec'd., late of Kent Co., MD, and Rachel Wood, dau. of Nathan Wood
and Rebeckah his wife, the former dec'd., m. at Wilmington Meeting
5-12-1803.
Joseph Richardson of Christiana Hundred, son of Richard Richardson, same
place, dec'd., and Sarah his wife and Ann Spackman, dau. of George
Spackman of Wilmington, dec'd., and Thomazin his wife, m. at Wilmington
Meeting 6-16-1803.
Christopher Hollingsworth of Wilmington, son of Christopher Hollingsworth,
same place, and Sarah his wife, the latter dec'd., and Elizabeth Horner, dau.
of Samuel Horner and Elizabeth his wife, late of Wilmington, both dec'd., m.
7-14-1803.
Daniel McPherson, son of John McPherson and Hannah his wife of Jefferson Co.,
VA, and Elizabeth Grubb, dau. of John and Hannah Grubb of Brandywine
Hundred m. 10-6-1803.
William Paxson of Philadelphia, PA, merchant, son of Joseph Paxson, late of

Bensalem Twp., Bucks Co., PA, dec'd., and Sarah his wife and Ann Canby, dau. of Samuel Canby and Frances his wife of Wilmington, m. at Wilmington Meeting 10-20-1803.

Caleb Harlan Jr. of Mill Creek Hundred, merchant, son of Caleb and Ann his wife and Edith Ferriss Jr. of Wilmington, dau. of Ziba Ferriss late of same place, dec'd., and Edith his wife, m. at Wilmington Meeting 12-22-1803.

Benjamin Ferriss of Philadelphia, PA, watchmaker, son of Ziba Ferriss, late of Wilmington, dec'd., and Edith his wife and Fanny Canby, dau. of William Canby of Wilmington and Martha his wife, m. at Wilmington Meeting 5-17-1804.

Eli Mendenhall of Wilmington, son of Benjamin Mendenhall, dec'd., and Hannah his wife of Wilmington and Mary Wayne of Brandywine Hundred afsd., widow, dau. of Jesse Jackson and Jane his wife of Marlborough Twp., Chester Co., PA, m. at Wilmington Meeting 10-11-1804.

William Walker of Wilmington, son of Samuel and Lettis Walker, late of Lower Chichester, Delaware Co., PA, dec'd., and Jane Sheward of borough afsd., dec'd., m. 10-17-1805.

Horton Howard of Belmont Co., OH, son of Bartholomew Howard of Craven Co., NC, and Ruth his wife, both dec'd., and Hannah Hastings, dau. of John Hastings of Wilmington and Sarah his wife, both dec'd., m. at Wilmington Meeting 12-5-1806.

Jeremiah Wollaston of Mill Creek Hundred, son of Thomas Wollaston and Hannah his wife, late of same place, dec'd., and Mary Chambers, dau. of Joseph Chambers and Eamy his wife, late of same place, also dec'd., m. at Stanton in Mill Creek Hundred on 1-14-1807.

Isaac Whitelock of Frankford, Philadelphia Co., PA, son of Daniel Whitelock, late of Lancaster, PA, dec'd., and Elizabeth his wife and Ann Marot, dau. of Joseph Marot, late of Wilmington, dec'd., and Elizabeth his wife, m. at Wilmington Meeting 5-14-1807.

Joshua Johnson of Mill Creek Hundred, son of Robert Johnson and Mary his wife and Margaret Carty, dau. of Joseph Chamberlain and Martha his wife of White Clay Creek Hundred, m. at Stanton on 5-13-1807.

John Morton Jr. of Philadelphia, PA, merchant, son of John Morton of said city, and Esther his wife, dec'd., and Margaret Canby, dau. of Samuel Canby and Frances his wife of Wilmington, m. at Wilmington Meeting 2-18-1808.

Albanins [Albanius?] Charles Logan of Stenton, Philadelphia Co., PA, farmer, son of George Logan and Deborah his wife of Stenton afsd. and Maria Dickinson, dau. of John Dickinson and Mary his wife, late of Wilmington, both dec'd., m. at Wilmington Meeting 4-28-1808.

Peter Mason of Mill Creek Hundred, son of William Mason, dec'd. and Sarah his wife and Martha Way, dau. of John Way of Wilmington, and Hannah his wife, the latter dec'd., m. at Wilmington Meeting 4-13-1809.

James Brian of Wilmington, son of Bernard Brian and Catherine his wife, both dec'd. and Mary Hastings, dau. of John Hastings of borough afsd. and Sarah his wife, both dec'd., m. at Wilmington Meeting on 4-20-1809.

Edward Tatnall of Brandywine Hundred, miller, son of Joseph Tatnall, same place, and his late wife Elizabeth, dec'd., and Margery Paxson, dau. of Joseph Paxson, late of Bensalem Twp., Bucks Co., PA, dec'd., and Sarah his wife, m. at Wilmington Meeting 10-12-1809.

Clement Biddle Jr. of Philadelphia, PA, son of Owen Biddle and Sarah his wife, both late of sd. city, dec'd., and Mary Canby, dau. of William Canby and Martha his wife of Wilmington, m. at Wilmington Meeting on 11-22-1810.

Joseph Hance of Salem, Salem Co., NJ, son of Isaac Hance, late of same place, dec'd., and Mary his wife, and Martha Pyle, dau. of Isaac and Mary Pyle, dec'd., late of Bethel Twp., Delaware Co., PA., m. at Chichester Meeting on 12 13-1810.

Caleb Stroud of Stanton, DE, son of Joshua Stroud of same place, and Martha his wife, and Esther Stapler, dau. of Thomas Stapler of same place, and Margaret his wife, the former dec'd., m. at Stanton, DE, on 1-23-1811.

Barrett Mason of Wilmington, son of James Mason of Salem Co., NJ, and Rebecca his wife, both dec'd., and Ann Williamson, dau. of John Williamson of Philadelphia and Grace his wife, also dec'd., m. at Wilmington Meeting on 4-11-1811.

John Hewes of Lower Chichester Twp., Delaware Co., PA, son of Jacob Hewes of same place, and Esther his wife, the former dec'd., and Mary Megear, dau. of Hugh Megear of Kent Co., DE, and Elizabeth his wife, m. at Wilmington Meeting on 6-20-1811.

Peter Askew of Cecil Co., MD, son of Parker Askew of New Castle Co., DE, and Hannah his wife, and Hannah Wilkinson, dau. of Joseph Wilkinson, late of Queen Anne's Co., MD, dec'd., and Margaret his wife, m. at Wilmington Meeting on 1B17-1811.

Asa Moore of Waterford, VA, son of Thomas Moore, same place, and Elizabeth his wife, both dec'd., and Ann Littler, dau. of Jacob Broom of Wilmington, and Rachel his wife, the former dec'd., at Wilmington Meeting on 10-24-1811.

Daniel Dawson of Caroline Co., MD, son of Elisha Dawson, same place, and Lydia his wife, and Sarah Stapler, dau. of Thomas Stapler of Mill Creek Hundred, and Margaret his wife, the former dec'd., m. at Stanton, DE, 4-15-1812.

Josiah F. Clement of Gloucester Co., NJ, son of Samuel Clement, and Mary his wife of Haddonfield, Newton Twp., co. and state afsd., and Esther Canby, dau. of Samuel Canby and Frances his wife of Wilmington, Christiana Hundred, m. at Wilmington Meeting on 5-6-1813.

John Richardson of Wilmington, son of Richard Richardson, dec'd., late of state afsd., and Sarah his wife, and Margaret Paxson, dau. of Joseph Paxson, late of Bensalem, Bucks Co., PA, dec'd., and Sarah his wife, m. at Wilmington

Meeting on 5-13-1813.

Samuel Malin of Upper Providence, Delaware Co., PA, son of William Malin, same place, and Elizabeth his wife, both dec'd., and Susanna P. Harvey of Wilmington, dau. of William Harvey of Birmingham Twp., Delaware Co., PA, and Susannah his wife, also dec'd., m. at Wilmington Meeting on 9-16-1813.

Jacob Pusey of Christiana Hundred, son of Joshua Pusey and Hannah his wife, the former dec'd., and Hannah Nichols, dau. of Samuel Nichols and Ruth his wife of Wilmington, m. at Wilmington Meeting on 11-4-1813.

John W. Sherwood of Easton, MD, son of Henry Sherwood, same place, and Elizabeth his wife, both dec'd., and Elizabeth Askew, dau. of Parker Askew of Brandywine Hundred, and Hannah his wife, m. at Wilmington Meeting on 12-8-1814.

Evan Lewis of Wilmington, son of Evan Lewis, late of Radnor, PA, and Jane his wife, both dec'd., and Sidney Ann Gilpin, dau. of James Gilpin, late of Christiana Hundred, and Sarah his wife, the former dec'd., m. at Wilmington Meeting on 3-9-1815.

David Smyth of Wilmington, son of Thomas Smyth, same place, and Mary his wife, both dec'd., and Anna Canby, dau. of William Canby, afsd. place, and Martha his wife, m. at Wilmington Meeting, on 10-12-1815.

Thomas Rudolph of Upper Darby, Delaware Co., PA, son of John Rudolph and Judith his wife, same place, the former dec'd., and Hannah Powel, dau. of George Powell and his wife of Haverford Twp., Delaware Co., PA, both dec'd., m. at Wilmington Meeting on 3-7-1816.

Daniel Byrnes, Wilmington, son of Caleb Byrnes and Mary his wife, same place, both dec'd., and Esther Fussel, dau. of Jacob Fussel and Esther his wife, same place, both dec'd., m. at Wilmington Meeting on 5-9-1816.

Ziba Ferris of Wilmington, watchmaker, son of Ziba Ferris and Edith his wife, same place, both dec'd., and Eliza Megear, dau. of Michael Megear of Wilmington afsd., and Phebe his wife, m. at Wilmington Meeting 11-14-1816.

John Sellers Jr. of Upper Darby, Delaware Co., PA, son of John Sellars, same place, and Mary his wife now dec'd., and Elizabeth Poole, dau. of William Poole of Wilmington and Sarah his wife, m. at Wilmington Meeting on 4-10-1817.

Reuben Webb of Wilmington, son of James Webb of Lancaster Co., PA, and Sarah his wife (dec'd.), and Sarah Jones, dau. of John Jones of Wilmington and Sarah his wife, m. at Wilmington Meeting on 5-18-1817.

Jacob Pusey of Christiana Hundred, son of Joshua Pusey and Hannah his wife, dec'd., and Hannah Mendenhall, dau. of Eli Mendenhall and Phebe his wife (dec'd.) of Wilmington, m. at Wilmington Meeting on 5-7-1818.

George Robinson of Philadelphia, PA, son of Stephen Robinson, late of Liverpool, Great Britain, and Elizabeth his wife, both dec'd., and Elizabeth

Barker of Wilmington, dau. of John Barker of Burlington Twp., Burlington Co., NJ, and Elizabeth his wife, both dec'd., m. at Wilmington Meeting on 10-8-1818.

Mahlon Betts of Wilmington, son of Jesse Betts and Hannah his wife, same place, and Mary Seal, dau. of Joshua Seal, late of borough afsd., dec'd., and Lydia his wife, m. at Wilmington Meeting, on 10-8-1818.

James R. Squibb, Wilmington, son of Robert Squibb of Stanton, DE, and Mary his wife and Catharine H. Bonsall, dau. of Vincent Bonsall, late of Baltimore, MD, and Sarah his wife, m. at Wilmington Meeting on 10-15-1818.

Jonathan Lamborn of Wilmington, son of Thomas Lamborn of New Garden Twp., Chester Co., PA, and Dinah his wife, both dec'd., and Martha Squibb, dau. of Thomas Squibb of Brandywine Hundred, and Rebecca his wife (dec'd.), m. at Wilmington Meeting on 11-5-1818.

Aaron Hewes, Wilmington, son of Edward Hewes and his wife, same place, and Hannah Commons, dau. of John Commons, late of New Garden Twp., Chester Co., PA, and Sarah his wife, both dec'd., m. at Wilmington Meeting on 4-8-1819.

Stephen Bonsall, Wilmington, son of Philip Bonsall, late of afsd. place, dec'd., and Hannah his wife, and Mary Stroud, dau. of Samuel Stroud, same place, and Elizabeth his wife, m. at Wilmington Meeting on 4-15-1819.

Stephen Pancoast, Delaware Co., PA, son of Seth Pancoast, late of afsd. co., dec'd., and Abigail his wife and Ann Stroud, dau. of Samuel Stroud, Wilmington, and Elizabeth, m. at Wilmington Meeting 11-16-1820.

William Chandler of New Garden Twp., Chester Co., son of John Chandler of co. afsd. and Susanna his wife, both dec'd., and Lydia Seal of Wilmington, dau. of Isaac Richards of New Garden Twp., Chester Co., PA, and Mary his wife (dec'd.), m. at Wilmington Meeting 3-8-1821.

William Cranston of Mill Creek Hundred, son of Simon Cranston, same place, and Mary his wife, and Mary Johnson, dau. of Joshua Johnson, same hundred, and Ann his wife (dec'd.), m. at Stanton on 4-12-1821.

Charles Canby, Wilmington, son of Thomas Canby, formerly of Philadelphia, PA, and Catharine his wife (dec'd.,) and Ann Richards, dau. of Nathaniel Richards, borough afsd., and Lydia his wife, m. at Wilmington Meeting on 10-11-1821.

Henry Latimer, Wilmington, son of Henry Latimer, same place, dec'd., and Ann his wife, and Sarah Ann Baily, dau. of Joseph Baily, same borough, and Elizabeth his wife (dec'd.) m. in Wilmington Meeting, on 6-6-1822.

John Quinby of Mill Creek Hundred, son of Moses Quinby, same place, and Jane his wife, the latter dec'd., and Elizabeth Phillips, dau. of William D. Phillips and Phebe his wife of Christiana Hundred, m. at Stanton, DE, 6-6-1 822.

Joshua Harlan of Mill Creek Hundred, son of Caleb Harlan, same place, and Ann his wife, both dec'd., and Ann Quinby, dau. of Moses Quinby, now of same place, and Jane his wife (dec'd.), m. at Stanton Meeting on 11-7-1822.

James Webb, Wilmington, son of James Webb of London Grove, Chester Co.,
PA, and Sarah his wife (dec'd.) and Lydia P. Richards, dau. of Nathaniel
Richards of borough of Wilmington and Lydia his wife, dec'd., m. at
Wilmington Meeting on 11-14-1822.

Henry Battin, Greenwood Twp., Columbia Co., PA, son of John and Susanna
Battin, and Rachel Yarnall of Wilmington, DE, dau. of John and Elizabeth
Yarnall, the former dec'd., m. at Wilmington Meeting on 12-5-1822.

Daniel Wilson of the village of Cantwell's Bridge, St. Georges Hundred, son of
David Wilson, same place, and Mary his wife, both dec'd., and Mary Poole,
dau. of William Poole, Wilmington, and Sarah his wife, m. at Wilmington
Meeting on 5-8-1823.

Simon Cranston of Mill Creek Hundred, son of William Cranston, late of
Delaware Co., PA, and Ann his wife, both dec'd., and Hannah Cope, dau. of
Caleb Cope, now of Philadelphia, PA, and Mary his wife (dec'd.), m. at
Wilmington Meeting on 5-15-1823.

William Marot, Philadelphia, PA, son of Joseph Marot of Wilmington and
Elizabeth his wife, both dec'd., and Deborah Bassett, dau. of Nathan Bassett
of Wilmington, and Sarah his wife, m. at Wilmington Meeting on 3-4-1824.

John W. Tatum of Wilmington, son of John Tatum of Gloucester Co., NJ, and
Hannah his wife (dec'd.), and Mary Canby, dau. of Samuel Canby of
Wilmington, and Frances his wife (dec'd.), m. at Wilmington Meeting on
6-10-1824.

Stephen M. Stapler of Mill Creek Hundred, son of William Stapler, same place,
and his wife (dec'd.) of Brandywine Hundred and Mary his wife, former
dec'd., m. at Wilmington Meeting on 6-17-1 824.

Joseph Ballance Jr. of Little Britain Twp., Lancaster Co., PA, son of Joseph
Ballance, same place, and Anna his wife, and Mary L. Betts, dau. of Samuel
C. Betts, Wilmington and Grace his wife, m. at Wilmington Meeting on
11-4-1824.

William Richards of New Garden Twp, Chester Co., PA, son of Isaac Richards,
same twp., and Ann his wife (dec'd.) and Lydia Seal, dau. of William Seal,
Wilmington and Rachel his wife, m. at Wilmington Meeting on 12-9-1824.

Samuel P. Johnson, Mill Creek Hundred, son of Joshua Johnson, same place, and
Ann his wife (dec'd.) and Mary Ann Cranston, dau. of Simon Cranston of
Mill Creek Hundred and Mary his wife (dec'd.), m. at Stanton Meeting on
3-10-1825.

Richard Clement of borough of Wilmington son of Samuel Clement of
Philadelphia and Mary his wife and Frances Canby, dau. of Samuel and
Fanny Canby of Wilmington m. on 5th mo. 13th [18th?], 1826 at
Wilmington. Hicksite

William Marshall of Wilmington son of John Marshall (dec'd.) of Kennett Twp,
Chester Co., PA and Susanna his wife and Margaret McCamon dau. of
Richard McCamon of Wilmington and Jane his wife (both dec'd.) m. on 11th

mo. 9th, 1826 at Wilmington. Hicksite

Samuel Buzby of Wilmington son of Joseph and Beulah (dec'd.) his wife and Maria Tatum dau. of David Tatum late of Wilmington (dec'd.) and Hephzibah his wife m. on 3rd mo. 8th, 1827 at Wilmington. Hicksite

Joel Fisher of Delaware Co., PA, son of Samuel Fisher of Frederick Co., MD, and Susannah (dec'd.) his wife and Mary Brooks dau. of Edward Brooks of Wilmington and Margaret his wife m. on 5th mo. 10th, 1827. Hicksite

John Clark of Mill Creek Hundred, New Castle Co., son of John Clark late of Red Lion Hundred, New Castle Co. and Mary his wife (both dec'd.) and Ann Harlan dau. of Caleb Harlan [Harlow?] of Mill Creek Hundred and Ann his wife (both dec'd.) m. on 10th mo. 4th, 1827 at Wilmington. Hicksite

John Bancroft, Jr. of Wilmington, son of John Bancroft of Delaware C., PA and Elizabeth his wife and Susannah Brookes, dau. of Edward Brookes (dec'd.) and Margaret his wife of Wilmington m. on 6th mo. 12th, 1828 at Wilmington. Hicksite

Ezra Hoopes of Wilmington son of John Hoopes of East Caln Twp, Chester Co., PA and Jane his wife (both dec'd.) and Ann Warner dau. of William Warner of Wilmington and Esther his wife m. on 6th mo. 4th, 1829 at Wilmington. Hicksite

Joseph Bancroft of Brandywine Hundred, New Castle Co., son of John Bancroft of Upper Providence Twp, Delaware Co., PA and Elizabeth his wife and Sarah Poole dau. of William Poole of Wilmington and Sarah his wife (both dec'd.) m. on 6th mo. 25th, 1829 at Wilmington. Hicksite

Thomas Garrett, Jr. of Wilmington son of Thomas Garrett of Delaware Co., PA and Sarah his wife and Rachel Mendenhall dau. of Eli Mendenhall and Phebe his wife (dec['d.) m. on 1st mo. 7th, 1830 at Wilmington. Hicksite

Edward Grubb of Wilmington, son of Joseph Grubb of same and Esther his wife and Elizabeth P. Seal dau. of William Seal and Rachel his wife m. on 5th mo. 6th, 1830. Hicksite

Merrit Canby of city of Philadelphia, son of William Canby of borough of Wilmington and Martha his wife (both dec'd.) Eliza T. Sipple, dau. of Thomas Sipple of Kent Co., DE and his wife Ann m. on 5th mo. 20th, 1830. Orthodox

Jesse Mendinhall of Wilmington son of Eli Mendenhall of same and Phebe his wife and Sarah R. Stroud dau. of Samuel Stroud of Wilmington and Sarah his wife m. on 11th mo. 4th, 1830 at Wilmington. Hicksite

Thomas Baynes of Wilmington son of John Barzote(?) Baynes of Brandywine Hundred, New Castle Co. and Merian his wife (dec'd.) and Sarah Wetherald dau. of Joseph Wetherald of Wilmington and Mary his wife m. on 11th mo. 8th, 1832. Hicksite

Henry Gibbons of Wilmington son of William Gibbons of Wilmington and Rebecca his wife and Martha Poole dau. of William Pool of Wilmington and Sarah his wife (both dec'd.) m. on 5th mo. 9th, 1833 at Wilmington. Hicksite

William E. George of Bl..., Philadelphia Co. son of Amos George late of same place and Rebecca his wife and Hannah Poole dau. of William Poole of Wilmington and Sarah his wife also dec'd. m. 5th mo. 23rd, 1833. Hicksite

Isaac Pyle, son of Isaac Pyle and Jane his wife, late of Delaware Co., PA, both dec'd., and Ann Stern, dau. of Thomas Owen and Elizabeth his wife, late of Radnershire, South Wales, Great Britain, both dec'd. m. on 8th mo. 8th, 1833. Orthodox

Jacob Balderston of city of Baltimore, MD, son of Hugh Balderston of Baltimore and Margaret his wife, and Ruth Ann Dawson, dau. of Thomas H. Dawson and Edith his wife of Easton MD m. on 5th mo. 13th, 1834 at the house of Thomas H. Dawson in Easton. - Orthodox. [*This is the only Quaker marriage having taken place in Talbot Co. deposited in the Wilmington Monthly Meeting (orthodox).*]

William S. Poole of Wilmington son of William Poole and Sarah his wife (both dec'd.) and Lydia Mendenhall dau. of Eli Mendenhall (dec'd.) and Mary his wife m. on 12th mo. 11th, 1834. Hicksite

Abner Chalfant of East Marlborough Twp., Chester Co., PA, son of Henry Chalfant of said twp and Susanna his wife (both dec'd.) and Mary W. Betts dau. of Joshua Wollaston late of Wilmington and Catharine his wife m. on 4th mo. 9th, 1835. Hicksite

William Hodgson, Jr., of Philadelphia, son of William Hodgson of Philadelphia and Mary his wife and Elizabeth Richardson, dau. of Ashton Richardson near Wilmington and Mary his wife on 5th mo. 14th, 1835 at Wilmington. Orthodox

Benjamin Ferris of Wilmington son of Ziba Ferris late of Wilmington and Edith his wife and Hannah Gibbons dau. of Abraham Gibbons late of Lampeter Twp, Lancaster Co., PA (both also dec'd.) m. on 10th mo. 15th, 1835. Hicksite

Harlan Baker of London Grove Twp, Chester Co., PA son of Aaron(?) Baker of same and Hannah his wife and Hannah Eastburn dau. of David Eastburn late of Mill Creek Hundred, New Castle Co. (dec'd.) and Elizabeth his wife m. on 12th mo. 10th, 1835. Hicksite

Jeremiah Hartley of Philadelphia son of Joseph Hartley of Wilmington and Phebe (dec'd.) his wife and Elizabeth Wetherald dau. of Joseph and Mary Wetherald of Wilmington m. on 6th mo. 9th, 1836. Hicksite

Thomas Stapler of the village of Stanton, New Castle Co., son of William Stapler and Mary his wife, both dec'd., and Sarah Webb, dau. of James Webb of London Grove Twp, Chester Co., PA and Sarah his wife m. on 12th mo. 7th, 1837 at Wilmington. Orthodox

James A Wright of Philadelphia son of Peter Wright of Philadelphia and Mary his wife and Martha Tatum dau. of David Tatum (dec'd.) of Wilmington and Hephzibah his wife m. on 6th mo. 7th, 1838. Hicksite

William Kite of city of Philadelphia, son of Thomas Kite of city of Philadelphia and Elizabeth his wife (dec'd.) and Mary F. Clemens, dau. of Josiah F. Clemens (dec'd.) and Esther his wife m. on 11th mo. 8th, 1838 at Wilmington. Orthodox

Alban Buckingham of Mill Creek Hundred son of Richard Buckingham of Mill Creek Hundred and Mary his wife and Mary E. Jeanes (Jeames?) Dau. of David Eastburn late of said hundred (dec'd.) and Elizabeth his wife m. on 2nd mo. 6th, 1839. Hicksite

Albert M. Smith of Poughkipsie Co., NY son of Samuel Smith and Sarah his wife and Elizabeth Wollaston dau. of Samuel Wollaston and Elizabet his wife (dec'd.) m. on 6th mo. 6th, 1839 at Wilmington. Hicksite

Ellwood Garrett of Wilmington son of Thomas Garrett and Mary (dec'd.) his wife and Catharine K. Wollaston dau. of Samuel Wollaston and Elizabeth his wife (dec'd.) on 6th mo. 6th, 1839. Hicksite

Lindley Smyth of Philadelphia son of David Smyth of Wilmington and Anna his wife and Elizabeth S. Ferris dau. of Ziba Ferris of Wilmington and Elizabeth his wife m. on 10th mo. 3rd, 1839. Hicksite

Lloyd Oakford of Darby, Delaware Co., PA son of John Oakford of same and Hannah his wife and Rachel Wilkinson dau. of Hobert (?) Wilkinson of Wilmington and Rachel his wife on 10th mo. 10th, 1839. Hicksite

Henry H. Paschall of K..., Philadelphia Co. son of John and Sarah his wife and Mary Anna Dixon dau. of John Dixon and Mary his wife of Wilmington m. on 12th mo. 3rd, 1840. Hicksite

Joseph Tatnall of New Castle Co., son of Edward Tatnall of same place and Margery his wife (dec'd.) and Sarah Richardson, dau. of Ashton Richardson of co. afsd. and Mary his wife m. on 6th mo. 10th, 1841 in Wilmington. Orthodox

Edward C. Hewes of New Castle Co. son of Aron(?) Hewes and Hannah C. his wife and Sarah S. Garrett dau. of Thomas Garrett and Mary S. (dec'd.) his wife m. on 9th mo. 9th, 1841 at Wilmington. Hicksite

Samuel Richardson of Christiana Hundred, New Castle Co. son of Joseph Richardson (dec'd.) of same and Ann his wife and Susanna Robinson dau. of William Robinson (dec'd.) and Elizabeth his wife of Wilmington m. on 10th mo. 14th, 1841 at Wilmington. Hicksite

Norris W. Palmer of city of Wilmington, son of Moses Palmer and Sarah his wife (dec'd.) and Martha Webb, dau. of Benjamin Webb and Catherine his wife m. on 4th mo. 7th, 1842 at Wilmington. Orthodox

Joshua L. Pusey of Wilmington, son of Jonas Pusey of Wilmington and Hannah his wife (dec'd.) and Sarah W. Pyle, dau. of Isaac Pyle of Mill Creek Hundred in New Castle Co. and Ann his wife (dec'd.) m. on 9th mo. 8th, 1842 at Wilmington. Orthodox

Joseph Bringhurst of Wilmington son of Joseph Bringhurst of Wilmington (dec'd.) and Deborah his wife and Anna Richardson dau. of John Richardson of Christiana Hundred and Margaret his wife m. on 10th mo. 6th, 1842 at the house of John Richardson in Christiana Hundred. Hicksite

Moses Brinton of Coleran Twp, Lancaster Co., PA, son of Caleb Brinton and Ann his wife (dec'd.) and Margaret Ann Hallowell dau. of Jesse Hallowell of Christiana Hundred and Jane his wife m. on 3rd mo. 9th, 1843. Hicksite

Charles Warner of Wilmington son of William Warner of Wilmington and Esther his wife and Mary R. [*could be Margaret*] Richardson dau. of D .... ? on and .?.. his wife of Christiana Hundred m. on 6th mo. 22nd, 1843. Hicksite

Charles W. Howland of Cayuga Co., New York, son of George Howland of city of New Bedford, MA, and Susan his wife and Gulialma Maria Kelly [Hilles?], dau. of Samuel Kelly [Hilles?] of Wilmington and Margaret H. his wife m. on 9th mo. 7th, 1843 at Wilmington. Orthodox

William P. Woodward of Chester Co., PA, son of Eli Woodward of Chester Co. and Elizabeth his wife and Rachel England, dau. of Thomas England and Mary his wife of Wilmington m. on 1st mo. 4th, 1844 at Wilmington. Orthodox

Joshua T. Heald of Wilmington son of Joseph Heald of Mill Creek Hundred, New Castle Co. and Hannah his wife and Hannah Pusey dau. of Jonas Pusey of Wilmington and Hannah (dec'd.) his wife m. on 4th mo. 18th, 1844. Hicksite

Jesse T. Bonsall of Kennett Square, Chester Co., son of Abraham Bonsall late of Wilmington (dec'd.) and Elizabeth his wife and Mary Ann England m. on 5th mo. 9th, 1844 at Wilmington. Orthodox

George S. Grubb of Wilmington, son of Joseph Grubb and Esther his wife both dec'd.), and Mary T. Seal, dau. of William Seal (dec'd.) and Rachel his wife of Wilmington, m. on 5th mo. 23rd, 1844. Hicksite.

Edward Tatnall, Jr. of New Castle Co., son of Edward Tatnall of New Castle Co. and Margery his wife and Rachel Webb, dau. of James Webb of Wilmington and Lydia P. his wife m. on 9th mo. 12th, 1844 at Wilmington. Orthodox

Benjamin Poultney of New York, NY, son of Thomas (dec'd.) and Ann Poultney of Baltimore, MD and Eliza Ellicott, dau. of Andrew and Hannah Ellicott (both dec'd.) m. on 10th mo. 8th, 1844 at Wilmington. Orthodox

Ellis P. Wilkinson of London Grove Twp, Chester Co., PA son of Francis (?) Wilkinson and Phebe his wife and Sarah R. Cranston of Mill Creek Hundred, New Castle Co. Dau. of Simon Cranston and Mary (dec'd.) his wife m. on 12th mo. 4th, 1844 at the house of Simon Cranston of Mill Creek Hundred. Hicksite

William Ferris of Harford Co., MD, son of Benjamin Ferris of Wilmington but now of Harford Co., MD, and Fanne his wife and Mary Wetherald, Jr. Dau. of Joseph Wetherald (dec'd.) late of Wilmington and Mary his wife m. on 1st mo. 2nd, 1845. Hicksite

Henry Drinker of Susquehanna Co., PA, son of Henry S. Drinker late of Philadelphia and Hannah his wife (both dec'd.) and Frances C. Morton, dau. of John Morton Jr. (dec'd.) and Margaret his wife m. on 6th mo. 5th, 1845 at

Wilmington. Orthodox

Aron Hewes of Wilmington and Hannah Wollaston dau. of Joshua Wollaston and [blank] his wife of Wilmington (both dec'd.) m. on 7th mo. 3rd, 1845 at Wilmington. Hicksite

Nathaniel Wilkinson son of New Garden Twp, Chester Co., PA, son of Joseph Wilkinson and Hannah his wife and Mary Woodward of Wilmington dau. of Nathan(?) Bane and Margaret his wife m. on 12th mo. 4th, 1845 at the house of Rachel Wilkinson in Wilmington. Hicksite

William Canby of New Castle Co., son of James Canby of New Castle Co. and Elizabeth his wife and Ann Tatnall, dau. of Edward Tatnall and Margery (dec'd.) his wife m. on 4th mo. 13th, 1846 at Wilmington. Orthodox

Henry Garrett of Wilmington son of Thomas Garrett of Wilmington and Mary S. his wife (dec'd.) and Catharine Ann Canby dau. of Charles Canby of same and Ann his wife m. on 5th mo. 7th, 1846 at Wilmington. Hicksite

John C. Deacon of Burlington Co., NJ, son of John Deacon and Hannah his wife (both dec'd.) and Maria W. Buzby, dau. of William Buzby (dec'd.) and Ann his wife m. on 9th mo. 17th, 1846 at Wilmington. Orthodox

Daniel Corbit of Cantwell Bridge, New Castle Co., son of William Corbit of same place and Mary his wife (both dec'd.) and Mary C. Wilson, dau. of David Wilson of Richmond, Wayne Co., IN and Ann his wife (dec'd.) m. on 4th mo. 15th, 1847 at Wilmington. Orthodox

William C. Smyth of Wilmington son of David (?) Smyth and Anna C. his wife and Emily Betts dau. of Mahlon Betts and Mary his wife m. on 9th mo. 28th, 1847. Hicksite

Joseph Davis of Chester Co. PA son of William Davis and Cramus(?) his wife (both dec'd.) and Elizabeth M. Peart dau. of Joshua (?) and Rebecca his wife m. 8th mo. 31st, 1848. Hicksite

Frederick Paxson of Philadelphia son of Charles Paxon and Mary his wife and Lydia Betts dau. of Mahlon Betts and Mary his wife m. on 12th mo. 6th, 1848. Hicksite

Caleb Hood of Bart Twp, Lancaster Co., PA, son of Thomsa Hood and Margaret his wife and Mary E. Hallowell dau. of Jesse Hallowell of Christiana Hundred, New Castle Co. and Jane his wife m. on 3rd mo. 8th, 1849 at the house of Jesse Hallowell. Hicksite

Clement H. Smith of city of Philadelphia, son of Stephen W. Smith late of same place (dec'd.) and Mary his wife and Mary C. Emlen, dau. of Samuel Emlen late of said city (dec'd.) and Beulah S.(?) his wife m. on 4th mo. 12th, 1849 at Wilmington. Orthodox

William Sellers of Philadelphia son of John Sellers of Delaware Co., PA, and Elizabeth his wife and Mary Ferris dau. of Ziba Ferris of Wilmington and Eliza his wife m. on 4th mo. 19th, 1849. Hicksite

William R. Bullock of city of Philadelphia, son of John Bullock late of city of Wilmington and Rachel his wife (both dec'd. ?) and Elizabeth A. Emlen, dau.

of Samuel Emlen late of Philadelphia (dec'd.) and Beulah S. his wife m. on
10th mo. 17th, 1850. Orthodox

Joseph Z. Lippincott of Gloucester Co., NJ son of Samuel Lippincott of same and
Sarah Z. his wife (dec'd.) and Elizabeth C. Tatum dau. of David Tatum
formerly of Wilmington and Hephzibah his wife (both dec'd.) m. on 10th mo.
31st, 1850. Hicksite

Samuel B. Regester of Philadelphia son of Robert Regester (dec'd.) and Lydia his
wife and Mary S. Denny dau. of Collins Denny formerly of Wilmington and
Ann his wife (both dec'd.) m. on 11th mo. 26th, 1850 at the residence of
William B. Hinton(?). Hicksite

Births and Deaths of Wilmington Monthly Meeting

A child of John Ferriss (son of Ziba and Edith Ferris) and Sarah his wife. John
their son, b. 21-9-1801. John Ferriss d. age 26-10-21 on 1-11-1802.

Children of Jesse Shenton Zane and Susannah his wife, dau. of Timothy Hanson.
Mary Hanson, b. 19-12-1795. Mary Hanson b. 18-3-1797. Hester Hanson b.
18-7-1798. Timothy Hanson b.19 -4- 1800.   Susannah mother of afsd.
children d. 26-4-1800.

Children of William Warner (son of Joseph) and Esther his wife dau. of Joseph
Tatnall. Joseph Tatnall, b. 30-4-1800; Ann Tatnall b. 3/1-1802.

Children of Robert and Mary Squibb James Robinson b. 11-6-1796; Samuel b.
27-3-1799; Jacob Hewes b. 29-1-1801

Joseph son of Thomas and Mary Shipley, b. 11-11-1752, d. 20-7-1832.

William, son of Charles and Mary West, b. Wilmington 26-9-1771, d. 1856

Children of Nathan Wood, son of Nathan and Rebekah Trimble

    Nathan Wood d. 11-1--1793

    Hannah Wood d. 23-6-1780

    William Wood d. 13-4-1780

Jane Starr d. 16-5-1812

Hannah Troth dau. of Wm. and Jane Starr d. 11-3-1828

Elizabeth Starr d. 21-11-1776

Isaac Starr, the father d. aged 83 and upwards 1811

John Richardson d. 30-9-1859

Rachel Byrnes, dau. of Caleb Brynes (son of Daniel) and wife Mary, d. 1804

Philip Bonsall d. 1803.

Child of John Ferriss (son of Ziba and Edith Ferriss) and Sarah his wife d. aged
26-10-21 on 1-11-1802

Hester Warner d. 12-9-1802

John Kendall d. aged 79-5-11 on 12-1-1845

Rachel Richards d. age 29 on 9-10-1818

Lydia Richards d. aged 60-10-21 on 2-8-1822

Ann Canby formerly Richards d. 2-10-1826

Children of Thomas Robinson (son of James and Elenor Robinson) and Mary his
    wife dau of Jacob and Betty Wilson. Samuel b. 15-6-1788; John b. 8-2-1790;
    William b. 4-4-1792; Elizabeth b. 26-3-1794; Thomas Wilson Robinson b.
    6-8-1799; Mary b. 20-3-1802; Ellinor b. 28-12-1805, James b. 8-2-1808

Phebe dau. of Eli Mendenhall, son of Benjamin Mindeinhall and Hannah his wife
    and Phebe his wife dau. of John Pritchett late of Brandywine Hundred, b.
    8-1-1802

Children of Eli Mendenhall and Mary his wife: Lydia b. 6-9-1805; Samuel b.
    26-4-1810; Mary b. 31-10-1807. Phebe Mendenhall the mother d. 36-3-11 on
    30-9-1802.Mary d. 15-7-1829.

Children of William Poole and Elizabeth his wife: Elizabeth b. 28-4-1792;
    Rebeckah b. 21-8-1793, d. 13-8-1794; Mary b. 21-2-1795; Samuel S. B.
    13-11-1796; Hannah b. 10-10-1798; William Shipley Poole b. 4-1-1801;
    Sarah b. 28-1-1804.

Sarah Brian, wife of James d. 23-10-1802

Children of William Warner (son of Joseph) and Esther his wife, dau. of Joseph
    Tatnall: Joseph Tatnall, b. 30-4-1800; Ann b. 3-1-1802

Jacob Hewes b. 29-1-1801

Rebecca Askew, b. 5-6-1781, d. at the Asylum 26-12-1826; William Askew d. in
    OH 7-12-1860

Sarah Ann Baily b. 15/2/1801

Children of Thomas and Sarah Wickersham: James b. 2-12-1796; Elijah, b.
    29-11-1798; Samuel, b. 15-3-1801; Samuel Wickersham d. 17-6-1802.

Children of Nathan and Lydia Sharples: Edith b. 2-2-1797; Joseph P. 19-3-1799;
    Elizabeth b. 17-8-1801

Joseph son of Mordecai and Elizabeth Yarnall b. 3-2-1802

Children of Joseph Richardson and Ann: Jane b. 5-6/1805. Samuel b. 11-10-1806

Child of Samuel Hooton and Sarah: Charles Ballinger Hootton b. 15-8-1801

Children of Jacob Alricks and Lydia (d. 7-11-1825): William b. 7-4-1800, d.
    17-10-1823; Mary Ann b. 18-4-1801, d. 2-3-1812; Sidney Ann b. 8-9-1803;
    Henry Sigpedus b. 30-5-1806; Sarah b. 28-8-1802

Lydia Warner, widow of John Warner d. 15-10-1802.

Margaret Nichols, widow of Joseph Nichols d. aged about 87, 24-12-1802

John Grubb of Brandiwine Hundred d 11-2-1804

Mary Commons d. 3-9-1803

David Wet d. 12-1-1804

Hannah Starr, wife of Jacob, d. 6-5-1803

James Marshall d. 28-6-1805

Robert Higgins or Hagins wife d. 6-9-1803

Zachariah Jess d. 5/7/1805

Rebekah Jess d. 15-1-1807

Mary Gray d. [no date]

Mary Niles, widow of Hezekiah b. 2-11-1806

Sarah Hastings, widow, d. age 57 on 6-8-1806

Margaret, wife of Barrett Mason, d. 0-8-1806

Ann Cloud, widow of Mordecai, aged 67, d. 14-11-1806

Hannah West, widow of Joseph West d. 4 1-1806 in her 74th year, an elder from 1771 until her death.

Ann Harlan, elder of Stanton Particular Meeting, d. 16-6-1804, aged upwards of 64.

Ann Johnson, an elder of Stanton P.M. d. 25-11-1804, age 32

Joseph Chambers an elder of Stanton P.M. d. 8-10-1804, aged near 60 years

Zachariah Ferriss, minister, d. 6-1-1803 in 86th year of his age, member of Wilmington MM from the first settlement thereof which was allowed and established by Concord Quarterly Meeting on 14 -3-1750

Abigail Harland, wife of William, d. age 77, 27-1-1807

Mary Dickinson, wife of John, d. 23-7-1803

Susannah Fussell d. 2nd mo. 1805

Rachel Wilson d. 9-11-1804

Thomas Baldwin d. 5-11-1805

Ann Johnson d. 25-11-1804

DEATHS
Date of Burial

Alice Platt, 7/14/1806, at Wilmington.

Elizabeth Robinson, 2/7/1807, at Wilmington.

Mordecai Yarnall, 1/23/1808, at Wilmington.

James Kendall, 3/14/1808, at Wilmington.

Wm. Garrison, 4/10/1808, at Wilmington.

Elizabeth Baily, 10/28/1808, at Wilmington.

Grace Smith, 11/28/1808, at Wilmington.

Jane Shipley, 12/1/1808, at Wilmington.

Lydia Webster, 1/19/1809, at Wilmington.

Esther Yarnall, 1/24/1809, at Wilmington, aged about 73 years.

Rebeccah Wood 1/25/1811, at Wilmington, aged 69.

Thomas Robinson, 6/11/1809, near Wilmington.

Elizabeth Brinton, 6/11/1809, at Wilmington.

Susanna Cloud, 8/15/1809, at Wilmington.

Ann Way, 9/3/1809, at Wilmington, daughter of John Way.

Hannah Wilkinson, 10/20/1809, at Wilmington, daughter of Robert Wilkinson.

Mary Lea, 3/5/1810, at Wilmington, daughter of Thomas, 23 years nearly.

Hannah Mendenhall, 3/27/1810, at Wilmington, widow of Benjamin, 81 years.

Priscilla Jones, 5/19/1810, at Wilmington, daughter of John, aged 19 years.

—— Grubb, 7/2/1810, at Wilmington, son of Joseph, under 1 year.

Hannah Bassett, 9/15/1810, at Wilmington, daughter of Nathan, aged 21 years 6 months, 24 days.

Samuel N. Mendenhall, 10/16/1810, at Wilmington, son of Eli, under 1year.

Rachael Byrnes 12/28/1810, at Wilmington, wife of Daniel, 28th year.

Ann Sanders, 11/11/1810, at Stanton, wife of John.

Hannah Baldwin, 4/21/1811, at Wilmington.

William Hillis, 7/8/1811, at Wilmington, son of Eli, 2nd year.

Joseph Bringhurst, 8/4/1811, at Wilmington, 79th year, late of Phila Southern District.

Dickinson Logan, 8/16/1811, at Wilmington, son of Albanus C, under 1year.

Sarah Elizabeth Allen, 8/25/1811, at Wilmington, daughter of Charles, Phila.

Joseph Baldwin, 9/7/1811, at Wilmington.

Isaac Starr Senr, 11/26, 1811, at Wilmington, in 84th year.

John P Hanson, 1/13/1812, at Wilmington, son of Thomas, in 3rd year.

Mary Ann Alricks, 3/3/1812, at Wilmington, daughter of Jacob.

James Walker, 4/11/1812, at Wilmington.

John Johnson, 5/11/1812, at Wilmington.

Jane Griffith, 8/11/1812, at Wilmington, in her 82nd year.

Samuel T. Hanson, 8/29/1812, at Wilmington, son Thomas in 2nd year.

Jane Starr, 5/16/1812, at Wilmington, widow of William, in her 80th year.

Frances Ford, 11/26/1812, at Wilmington, wife of Abraham, of Wilmington.

Rachel Hayes, 4/3/1813, at Wilmington, wife of John of Wilmington.

Joseph Tatnall, 5/9/1813, at Brandywine, son of Edward, under 1 year.

Thomas Shipley, 6/1/1813, at Wilmington, son of Joseph and Mary, of Brandywine, in 33rd year of his age.

Mary Gregg, 7/18/1813, at Wilmington, wife of Harmon, of Wilmington.

Susannah Hanson, 7/29/1813, at Wilmington, of Wilmington.

Edward Hilles, 8/1/1813, at Wilmington, son of Eli of Wilmington, near 10 months.

Ann White, 8/5/1813, at Wilmington, daughter of John Wilmington, 14 years 4 mo. 21 days.

Elizabeth Stroud, 2/7/1813, at Wilmington, daughter of Samuel of Wilmington, 5th year.

Hannah Commous, 11/26/1813, at Wilmington, wife of Isaac, of Brandywine.

Joseph Tatnall, 8/5/1813, at Wilmington, in 73rd year, of Wilmington.

Rebecca Manle, 5/7/1812, at Phila, wife of Joshua, of Wilmington 37 years 2 months, 3 days.

Joshua Maule, 8/30/1812, at Middletown Bucks Co, of Wilmington, aged 35 years, 8 months 2 days.

Elizabeth Harlan, 11/19/1814, at Stanton, wife of John of Milltown.

Grace Sanders, 6/16/1805, at Stanton, wife of Amos.

Frances Canby, 2/10/1814, at Wilmington, wife of Samuel of Brandywine, aged 57 years.

William Savory Hanson, 4/1/1814, at Wilmington, 2nd year, child of Thomas of

Wilmington.

Mary Ford, 5/5/1814, at Wilmington, wife of Samuel of Wilmington, in her 36th year.

James Bellach, 7/21/1814, at Wilmington, son of John of Namons Creek.

George P.[?] Hallowell, 8/27/1814, at Wilmington, ch. of Wm., of Wilmington, 2nd year.

Nicholas Robinson, 8/24/1814, at Wilmington, in 86th year of Wilmington.

Sarah Canby, 9/11/1814, at Wilmington, dau of Saml. of Brandywine, 26y, 6 mos.

Anna Ferris, 9/29/1814, at Wilmington, ch of Benj of Brandywine, aged 2y 10m.

Esther Fussle, 1/21/1815, at Wilmington, wife of Jacob, of Wilmington, 77th year.

Mary Sharpless, 6/12/1812, of Wilmington, not a member of this meeting.

Edith Ferris, 2/10/1815, at Wilmington, widow of Ziba of Wilmington, 73rd year.

Robert Wilkinson, 3/21/1815, at Wilmington, 36th year of his age, of Wilmington.

John White, 5/12/1815, of Wilmington, son of Jno. and Mary, of Wilmington, 14th year.

Elizabeth Bane, 7/21/1815, of Wilmington, dau of Nathan and Margt of Wilmington, 24th year.

Isaac Lambs child, 9/21/1815, at Wilmington, under 1 year, of Wilmington.

Wm Barret Mason, 10/28/1815, of Wilmington, son of Barret and Ann, of Wilmington, 2nd year.

Abigail Gilpin, 11/11/1815, of Wilmington, wife of Vincent, of Wilmington, 78th year.

Pinder Antrim's child, 12/24/1815, at Wilmington, not a member, of country.

Joseph White, 12/25/1815, of Wilmington, son of Jno. and Mary of Wilmington, 16th year.

Gerrard Blackford, 1/19/1816, of Wilmington, in 87th year, of Wilmington.

William Shipley, 2/14/1816, of Wilmington, in 70th year, of Brandywine, son of Thomas and brother of Joseph.

Aquilla Strarr, 3/8/1816, at Wilmington, son of Isaac, of Wilmington, in 49th year.

Elizabeth Blackford, 3/15/1816, at Wilmington, widow of Garret, in 83rd year.

Hannah McConnel, 5/5/1816, at Wilmington, wife of Thos of Wilmington, 41st year.

Elizabeth Baldwin, 6/17/1816, at Wilmington, wife of Thos of Wilmington.

Martha Mason, 6/26/1816, at Wilmington, wife of Peter of Wilmington, in 55th year.

Rest Sheward, 7/20/1816, at Wilmington, wife of James of Wilmington and dau of John Perry.

Lydia Nichols, 7/28/1816, at Wilmington, dau of Saml. of Wilmington, 30th year.

Eliza Nichols, 8/2/1816, at Wilmington, dau of Saml. of Wilmington, 18th year.

Alfred Bonsal, 9/11/1816, of Wilmington, son of Isaac of Wilmington, 2nd year.

Ann Bellach, 10/5/1816, at Wilmington, wife of John of Namons Creek, 42nd year.

Job Harvey, 10/19/1816, at Wilmington, in 79th year of Wilmington.

Nathan Bane Jr, 11/26/1816, at Wilmington, son of Nathan of Wilmington, 20th year.

Nathan Bane Jr, 11/26/1816, at Wilmington, son of Nathan of Wilmington, 20th year.

Isaac Dixon, 12/20/1816, of Wilmington, in 63rd year, of Wilmington.
Amy Chambers, 3/3/1806, at Stanton, of Stanton.
Mercy Johnson, 3/31/1808, at Stanton, of Stanton.
Lewis Sanders, 1/23/1809, at Stanton, of Stanton.
William Marshal, 5/4/1808, at Stanton, of Stanton, abt 78 years.
Robert Johnson, 8/19/1809, at Stanton, of Stanton, 75th year.
Joshua Sanders, 10/21/1809, at Stanton, of Stanton.
Mary Marshal, 1/1/1810, at Stanton, 78 years, of Stanton, dau of Edwd. Tatnall.
Alice Wollaston, 6/29/1810, at Stanton, of Stanton.
Thomas Stapler, 1/22/1812, at Stanton, of Stanton.
Thomas Stroud, 1/20/1812, at Stanton, of Stanton.
Thomas Meteer, 11/11/1812, at Stanton, of Stanton.
Jacob Starr, 11/11/1812, at Stanton, of Stanton, 79th year.
Joseph Chamberlin, 4/21/1813, at Stanton, of Stanton.
Margt. Allen Stapler, 7/24/1813, at Stanton, of Stanton.
Mary Jane Phillips, 9/12/1814, at Stanton, of Stanton.
Elizabeth Harlan, 11/22/1814, at Stanton, of Stanton.
Caleb Harlan, 7/8/1815, at Stanton, of Stanton, 87th year.
Sarah Bayley, 7/28/1815, at Stanton, of Stanton.
Joseph Stapler, at Stanton, of Stanton.
Samuel Meteer Jr, 9/15/1815, at Stanton, of Stanton.
Martha Meteer, 10/3/1815, at Stanton, of Stanton.
Elizabeth Yarnall, 3/9/1816, at Stanton, widow of Benj of Wilmington, 83rd year.
Elizabeth Robinson, 1/28/1817, dau of Wm and Eliz of Wilmington, under 1 year.
William Wollaston, 6/3/1817, at Stanton, of Stanton.
William Ferris, 11/21/1817, at Stanton, son of Nathan from Easton, Maryland.
Luerane Gray, 2/20/1818, at Stanton, of Stanton.
Lueranah Ferris, 5/13/1818, at Stanton, of Stanton, widow of William.
Rachel Lamborn, 6/25/1817, at Wilmington, wife of Jona. in 39th year.
Lydia Baldwin, 7/19/1817, at Wilmington.
Caleb Sheward, 11/14/1817, at Wilmington, 40 years, 6 mos.
Samuel Nichols, 11/30/1817, at Wilmington, in 69th year.
Rachel Starr, 11/20/1817, at Concord, widow of Isaac of Wilmington, 77th year.
John Tatum, 4/16/1818, at Wilmington, son of David.
Robt Phillips Jr., 10/14/1815, at Stanton, son of Wm D and Phebe, in 7th year.
Mary Jane Phillips, 9/11/1814, at Stanton, dau of Wm D and Phebe, in 2nd year.
Nathan Bane, 1/30/1817, in Wilmington, in 60th year, of Wilmington.
Phebe Hull, 1/29/1817, in Wilmington, of Wilmington.
Rachel Richards, 10/11/1818, at Wilmington, in 29th year, dau of N & L of Wilmington.
William Bringhurst, 6/14/1818, at Wilmington, son of Jos and Sarah, in 18th year,

of Wilmington.

Elizabeth Kinsey, 1/4/1819, of Stanton, wife of John Jr., Country.

Benjn Ferris Jr., 1/11/1819, of Stanton, a minor son of Wm, nearly 10 years old.

John Lea, 11/9/1818, of Wilmington, son of Thomas and Sarah of Brandywine, aged 24 years and 7 mos.

Mary Hollowell, 1/7/1819, at Wilmington, wife of Wm of Wilmington.

Mary Stapler, 2/15/1819, at Stanton, wife of Wm of Stanton, aged 65.7.4.

Phebe Wolley, 2/21/1819, at Wilmington, of Wilmington aged 77 years 3 mos nearly.

Wm. Megear Ferris, 2/21/1819, at Wilmington, son of Ziba and Eliza of Wilmington, 2nd year.

Newton Lamborn, 7/20/1819, at Wilmington, of Wilmington, son of Eli and Rebecca, 2nd year.

Sarah Dawson, 9/10/1819, at Stanton, of Stanton.

William Harlan, 9/30/1819, at Wilmington, of Wilmington aged 95.4.15.

Caleb Johnson, 11/28/1819, at Wilmington, in 82nd year.

Thomas Hanson, 12/5/1819, at Wilmington, son of Thomas of Mary, 2nd year.

Mary Pierce Hallowell, 12/24/1819, at Wilmington, under 1 year.

Lucy Hurnard, 1/11/1820, at Wilmington, daughter of Robert and Hannah, 19th year.

Sarah Lea, 1/30/1820, at Wilmington, daughter of Thomas and Sarah of Brandywine 18th year.

Isaac Lamb Jr. 2/18/1820, at Wilmington, son of Isaac, of Wilmington.

Ruth Rowland, 5/2/1820, at Wilmington, wife of John, of Wilmington.

Hannah Eastburn, 7/26/1820, at Stanton, wife of Saml., of Wilmington.

Thomas Stapler, 9/7/1820, at Wilmington, son of Jno. and Ann of Wilmington, 2nd year.

John Smith, 9/18/1820, at Wilmington, of Phila, not of this meeting.

Mary Johnson, 10/22/1820, at Wilmington, wife of Caleb of Wilmington, 81st year.

John Sanders, 11/6/1820, at Stanton, son of Benjamin, of Stanton, 8th year.

Ann Wollaston, 12/19/1820, at Wilmington, daughter of Jos., of Wilmington.

Edward Lea, 12/20/1820, at Wilmington, son of Thomas of Brandywine, 23rd year.

Ann Saunders, 12/24/1820, at Stanton, daughter of Benj., of Stanton, 2nd year.

Mary Bonsall, 4/20/1821, at Wilmington, wife of Stephen, 24th year.

Mary Cranston, 5/1/1821, at Stanton wife of Simon of Stanton, 47 nearly.

Dinah Jackson, 7/17/1821, at Wilmington, wife of Joshua, of Wilmington, 73 years.

John Sanders, 9/16/1821, at Stanton, a valuable minister of Stanton, 84 years.

Mary Williamson, 10/2/1821, at Wilmington, wife of Adam of Brandywine Hundred.

Ann Thistlethwaite, 10/7/1821, at Wilmington, deceased at John Richardson's,

Country.

Harriot Williamson, 12/8/1821, at Wilmington, daughter of Adam, Brandywine hundred, 37 years.

Jonas Canby, 2/1/1822, at Wilmington, in 87th year, of Wilmington.

Beulah Eastburn, 2/22/1822, at Stanton, of Stanton.

Ann White, 4/1/1822, at Wilmington, mother of John, of Wilmington.

Samuel Eastbourn, 4/5/1822, at Stanton, of Stanton.

Hannah Bonsal, 4/17/1822, at Wilmington in 69th year, of Wilmington.

Ann Ferris, 6/18/1822, at Wilmington, wife of John, of Wilmington, aged 61.

Nicholas Way, 6/27/1822, at Wilmington, son of John near Wilmington.

Lydia Richards, 8/2/1822, at Wilmington, aged 60 years, 10 months, 21 days, of Wilmington.

John Dixon, 9/2/1822, at Wilmington, aged 46 years, of Wilmington.

Phebe Phillips, 9/23/1822, at Stanton, wife of William. D, of Country in 50th year.

Ann Richardson, 10/14/1822 at Wilmington, daughter of Ashton

Rachel Ashburnham, 11/23/1822, at Wilmington, wife of Jos., Wilmington, 73rd year.

David Tatum, 11/27/1822, at Wilmington,

Rebecca Lamborn, 12/10/1822, at Wilmington, wife of Eli of Wilmington.

Elizabeth Beeson 2/10/1823 at Wilmington, dau. of Samuel Shipley, wife of Jonathan Beeson of BW Hundred.

William Robinson, 3/2/1823 at Wilmington, son of Nicholas dec'd, resided at Wilmington, in 60th year.

----- Mitchell, 8/12/1823, at Wilmington, wife of John, of N.C. Hundred.

Thomas Lea, 9/4/1823, at Wilmington, B. Wine, Hundred.

Alice Seeds, 9/7/1823, at Wilmington, wife of Adam of N. Castle, 85 years.

Sarah Poole, 9/13/1823, at Wilmington, wife of William Poole of B. Wine aged 52 years. 11 mos. 18 days.

Martha Whitelock, 9/14/1823, at Wilmington, of Wilmington.

Adam Seeds, 10/1/1823, at Wilmington, in 79th year, of New Castle.

— Bullock, 10/15/1823, at Wilmington, under 1 year, child of John of Wilmington.

William Alrich, 10/17/1823, at Wilmington, son of Jacob and Lydia of country aged 24 years.

Moses Palmer's child, 11/6/1823, under 1 year.

Ferris Harlan, 11/7/1823, at Stanton, son of Caleb and Edith of Millstown.

Stephen Shapler, 11/18/1823, at Stanton, of Stanton.

Hannah Bonsal, 11/14/1823, at Wilmington, 64th year, of Wilmington.

A. Richardson's child, no date, at Wilmington, under 1 year.

Martha Hanworth Wetherald, 1/28/1824, at Wilmington nearly 2 years. Joseph and Mary.

David Eastborn, 6/29/1824, Stanton, aged 52 years, of Stanton.

Caleb P Kinsey, 7/3/1824, Stanton, of Stanton.

John Kinsey, 7/19/1824, Stanton, of Stanton.

Francis Bullock, 7/30/1824, Wilmington, 3rd year, of Wilmington.

Mary Mendinhall, 8/12/1824, Wilmington, 17th year, daughter of Eli and Mary.

Moses Quimby, 9/1/1824, Stanton, of Stanton.

Phebe Hartley, 9/4/1824, Wilmington, wife of Joseph of Nottingham, 52 years.

Sarah Grubb, 9/8/1824, Wilmington, daughter of Joseph, of Wilmington. 9 years.

Mary Buck, 9/30/1824, Wilmington, wife of George, of Wilmington.

Rachel Burgess, 3/29/1824, Wilmington, wife of John, of Wilmington.

Benjamin Betts, 4/16/1824, Wilmington, in 32nd year, of Wilmington.

Cyrus Newlin, 4/16/1824, Wilmington, in 75th year, of Wilmington.

Caleb Seal, 4/18/1824, Wilmington, in 93rd year, of Wilmington.

Sarah Newlin, 4/21/1824, Wilmington, in 69th year, of Wilmington.

Franklin C. Wilson, 7/9/1824, Wilmington, under 1 year, of Wilmington.

John Jones, 1/13/1825, Wilmington, in 67th year, of Wilmington.

Jeremiah Wollaston, 3/30/1825, Wilmington, in 60th year, of Wilmington.

Erevin, 6/15/1825, Wilmington, daughter of John Erwin, of Stanton.

Rhoda Price, 6/25/1825, Wilmington, daughter of Hannah Price, of Wilmington.

Hannah Nichols, 7/4/1825, Wilmington, in 73rd year, of Wilmington.

Mary Bonsal, 7/19/1825, Wilmington, in 83rd year, of Wilmington.

Amy Dixon, 7/25/1825, Wilmington, in 70th year, of Wilmington.

Emily Quinby, 8/8/1825, Wilmington, daughter of John, of Stanton.

Elizabeth Kinsey, 9/13/1825, of Wilmington.

Mary Woodward, 9/27/1825, Wilmington, of Centre.

Lydia Alrich, 11/8/1825, Wilmington, 55th year, of Wilmington.

Evan Thomas, 11/25/1825, Wilmington, of Wilmington.

Josiah Rowland, 3/21/1826, Wilmington, of Wilmington.

Sarah Jones, 4/5/1826, Wilmington, 67th year, of Wilmington.

Edward Hewes, 4/18/1826, Wilmington, 85th nearly, of Wilmington.

Sarah M. Smyth, 6/5/1826, Wilmington, 8th year, daughter of David and Anne.

William Warner Junr, 7/15/1826, Wilmington, 12th year, of Wilmington.

Skidmore Wilson, 6/18/1825, Wilmington, under 1 year, son of William, of Wilmington.

Sarah Wilson, 6/25/1825, Wilmington, under 1 year, daughter of William, of Wilmington.

Martha Canby, 8/18/1826, 79 year, wife of William,

Susan Swayne, 8/20/1826, wife of Huson.

Mary Brown, 9/1/1826, Wilmington,

Sarah Bassett, 9/15/1826, Wilmington, 55 year 11 months 17days.

Ann Canby, 10/2/1826, Wilmington, 29th year, wife of Charles.

John Mitchell, 10/12/1826, Wilmington

Samuel Kirby, 11/7/1826, Wilmington, son of Mark Kirby.

Elizabeth Wilson, 7/5/1827, Wilmington, under 1 year, daughter of Wm. Wilson.

Jacob Webb, 7/14/1827, Wilmington, [*from London Grove with his brother Benjamin 1817/8.*]

Henry Richardson, 7/16/1827, Wilmington, under 1 year, child of John.

William Henry Hewes, 8/30/1827, Wilmington, under 1 year, son of Aaron of Wilmington.

Margaret Marshall, 9/2/1827, Wilmington, 79th year, of Wilmington.

Mary Hanson, 12/17/1827, Wilmington, 85th year, of Wilmington.

Sarah Tatnall, 1/7/1828, Wilmington, 75th year, wife of Joseph, nr Wilmington.

Robert Squibb, 2/25/1828, Wilmington, 67th year, of Staunton.

Elizabeth Breaer, 4/2-0/1828, Wilmington, dau. of Mark, 2nd year, Wilmington.

Mary Awmack, 5/4/1828, 74 years, of Wilmington

Sarah Ann Pusey, 6/30/1828, Wilmington, dau. of Joseph G., of Wilmington.

Hannah F. Rowland, 7/30/1828, Wilmington, 74 years, of Wilmington.

Susan Pusey, 7/9/1828, Wilmington, 6 months dau. of Jonas, of Wilmington.

Mary Garrett, 7/13/1828, Wilmington, wife of Thomas, of Wilmington.

Sally Ann Poole, 7/17/1828, Wilmington, wife of Samuel, of Wilmington.

Elizabeth Mason, 9/21/1838, Wilmington, dau. of Barrett, 17th year, of Wilmington.

Deborah Betts, 10/25/1828, Wilmington, dau. of Jesse, 38th year, of Wilmington.

John Ferris, 10/24/1828, Wilmington, son of Zachariah, 83rd year, of Wilmington.

Elizabeth Yarnall, 10/28/1828, Wilmington, 87th year, of Wilmington.

William Richards Sr 1/5/1829, Wilmington, 68th year, of Wilmington.

John White, 2/5/1829, Wilmington, 67th year, of Wilmington.

Amy Lewis, 10/8/1826, Wilmington, 75th year.

Joshua Johnson, 2/15/1828, Staunton, 1y, 2 m, 19 d, 13 h, son of Saml. and Mary Ann, of Wilmington.

Ann Phillips, 4/11/1828, Staunton, 92nd year, wife of Robert, Staunton.

Margaret Kinsey Sr., 1/15/1829, Staunton.

Sarah Latimer, 3/19/1829, Wilmington, 38th year of Wilmington.

Hannah Hedges, 4/16/1829, Wilmington, 86th year, of Wilmington.

William Poole, 5/25/1829, Wilmington, 65th year, of Wilmington.

Isaac Bonsall, 6/30/1829, Wilmington, aged 51 years of Wilmington.

John Hirons, 7/27/1829, Wilmington, 77th year of Wilmington.

John Lukens, 8/16/1829, Wilmington, 33rd year, of Wilmington.

Mary Berry, 11/19/1829, Wilmington, member of another meeting.

Martha Hartley, 12/25/1829, Wilmington, dau. of Joseph, 28th year, of Wilmington.

Rebecca Askew, 12/26/1826, Frds' Asylum, dau. of Parker, 46th year, of Wilmington.

William Stapler, 1828, Staunton, aged 77 years., of Staunton.

Robert Phillips, 11/10/1828, Hockessin, abt. 85, of Wilmington.

Edwin Dixon, 7/25/1828, 20th year, son of Isaac and Margt.

Martha Wiley, 1828, about 76 years

Sarah Palmer, [*no date given*] Wilmington, wife of Moses, of Wilmington.

Edith Harlan, 4/20/1827, Staunton, wife of Caleb, of Milltown, 49 years.

Hannah Hart, 1/29/1830, Wilmington, of Wilmington.

Henry Lea, 2/19/1830, Wilmington, son of Thos., aged 18 years., of Wilmington.

Mary Hewes, 3/20/1830, Wilmington, wife of Edward, 79th year, of Wilmington.

William Canby, 4/3/1830, Wilmington, in 82nd year, of Wilmington.

Margaret Dixon, 6/30/1830, Wilmington, wife of Isaac, 45th year, of Wilmington.

Samuel S. Grubb, 8/31/1830, Wilmington, son of Joseph and Esther, 27th year, of Wilmington.

Joseph Grubb, 10/25/1830, Wilmington, of Wilmington.

Michael Megear, 1/1/1831, Wilmington, aged 65 years, of Wilmington.

Hannah Sanders, 1/23/1831, Staunton, of Staunton.

Joshua Johnson, 2/6/1831, Staunton, 65th year, of Staunton.

Martha Chamberlain, 2/20/1831, Staunton, in 76th year, of Staunton.

Lydia Gilpin, 5/4/1831, at Wilmington, wife of Edward of Wilmington.

John Shallcross, 10/8/1831, at Wilmington, aged nearly 75 years, of Wilmington.

Mary Rogers, 10/23/1831, at Wilmington, wife of Thomas A., of Wilmington.

Benjamin Ferris Jr, 10/29/1831, at Wilmington, in 15th year, son of Benj., of Wilmington.

Ann Mason, 11/11/1831, at Wilmington, widow of Barrett, of Wilmington.

Elizabeth Hirons, 11/16/1831, at Wilmington, widow of John, abt 76 years, of Wilmington.

Sarah Squibb, 11/29/1831, at Wilmington, dau. of Jas. and Catharine, 12th year, of Wilmington.

Ellen B. Squibb, 11/30/1831, at Wilmington, dau. of Jas. and Catharine, 3 mos., of Wilmington.

Mary H. Squibb, 12/6/1831, at Wilmington, dau. of Jas. and Catharine, 6 years, of Wilmington.

Lydia Webb, 12/5/1831, at Wilmington, aged 40 years, of Wilmington.

Phoebe Ferris, 3/8/1832 at Wilmington, dau. of Ziba and Eliza., 6 yrs.

Thomas Betts, 4/21/1832, at Wilmington, son of Mahlon and Mary, 3rd ye, of Wilmington.

John Robinson, 5/2/1832, at Wilmington, of Wilmington.

Abraham Ford, 6/23/1832, at Wilmington, in 85th year, of Wilmington.

Joseph Shipley, 7/20/1832, at Wilmington, in 80th year, of Wilmington.

Samuel Stroud, 7/23/1832, at Wilmington, of Wilmington.

Thomzin Spackman, 7/29/1832, at Wilmington, in 77th year, of Wilmington.

Phebe Hartley, 8/29/1832, at Wilmington, dau. of Joseph, of Wilmington.

Hester Grubb, 3/27/1833, at Wilmington, nearly 51 years, of Wilmington.

Catharine Squibb, 5/8/1833, at Wilmington, in 35th year, of Wilmington.

Joseph Wetherald Jr, 7/6/1833, at Wilmington, in 3rd year, of Wilmington.

John Way, 7/31/1833, at Wilmington, aged 70 years, of Wilmington.

Fanny Ferris, 8/3/1833, at Wilmington, in her 56th year, of Wilmington

Elizabeth Robinson, 9/12/1833, at Wilmington, member of another meeting of Phila.

Edith Yarnall, 9/15/1833, at Wilmington, in her 54th year, of Wilmington.

Isaac Richards, 10/4/1833, at Wilmington, in his 42 year, of Wilmington.

Elizabeth Wollaston, 10/13/1833, at Wilmington, wife of Samuel, of Wilmington.

Joseph Richardson, 12/24/1833, at Wilmington, in his 67th year, nr Wilmington.

John C. Moore, 1/15/1834, at Wilmington, in his 24th year, of Wilmington.

Ann Tatum, 2/3/1834, at Wilmington, of Wilmington.

Margaret Bane, 5/5/1834, at Wilmington, of Wilmington.

Mary West, 5/19/1834, at Wilmington, in her 65th year, of Philadelphia.

Eli Mendinhall, 6/10/1834, at Wilmington, nearly 77 years, of Wilmington.

Ann Hewes, 6/13/1834, at Wilmington, in her 59th year, of Baltimore.

Mary W. Rowland, 7/3/1834, at Wilmington, member of another monthly meeting, of Wilmington.

Elizabeth Dixon, 7/6/1834, at Wilmington, of Wilmington.

Joseph Bringhurst, 7/26/1834, at Wilmington, in his 67th year, of Wilmington.

Sarah Richardson, 9/6/1834, at Wilmington, widow of Richd. aged 89 years, of Wilmington.

Parker Askew, 10/14/1834, at Wilmington, in his 79th year, of Wilmington.

Jane Alderdice, 6/2/1835, at Wilmington, of Wilmington.

Margaret Brookes, 6/26/1835, at Wilmington, aged 75 years, of Wilmington.

Ellen Rowland, 7/4/1835, at Wilmington, member of another Monthly Meeting of Wilmington.

Ann Rowland, 4/5/1835, at Wilmington, wife of Joseph G., of Wilmington.

Elizabeth Mifflin, 8/31/1835, at Wilmington, not a member here. of Camden, DE

Thomas Squibb, 9/16/1835, at Wilmington, in 74th year.

Elizabeth Dawson, 3/7/1836, at Wilmington, of Wilmington.

Jeremiah Wollston, 3/23/1836, at Wilmington, in 75th year, of Wilmington.

Mary W. Chalfant, 5/8/1836, at Wilmington, a member of Kennet Mo. Mtg.

Mary White, 7/10/1836, at Wilmington, in 70th year.

William Wilson, 7/10/1836, at Wilmington, of Wilmington.

Martha B. Hayhurst, 8/20/1836, at Wilmington, dau. of Thomas, 2nd year, of Wilmington.

William R. Canby, 10/9/1836, at Wilmington, son of Charles, 11th year, of Wilmington.

Rachel Squibb, 12/20/1836, at Wilmington, in 70th year, near Chester Pa.

Mary E., Hollingsworth, 1/31/1837, at Wilmington, in 1st year, of Wilmington.

John Reynolds, 2/14/1837, at Wilmington, in 73rd year, of Wilmington.

Moses Rea, 4/14/1837, at Wilmington, in 86th year, of Wilmington.

Sarah Barker, 5/26/1837, at Wilmington, dau. of Joshua, of Wilmington.

Mary Warner, 6/11/1837, at Wilmington, dau. of William, of Wilmington.

Hannah Pusey, 7/29/1837 at Wilmington, wife of Jonas, 48th year, of Wilmington.

Fanny Baynes, 8/18/1837, at Wilmington, dau. of James, in 1st year., of

Wilmington.
Mary M. Poole, 8/28/1837, at Wilmington, dau. of Wm. S., of Wilmington.
Rebecca Gibbons Jr., 9/27/1837, at Wilmington, dau. of Henry, 2nd year, of
Wilmington.
Hannah Seal, 2/16/1838, Frankfort, dau of Caleb, 70th year, buried Frankford.
Elizabeth Brearer, 3/25/1838, at Wilmington, dau of Mark, 7th year, of
Wilmington.
Francis Ferris, 4/20/1838, at Wilmington, 7th year, dau. of Ziba, of Wilmington.
Margta, Hayhurst, 7/27/1838, at Wilmington, dau. of Thomas, 6 1/6 year, of
Wilmington.
Susan Bancroft, 7/28/1838, at Wilmington, dau. of John, 1st year, of Wilmington.
Mary Curl, 10/12/1838, at Wilmington, of Wilmington.
Ann Latimer, 11/6/1838, at Wilmington, widow of Dr. Henry Latimer, 79th year,
of Wilmington.
Mary Miller, 11/12/1838, at Wilmington, in her 71st year, of Wilmington
Edward Poole, 11/25/1838, at Wilmington, son of Wm S., in his 3rd year, of
Wilmington.
Deborah Hewes, d. 11/27/1838, at Wilmington, in her 50th year, of Wilmington.
Rebecca Carpenter, 11/15/1838, at New Castle, aged 53 y, 9 m, 27 d, of New
Castle.
Thomas Robinson, 12/11/1838, at Wilmington, in his 40th year, of Wilmington.
Letitia Woodcock, 12/15/1838, at Wilmington, in her 74th year, widow of Wm. of
Wilmington.
Thomas Newlin, 12/15/1838, at Wilmington, not a member, of Phila.
Catharine Richards, 1/30?/1839, in her 71st year, of Wilmington.
Edward Bancroft, 4/26/1839, at Wilmington, in his 3rd year, of Wilmington.
Sarah Lea, 9/4/1839, at Wilmington, widow of Thos., 74th year, of Wilmington.
Jane Poole, 9/11/1839, at Wilmington, wife of Samuel S., in 35th year, near
Wilmington
Sarah Ann Webb, 10/1/1839, at Wilmington, dau. of James, abt 5 years, of
Wilmington.
Mary Craig, 10/18/1839, at Wilmington, in 38th year, of Wilmington.
Sarah Rea, 12/2/1839, at Wilmington, widow of Moses, in 88th year.
Sarah Richardson, 12/25/1839, dau. of Joseph in 32nd year, near Wilmington.
Orpha Hewes, 1/20/1840, at Wilmington, in 62nd year, of Wilmington.
Naomie Souy, 3/6/1840, at Wilmington, of Wilmington. Check
William R. Souy, 5/8/1840, at Wilmington, aged 1 year, nr Wilmington.
Lydia Tatum, 5/25/1840, at Wilmington, dau. of David, in 19th year, of
Wilmington.
Mary W. Wollaston, 10/6/1840, at Wilmington, dau. of Saml. in 1st year, of
Wilmington.
Hepziba Tatum, 12/17/1840, at Wilmington, widow of David, of Wilmington.
Abram Bonsall, 12/23/1840, in 77th year, of Wilmington.

Bencil Kendall, 12/28/1840, at Wilmington, dau. of Jesse in 1st year, of Wilmington.

Jane Way, 75th year, 3/16/1841, buried at Wilmington, widow of John, of Wilmington.

Rebecca Robinson, 3/31/1841, at Wilmington, 89th year, of Wilmington.

Wm. S. Rumford, 4/30/1841, at Wilmington, of Wilmington.

Phebe Chandler, 11/1/1841, at Wilmington, 91st year, of Wilmington.

Hannah Gilpin, 11/27/1841, at Wilmington, 77th year, of Wilmington.

Ruth Nichols, 12/11/1841, at Wilmington, 88th year, of Wilmington

George Burge, 1/4/1842, at Wilmington, from England, 77th year, of Wilmington.

Joseph Wetherald, 3/24/1842, at Wilmington, from England, in 55th year, of Wilmington.

Ann S. Richardson, 6/23/1842, at Wilmington, widow of Joseph, 65th year, of Wilmington.

Mary Marriott, 8/12/1842, at Wilmington, in 85th year, of Wilmington.

William Seal, 9/20/1842, at Wilmington, in 66th year, of Wilmington.

Philena Wollaston, 12/29/1842, at Wilmington, wife of Samuel, abt 49, of Wilmington.

Francis Ferris, 2/8/1843, at Wilmington, of Wilmington.

Jesse Hollingsworth, 3/8/1843, at Wilmington, of Wilmington.

Ferris Smyth, 4/2/1843, at Wilmington, aged 19 mos., of Phila.

Joseph Wetherald, 4/22/1843, at Wilmington, aged 86 years, from England, of Wilmington.

Isaac Kendall, 11/12/1843, at Wilmington, aged 80 years, of Wilmington.

Mary Shipley, 12/11/1843, at Wilmington, aged 87 years, of Wilmington.

Phebe Magear, 12/16/1843, at Wilmington, of Wilmington.

Lydia Poore, 2/11/1844, at Wilmington, of Wilmington.

Edward Gilpin, 4/14/1844, at Wilmington, aged 84 years, of Wilmington.

Hannah C. Hewes, 4/24/1844, at Wilmington, aged 56 years, wife of Aaron, of Wilmington.

Deborah Bringhurst, 8/20/1844, at Wilmington, aged 71 years. 5 months, 18 days, of Wilmington.

Tabitha Roberts, 12/19/1844, at Wilmington, of Wilmington.

Mary Wilkinson, 2/11/1845 at Wilmington, of Wilmington.

Edward Grubb, 2/20/1845, aged 41 years, at Wilmington, of Wilmington.

Ann Denny, 3/15, 1845, at Wilmington, of Wilmington.

Emily H. Kendall, 3/17/1845, at Wilmington, of Wilmington.

Anna Thomas, 4/24/1845, at Wilmington, of Wilmington.

Henry Warner, 6/3/1845, at Wilmington, of Wilmington.

Jonathan Byrnes, 7/6/1845, at Wilmington, age 78 years, of Wilmington.

Ann Richardson, 7/9/1845, at Wilmington, aged 64 years, of Wilmington.

William Gibbons, 7/25/1845, at Wilmington, of Wilmington.

Jacob Knight, 10/17/1845, at Wilmington, member of Bristol Mo. Mtg, of

Wilmington.

John Kendall, 12/1/1845.

Rebecca Miller, 2/2/1846, aged 85 years.

Margaret Richardson, 3/10/1846, aged 61 years 10 mos.

Sarah Gregg, 4/29/1846, member of Kennett Monthly Meeting

Hannah S. Walker, 8/9/1846

William Poole, 8/28/1846, child of Morton Poole.

James Thompson, 10/9/1846, member of another meeting

William Ford, 2/18/1847

Edith Speakman, 4/29/1847, aged 74 years.

Mary Robinson, 5/16/1847.

Eliza Webster, 6/11/1847.

Nathan Bassett, 8/9/1847.

Elizabeth Reynolds, 10/28/1847.

Elizabeth Stroud, 11/5/1847.

Robert Graves, 3/3/1848, aged 4 years.

Ann Robinson, 9/8/1848, aged 69 years, from England.

Ann Hartley, 11/18/1848.

Milton Hartley, 11/23/1848, aged 33 years

Harriet Edwards, 1/17/1849.

Chas. Franklin Edwards, 1/26/1849.

Joseph Hartley, 4/4/1849.

Lydia Emmerson, 5/22/1849.

Isaac H. Starr, 6/15/1849.

Rebecca Martin, 6/15/1849, 93 years old, widow of John.

Maria Graves, 7/20/1849.

Alvina Williamson, 7/24/1849.

Wm. S. Woodward, 8/2/1849.

Mary W. Oakford, 9/18/1849, aged 4 years, of Darby.

Martha Hilles, 11/25/1849, aged 75 years.

Deborah Brown, 2/20/1850, aged 77 years.

Rachel W. Oakford, 3/13/1850.

Nathaniel Richards, 5/25/1850, aged 94 years.

Wilmington Monthly Meeting Removals (issued)
1799-1851

9/11/1799 Richard Buckingham to Kennett.

12/11/1799 Thomas Jackson to Kennett.

2/12/1800 Joseph Hewes to Baltimore.

6/11/1800 Joseph Blackford (a youth bound an apprentice to Samuel Shin) to Phila for Southern District.

8/13/1800 Mary Canby (a minor) to Bradford. apprentice

8/13/1800 Samuel Hollingsworth (a minor) to Kennett.

9/10/1800 Betty Shallcross to Phila for Southern District.

9/10/1800 Joanna Wallaston to Uwchlan.

9/10/1800 Joshua Stroud, wife Martha and minor children Mary and Elizabeth to Phila for Southern District.

10/15/1800 Marib Yarnall to Kennett.

11/12/1800 Lydia Hussey to Pipe Creek (removed with her husband).

2/11/1801 Robert Booth to Redstone.

5/7/1801 Curtis Grubb to Indian Spring.

6/4/1801 John Hewes ("by his father" crossed out) to Baltimore.

6/4/1801 Samuel Harvey to Baltimore. Been absent several years.

6/4/1801 Charles Harvey to Phila (living with his brother Isaac).

6/4/1801 Benjamin Canby to Phila for Southern District.

6/4/1801 Jonathan Corbett (a minor who is placed an apprentice with William Preston) to Phila Southern District.

7/9/1801 Sarah Newlin (to friends in Eastern States) informed us that her mind had been brought to a state of resignation in the prospect of accompanying our friend Phebe Speakman in a religious visit to your parts, which obtaining our weighty consideration and sympathy is united with.

7/9/1801 Thomas Wickersham Jr. (who is placed with Joseph Merrifield) to Phila.

7/9/1801 Joseph Marott (a minor) to Concord.

8/6/1801 Mary Rudolph to Phila for Southern District.

8/6/1801 Lydia Milner daughter of John to Phila.

8/6/1801 John Milner, wife Phebe, and minor children Sidney, Beulah, Anna, John, and Harriett, to Phila.

8/6/1801 Samuel Sheppard (a minor at present residing with Benjamin Swett a member of your meeting having been recommended with his mother and brother by friends of Rich Hill of Northern Meeting in Ireland to the society in this country) to Haddonfield.

8/6/1801 Robert Minshall to Uwchlan.

9/10/1801 John Richardson (who is placed with Ebenezer Large) to Phila for the Southern District (a minor).

9/10/1801 Thomas Coarse (a minor) to Cissel [Cecil], Maryland.

11/5/1801 Rachel Byrnes to New Cornwall, New York. A copy sent 11/13/1808, the original being lost.

12/10/1801 John Laicock to Darby.

2/4/1802 Hannah Common (a minor) to Londongrove (she residing with her uncle James Wollaston).

3/4/1802 Thomas Meteer and son William to Baltimore.

4/8/1802 Thomas Thorp to Duck Creek.

5/6/1802 James Sheppard to Salem.

5/6/1802 Margaret Hagen and children Joseph and James to Monthly Meeting of Friends in New York. She had removed previously with her husband.

5/6/1802 Lydia Nicholson and five children to New York by endorsement on one she brought (she having removed with her husband).

5/6/1802 George Mercer, wife Rachel, and children Caleb, Mary, and John Mercer to Sadsbury.

6/10/1802 Joseph Register and wife Sarah to Chester.

6/10/1802 Thomas Spackman, wife Deborah, and children Samuel, Joseph, and George to Phila.

6/10/1802 William Askew a minor apprenticed to Joseph Corbett, to Phila for the Southern District.

7/8/1802 Elizabeth Sheppard to London Grove.

7/8/1802 William Stapler's son Joseph (who is an apprentice with his uncle John Mitchel) to Baltimore.

7/8/1802 William Warner and wife Esther and their two infant children Joseph Tatnall Warner and Ann Warner to Phila.

8/5/1802 Jacob Robinson (who has gone to reside with his father) a minor, to Westland

9/9/1802 Sarah Sharpless, a minor (who is placed with Samuel Emlen) to Burlington.

9/9/1802 Joseph and Mary Sharpless (minors and placed with Benjamin Sharpless) to Concord.

12/9/1802 Ziba Ferriss (a minor, he being placed with his brother) to Phila.

1/6/1803 Margaret Rasin, (wife of Warner Rasin) and her daughter Hannah Wilkinson to Cecil, Maryland.

1/6/1803 George Williamson to Cecil, Maryland.

3/10/1803 David Johnson to Kennett.

4/7/1803 Elizabeth Evans (wife of Jonathan) to Darby.

6/5/1803 Rebeckah Hoopes, and children Hannah and Frances to London Grove.

6/9/1803 Talor and William Seal (minors) to New Garden (removed to reside with their uncle).

7/7/1803 Ann Bellach (wife of John Ballach) to Kennett. (record contains both spellings).

8/4/1803 Samuel Sharpless to Third Haven.

8/4/1803 Thomas Hanson, an apprentice to John Poultney to Phila.

9/8/1803 Samual Starr to Duck Creek.

9/8/1803 Joseph Lea, an apprentice with Thomas English and Charles Holland to Phila.

10/6/1803 Nanny Warner to Phila for the Southern District.

11/10/1803 Elizabeth Price to Phila.

11/10/1803 Mary Wickersham to Phila.

12/8/1803 Elizabeth McPherson (wife of Daniel) to Hopewell, VA.

12/8/1803 Anne Evans to Phila.

12/8/1803 Ann Paxson, wife of William to Phila.

3/8/1804 Dinah Jackson, wife of Joshua, to Duck Creek.

3/8/1804 Robert Wilkinson and wife Rachel to New Garden.

4/5/1804 Merrit Canby, (an apprentice with Moses Gillingham) to Abington.

5/10/1804 Hugh Roberts to Abington.

5/10/1804 Joshua Harlan to Phila for Southern District.

5/10/1804 Nathan Sharpless, wife Lydia and children Edith, Joseph P, and Elizabeth to Concord.

6/7/1804 Mary Hollis to Phila.

6/7/1804 Robert Hagan's children George, Robert, Elizabeth, and Sarah Hagan to New York (minors).

6/7/1804 John Erwin and wife Elizabeth, and daughter Mary Ann to Pilesgrove.

7/5/1804 Cyrus Jones to Concord.

7/5/1804 John Hewes to Baltimore.

8/9/1804 Fanny Ferris to Phila (removed to reside with her husband).

8/9/1804 Samuel Stroud, wife Elizabeth, and children Ann, Mary, Edward, and Samuel to Murderkill Monthly Meeting.

2/7/1805 George Blackford a minor and apprentice to James Shin to Phila for the Southern District.

4/4/1805 William Darlington to Concord.

4/4/1805 Mary Horne (removed with her husband) to Phila for the Northern District.

8/8/1805 Isaac Bonsal to Baltimore.

8/8/1805 Aron Hewes, a minor, and apprentice with his brother, to Nottingham.

9/5/1805 Martha Edwards to Chesterfield New Jersey.

9/5/1805 John Acton to Salem.

10/10/1805 Susanna Hopper to Woodbury. Removed with husband.

12/5/1805 Martha Pierce to New Garden.

3/6/1806 Meary Stokely to Duck Creek.

4/10/1806 Christopher Hollingsworth Jr, wife Elizeabeth and son John Ferris Hollingsworth to Concord, Ohio.

4/10/1806 John Shallcross to Phila for the Southern District.

6/5/1806 William Hallowell to Chester.

6/5/1806 Hannah Stapler to Baltimore Md.

6/5/1806 Ann Jess (a minor) to Evesham N.J.

6/5/1806 Caleb Sheward to Phila for the Southern District.

8/7/1806 Rebecca Elliott, who resides with her son William Elliott, to Phila.

8/7/1806 Eleanor Bonsall to Baltimore.

10/9/1806 Ann West and son David (a minor) to Concord.

11/6/1806 Thomas Swain to Bradford.

11/6/1806 Miriam Chandler (wife of David) and son Aaron a minor to Redstone.

10/9/1806 Benjamin Harvey to Little Britain.

12/4/1806 Euniss Edmondson to Duck Creek.

12/4/1806 Ruth Jess to Phila for the Northern District.

12/4/1806 John Grubb to Short Creek Ohio.

12/4/1806 Hannah Grubb to Short Creek, Ohio. Removed to settle with her sons.

12/4/1806 Rebecca Mott to Cecil.

12/4/1806 Mary Grubb to Short Creek, Ohio, removed with brothers.

12/4/1806 Sophia Edmonson to Duck Creek.

12/4/1806 Jemimah Grubb to Short Creek, Ohio, who has removed to reside with her brother.

5/30/1806 Phebe Bennett from Phila. Endorsed to Kennett.

1/8/1807 Phebe Bennett endorsed to Kennett.

2/5/1807 Hannah, wife of Norton Howard to Concord, Ohio.

2/5/1807 Ann Seal to Kennett.

2/5/1807 Elizabeth Wollaston to Nottingham.

3/5/1807 Ann Hewes to Baltimore.

3/5/1807 Joseph Martin to Phila for the Northern District, apprentice.

4/9/1807 Ann Shepherd to Concord.

5/7/1807 Mary Moore, wife of Ansalem Moore, to Concord.

5/7/1807 Elizabeth Sheppard to Concord.

5/7/1807 Isaac Wickersham to Redstone.

5/7/1807 Evan Taylor to Alexandria, Virginia.

5/7/1807 Jacob Blackford residing with Samuel Smith to Phila for the Southern Dist.

7/9/1807 Ann Whitelock to Abington (having removed with her husband).

7/9/1807 Jocll Zane and Hester his wife, to Phila Northern District.

7/9/1807 Jesse S. Zane and minor children Mary Hanson, Nathan Shinton, Hester and Timothy Hanson Zane to Phila Northern District.

5/7/1807 William Chambers to New Garden.

6/4/1807 Joseph Askew (a minor and apprentice to A. Konigmacher & Co) to Phila

9/10/1807 Peter Askew to Nottingham.

10/8/1807 George Sharpless to Concord Ohio.

10/8/1807 Ann Armstrong (wife of John) to Baltimore, MD.

10/8/1807 Isaac Horne to Phila for the Northern District.

11/5/1807 Thomas Squibb, wife Rachel and children Nathl., John, Lydia and Samuel to Chester.

11/5/1807 Thomas Williams, wife Sarah and children Matilda Enos, Margarett and Mary to Concord.

11/5/1807 Joseph Way apprentice with Lindsey Nicholson to Phila Northern District.

11/5/1807 Thomas Lea to Phila for the Southern District, late apprentice in Phila.

12/10/1807 James Elliott to Goshen, apprentice

12/10/1807 Elizabeth Duncan, (wife of John) to Baltimore for the Eastern District.

12/10/1807 Elizabeth Hooten to Haddonfield.

1/7/1808 Caleb Stroud son of Joshua to Phila for Southern District.

9/17/1806 Benjamin Cocks from Westbury Long Island to Wilmington.
1/7/1808 Benjamin Cocks from Wilmington to Westbury.
3/10/1808 Rachel Gilpin, minor child of George Gilpin, to New York.
3/10/1808 Lydia Wollaston to Nottingham a minor
4/7/1808 Martin Green, wife Mary and children Hannah, Mary, Anthony, Arthur and Rachel to Pilesgrove.
4/7/1808 Jane Marshall to Center.
4/7/1808 Margaret Morton, wife of John, to Phila Southern District.
5/5/1808 Samuel Hooten, wife Sarah and son Charles (a minor) to Haddonfield N.J.
5/5/1808 Joseph Atherton to Middletown Bucks County.
5/5/1808 Isaac and Amey Dixon and daughter Mary to Concord.
6/9/1808 William Way an apprentice with Nathan Smith to Phila for the Northern District.
6/9/1808 Stephen Bonsall (a minor) to Baltimore.
6/9/1808 Samuel Griscom to Salem, returning.
7/7/1808 Rachel Yarnall to Mother-kiln.
7/7/1808 Kezia Vandver, and small children Thomas B. and Sally Ann Vandiver to Phila for Northern District (both spellings in record).
5/5/1808 Nicholas Robinson White, (a minor) to Phila Northern District. Apprentice - son of John White.
6/9/1808 Phebe Johnson to Nottingham, unmarried.
7/7/1808 Samuel Canby Jr, (who resides with John Morton Jr.) to Phila for the Southern District.
10/6/1808 Mary Shortledge, wife of Isaac Shortledge, to Little Britain.
10/6/1808 William Levis to Concord, unmarried.
10/6/1808 Joshua Peirce to Concord, returning.
10/6/1808 Isaac Wilkinson (a minor) to Milddletown Bucks County, apprentice.
11/10/1808 Robert Newlin, wife Mary and children, Saml., Abigail, Cyrus and Robert Newlin to Oswego N.Y.
11/10/1808 Isaac Newlin to Oswego New York, unmarried.
1/5/1809 Alice, wife of Nathan Sanders, to Kennett.
3/9/1809 Ann Humphreys, wife of Richard, to Duck Creek.
4/6/1809 Thomas Spackman, wife Deborah and minor children Samuel, Joseph, George, Anna and Thomas Spackman to Londongrove.
4/6/1809 Thomas Griffith, wife Christiana and small children Hannah Gibson and Charlotte Griffith, to Little Britain.
4/6/1809 Sarah Marriott to Middletown Bucks County.
4/6/1809 William White, an apprentice, to Phila for Northern District.
5/4/1809 Susanah Sawyer (removed with her husband) to Phila, for the Northern District.
8/10/1809 Isaac Lea, residing with his brother John Lea, to Phila, for the Southern District.

8/10/1809 James Lea, wife Elizabeth and children Margaret, Hannah Gibson, Eliza, Susannah and Henry to Phila for the Northern District.

10/5/1809 William Platt (a minor) to Phila for the Northern District.

7/7/1809 Aaron Hewes to Wilmington, from Nottingham.

12/7/1809 Aaron Hewes to Little Britain. By endorsement.

2/8/1810 Joseph Wilson to Wrightstown Bucks County.

2/8/1810 Abner Yarnall to New Garden, a minor.

2/8/1810 Joseph Yarnall to Chester, a minor.

2/8/1810 William Eliott to Goshen. ("Gotion")

2/8/1810 Lydia Jones to Middletown, Bucks County.

2/8/1810 Rachel Yarnall (daughter of Mordecai, deceased) to Goshen, minor.

2/8/1810 Mary Elliot to Phila for the Northern District.

2/8/1810 Deborah and Martha Kendall (minor children of James Kendall, deceased, to New Garden Monthly Meeting.

3/8/1810 John Lea Corbit to Phila Monthly Meeting.

3/8/1810 Charles Hilyard and children Lavinia, Thomas, Junia, Eliza, and Harriott, to Duck Creek.

4/5/1810 George Wollaston to Miami Monthly Meeting Ohio.

5/10/1810 Martha Wollaston to Baltimore Eastern District.

6/7/1810 Susannah Wilson to Wrightstown Bucks County.

6/7/1810 Amey Chambers to Kennett.

6/7/1810 Mary Jones to Phila for the Northern District.

6/7/1810 Elizabeth Jones to Phila for the Northern District.

6/7/1810 William P Richards to Phila, a minor.

4/5/1810 John Yarnall to Phila.

7/5/1810 John R Latimer to Phila for Southern District.

8/9/1810 Mary Kendall to London Grove, a minor.

9/6/1810 William Marshall to Center.

10/4/1810 Stephen Wilson, wife Mercy, and children Isaac, Elizabeth, and Joseph Wilson to Buckingham.

12/6/1810 John Sherwood to Third Haven.

12/6/1810 Phebe Yarnall to Phila.

1/10/1811 Mary Biddle wife of Clement Jr. to Phila.

1/10/1811 Levi Warner to Fairfield, Highland County Ohio.

2/7/1811 Elizabeth Thomas for self and children Amy, Jane, and Joseph Thomas to Kennet.

3/7/1811 Martha Hance (removed with husband) to Salem NJ.

4/4/1811 Joseph Hinchman Wilson to Phila.

5/9/1811 Esther Garretson to Phila for the Northern District.

5/9/1811 Parker Askew Jr. to Concord.

6/6/1811 Lydia Garretson (wife of Eliakim) for self and 4 children John D, Eliza Ann, George F, and Lydia to Phila for the Northern District.

9/5/1811 Mary Hewes to Concord to reside with husband.

9/5/1811 Robert Thomas (who removed from here about the year 1796) to Abington.

11/7/1811 Isaac Ford to Kennett.

11/7/1811 Mary Wilson Jr. to Phila for the Southern District.

11/7/1811 Elisha Starr, wife Ann and children, Margaret Hall, Isaac Walter, Mary Ann and Ashbridge Starr to Phila.

11/7/1811 Samuel Baily (an apprentice) to Baltimore for the Western District.

11/7/1811 Mary Hewes (residing with her father Joseph Hewes) to Little Britain, a minor.

12/5/1811 Ann Moore, wife of Asa, for self and two minor children Rachel and Sarah Ann Littler to Fairfax Monthly Meeting Virginia.

12/5/1811 Hannah W Askew, wife of Peter to Nottingham.

12/5/1811 Mary Miller, to Phila for the Northern District.

1/9/1812 Martha Johnson to Phila for the Southern District.

1/9/1812 Job Reynolds to Little Britain.

1/9/1812 John Lea to Phila for the Southern District.

2/6/1812 Caleb Johnson (a minor) who is placed with Richard Wier, to Phila for the Southern District.

3/5/1812 Isaac Jefferiss, Anne his wife and children Mercy, Joshua, Thomas, Anne and Isaac, to Duck Creek.

3/5/1812 David Seal, a minor to Phila for Northern District, apprentice.

3/5/1812 Caleb Seal, a minor to Phila for Northern District, apprentice.

5/7/1812 Jonas Preston to Goshen having removed many years ago.

5/7/1812 Sally Canby (a minor) daughter of Jonas Canby, to Center.

5/7/1812 Maria D Logan, for self and daughter Mary Nois Logan to Abington, (removed with her husband).

6/4/1812 Sarah Blackford for self and minor daughter Sarah to Phila Southern District.

7/9/1812 Mary Blackford to Phila.

7/9/1812 Luranna Gray to North West York Mo Meeting.

8/6/1812 Alice Jackson for self and minor children Mary Ann, Alice Anna, Catharine and Jonathan Morriss Jackson to Little Britain. (She having removed to reside with her husband).

6/28/1816 Daniel Offly Johns to Phila.

6/28/1816 Caleb Stroud, wife Esther and minor children Margaret and Joshua Stroud to New Garden.

8/2/1816 Elizabeth Marot to Phila for the Western District.

8/30/1816 John Hadley to London Grove.

8/30/1816 Joseph R. Martin to Baltimore for Western District.

8/30/1816 Edward Lea (a minor) to Phila Southern District. Apprentice to Emlen and Howell and lives with his brother Joseph Lea.

10/4/1816 Mary Miller to Duck Creek.

11/29/1816 Daniel Offley Johns to London Grove.

11/29/1816 Benjamin S Johnson to Phila for Northern District. Apprentice with Caleb Maule.

11/29/1816 George Platt to Phila. Left us in his minority.

1/3/1817 Josiah Bassett to Duck Creek.

1/3/1817 Elizabeth Sanders to Kennett, minor.

9/10/1812 Achsah Walton (a minor) to Phila.

10/8/1812 Abraham Walton's children, Hannah, Ruth, Eber, Abraham, Rachel and Amos to Richland Monthly Meeting.

12/10/1812 Samuel S Gilpin (a minor) with Samuel Smith to Phila for the Southern District.

12/10/1812 Hannah Walton, a minor, who resides with Thomas Parker, to Phila.

12/10/1812 Ruth Walton (a minor) to Horsham.

3/4/1813 Israel Yarnall to Goshen.

4/2/1813 Joseph Chambers, wife Deborah and three minor children, Lydia, Amy and Mary Ann to New Garden.

6/4/1813 Hannah Hart, to Center (having removed with her husband).

7/2/1813 Esther, wife of Josiah F. Clement, to Haddonfield (she having removed to reside with her husband).

7/2/1813 Joshua Vansant to Phila Northern District.

12/3/1813 John Wilson, wife Elizabeth and daughter Mary Ann (a minor) to Burlington.

12/3/1813 Margaret Wilson (who has removed with her parents) to Burlington.

12/3/1813 Lydia and Elizabeth Maule to Phila for the Northern District.

12/31/1813 Jonathan Dawes to Chester.

12/31/1813 Rachel Beaty to Concord.

2/4/1814 Septimus Roberts to Phila.

2/4/1814 James Bringhurst Jr. to Phila for the Southern District.

2/4/1814 Sarah Anna Bringhurst to Phila for the Southern District.

2/4/1814 Hannah Bonsall to Concord.

2/4/1814 Rumford Dawes to Chester.

3/4/1814 Jacob Pusey and wife Hannah to Center.

4/1/1814 Joseph Shipley Jr. (a minor) to Phila for the Southern District.

4/1/1814 Richard Peirce to Center Ohio.

4/29/1814 Devanport Marot to Abington, a minor.

4/29/1814 John Haddock, Sarah his wife and their two minor children James and John Haddock to Center Monthly Meeting.

4/29/1814 Isaac Dixon Jr. wife Margaret and four minor children Edwin Sanders, Amy, William Hirons and John Hadley Dixon to Concord.

6/3/1814 Joel Holloway, to Salem Ohio, returning.

6/3/1814 Anna Walton (a minor) to Richland.

6/3/1814 Ann Haydock (having removed with her parents), to Center Monthly Meeting.

7/1/1814 Sally Norris Dickinson to Phila.

9/2/1814 Mary Gibbons to Phila for the Western District.

9/30/1814 Elizabeth Yarnall to Goshen.

11/4/1814 Susannah P. Malin to Chester (having removed with her husband).

11/4/1814 William Marot to Phila for the Northern District.

12/30/1814 Elizabeth Black to Upper Springfield New Jersey.

2/3/1815 Elizabeth wife of John Sherwood to Third Haven, (removed with her husband).

6/2/1815 John Williamson to Haddonfield.

6/30/1815 Jane Pennal, to Chester.

8/4/1815 Merrit Canby to Phila for the Western District.

9/1/1815 William Johnson to Nottingham.

9/1/1815 Joseph Samuel Lovering (a minor) to Phila for the Southern District.

12/1/1815 William P. Palmer to Indian Spring.

12/1/1815 Jesse Gause, to Phila for the Northern District.

12/1/1815 Oliver Wilson to New Garden. Returning.

12/29/1815 Parker Askew Jr. to Nottingham.

12/29/1815 Martha Maule (a minor) who has removed to reside with her uncle Benjamin Johnson, to Phila for the Western District.

12/29/1815 Margaret Moore, a minor (who now resides with her grandfather David Moore) to New Garden.

12/29/1815 Thomas Pim to Bradford, returning.

12/29/1815 William Way to Phila for the Northern District.

12/29/1815 Caleb Sanders, a minor (having been placed with his grandfather Caleb Pennock) to Kennett.

12/29/1815 Joseph Seal to Phila for the Southern District.

2/2/1816 William Warner, wife Esther and children Joseph Tatnall Warner, Ann, Susan, John Edward, Henry, Elizabeth Tatnall Warner and William Welton Warner to Phila for the Southern District.

2/2/1816 Isaac Starr (a minor) to Phila for Southern District.

3/1/1816 Hester Yarnall to Goshen.

3/29/1816 John Ferriss Gilpin, (a minor) to Phila.

5/3/1816 Edith Sharpless to Phila.

5/3/1816 Nathan Pennell to Short Creek Ohio. Also Rosanna his wife and four minor children, ---- M., Ely Y., Lewis M. and Mary Ann.

5/3/1816 Ann Bassett, her sister Sarah Bassett (a minor) to Duck Creek Monthly Meeting.

5/3/1816 Hannah Rudolph to Darby, (having removed to settle with her husband.)

/1816 Mary Powell to Wilmington, endorsed to?.

5/31/1816 Joseph Marot to Phila for the Northern District. Cert. returned and addressed to Green Street.

5/31/1816 Mary Johnson to Phila.

5/31/1816 Elizabeth Johnson to Phila.

5/31/1816 Hannah, _____, Elizabeth and Rebecca Maula. Minors, (who reside with their aunts Mary and Elizabeth Johnson) to Phila.

5/31/1816 Hannah Johnson to Phila.

Volume II

1/3/1817 Mahlon Haines, Elizabeth his wife and 4 minor children Mary Ann, Maria, Clayton and Lydia Haines to Pilesgrove New Jersey.

1/3/1817 Deborah Keerans for self and 4 children, Anna Starr Rebecca, Samuel, Thomas and Jeremiah Starr Keerans to Sadsbury.

1/3/1817 Ann Saunders (minor) to Kennett.

2/28/1817 Sarah Russal to New Garden.

4/4/1817 Martha Wiley to Bradford.

5/2/1817 Elizabeth Ellison to Phila for the Northern District.

5/2/1817 Joseph Woodrow, wife Deborah and children Mary Ann, Rachel, Martha, Levi and Joseph to Chester.

5/2/1817 Joel Zane and wife Esther to Phila for the Northern District.

5/30/1817 Elizabeth P Sellars, having removed to reside with her husband to Darby.

7/4/1817 Samuel Hadley, (a minor) to London Grove.

7/4/1817 Hannah Briggs and six minor children, Deborah, Sarah, Isaac, Elizabeth, Margaret and Wm, Henry to Indian Spring.

7/4/1817 Mary Brooke Briggs to Indian Spring.

8/1/1817 Pindar Antrim to Chesterfield New Jersey.

8/1/1817 Joseph Ford to New Garden.

8/1/1817 Thomas Curle to London Grove.

8/1/1817 Elizabeth Lea (a minor residing with her father James Lea at Pittsburg,) to Redstone.

8/29/1817 Samuel Marot, (residing at Hamiltonville) to Phila for the Western District.

8/29/1817 Peter Mason to Center.

10/3/1817 Parker Askew Jr to Plainfield Ohio.

10/3/1817 Susannah Bartlett (a minor who now resides with her father) to Third Haven Maryland.

10/31/1817 James Wickersham to Redstone.

11/28/1817 Edward Needles to Baltimore for the Western District.

11/28/1817 Joseph Seal to Phila for the Southern District, returning.

11/28/1817 Mary Bassett to Duck Creek.

11/28/1817 George Bolton Lownes to Frankford.

1/30/1818 Cyrus N. Jones to Redstone. Cert. sent back: he not found.

2/27/1818 Mary Gause and eight minor children, Levi, William B., Lavinia, Ruth Anna, Lea W., Saml., Bayard and Washington to Kennett.

4/3/1818 Samuel Curle to New Garden (returning).

4/3/1818 Abigail Yearsley to Stillwater (removed with her husband).

5/1/1818 Sarah L. Gilpin to Frankford.

5/1/1818 Hannah James Gilpin to Frankford.

5/29/1818 Mary Sheward for self and three minor children, Ann, William and Isaac Garrett Sheward to Londongrove Monthly Meeting.

7/3/1818 Joseph Atherton to Phila for the Western District.

7/3/1818 Samuel Gause to Kennet (sent back by Kennet).

7/3/1818 Samuel S Gilpin to Cedar Creek, Virginia.

7/3/1818 Thomas Spackman's son George (a minor and apprentice) to Phila for the Northern District.

7/3/1818 Isaac Briggs to Bridgewater New York.

7/3/1818 Martha Buckingham to Center Monthly Meeting (removed with her husband).

7/3/1818 Henry Dickinson, wife Hannah and infant son Joseph to Sadsbury.

7/31/1818 Mary Worth Smith (a minor residing with her uncle Micajah Spackman) to Concord.

7/31/1818 Thomas Wickersham, Sarah his wife and minor son Elijah to Redstone.

7/31/1818 Hannah Pusey (having removed to reside with her husband) to Center.

9/4/1818 Mary Hope, (having removed to reside with her husband) to Chester.

9/4/1818 Ann J Hull, to Baltimore for the Eastern District.

10/2/1818 Rachel Tatum to Cincinnati Ohio.

10/2/1818 William Bane (a minor) to Center.

10/30/1818 Samuel Gause, to Center Monthly Meeting.

10/30/1818 William Coale, to Deer Creek.

12/4/1818 John Ferris, (a minor and apprentice) to Phila Southern District.

12/4/1818 William Shipley Poole (a minor) to Phila for the Northern District.

12/4/1818 Elizabeth Robinson, to Green Street, Phila to reside with husband.

1/1/1819 Stephen Stapler, wife Sarah, and minor children Mary and Rebecca to New Garden.

1/29/1819 Abraham V Mattson, to Baltimore for Western District.

1/29/1819 Sarah Heillman, to Salem.

2/26/1819 Samuel C Spackman, to Green Street Monthly Meeting.

2/26/1819 Mary L Betts (a minor) to Phila.

2/26/1819 Nathan Bassett's son Mark Bassett (a minor) to Egg Harbor.

4/2/1819 Elizabeth D Sheward, (who has removed with her husband and settled at Zanesville) to Stillwater Ohio.

4/30/1819 Margaret Raisin, to Nottingham.

4/30/1819 Isaac Wilkinson, to Nottingham.

4/30/1819 Thomas Commons, to Cincinnati.

4/30/1819 Ann Wilkinson, (a minor) to Sadsbury.

4/30/1819 Jane Webb, to Sadsbury.

4/30/1819 William Mendenhall, to New Garden.

4/30/1819 James Dawson, to North West Fork Monthly Meeting.

4/30/1819 John George, to Green Street Phila.

6/4/1819 Mary Warner, to Baltimore.

7/2/1819 Thomas I Hull, to Baltimore.

7/2/1819 Alexander McKever, wife Lydia and three minor children, Mary, Hannah and Eliza to Kennet.

7/30/1819 George Winslow to Windham Maine.

7/30/1819 Sarah Reed, having removed with her husband, to Darby Creek Monthly meeting Ohio.

9/3/1819 Sarah Ferris (a minor) to Kennett.

3/31/1820 Alexander Dirkin, to New Garden.

3/31/1820 Amasa Baker, wife Sarah and five minor children George H, John Y, Mary, Joseph and Nathan to Chester.

3/31/1820 Palmer Chamberlin, to New Garden.

4/28/1820 Rebecca Russel, to Alexandria.

6/2/1820 Charles Betts, to Concord, PA.

6/2/1820 Ann Humphreys, to Duck Creek.

6/2/1820 Rebecca Wilkinson, (a minor) to Darby.

6/30/1820 Robert Cain, to Phila for the Northern District.

8/4/1820 Charles Sanders, to Phila.

8/4/1820 Mary Jeanes, to Gwynedd.

9/1/1820 John L Gilpin to Chester.

9/1/1820 Robert Churchman to Chester.

9/1/1820 Caroline Price, a minor to Darby.

11/3/1820 Evan Price, a minor to Darby.

12/1/1820 Isaac Lamb, wife Rachel, and two minor children, John Emerson and Philina E Lamb to Baltimore for the Western District.

12/29/1820 Ann Pancoast, having removed to reside with her husband, to Darby.

12/29/1820 William Wetherald, a minor, who is placed as an apprentice with Thomas Marshall, to Concord.

12/29/1820 John Wetherald, to Muncy.

12/29/1820 George Wetherald, wife Joanna and children Catherine, Joseph, Mary, Henry, George, James and Joanna to Muncy.

12/29/1820 Jane Wetherald, to Concord.

2/2/1821 Isaac S Dixon, a minor to Philadelphia, who is placed as an apprentice with Timothy Abbott.

3/2/1821 Rececca Reynolds, to Phila.

3/30/1821 Daniel Megear to Duck Creek.

3/30/1821 Mary Saunders to Goshen.

3/30/1821 Martha Dilworth to Concord.

5/4/1821 Lydia Chandler, having removed to reside with her husband, to Kennett.

5/4/1821 Rachel Beaty, to Concord.

5/4/1821 Ann Denny and children Elizabeth, Sarah, William, Samuel and Daniel to Duck Creek.

5/4/1821 Phillip Millington Steel, to Nottingham.

6/1/1821 Rachel Hayes, to Philadelphia.

6/29/1821 William Alrichs, to New Garden.

8/3/1821 Elen Sanders, to Goshen.

8/3/1821 Rachel Quimby to Purchase Monthly Meeting. New York

9/1/1821 William Ferris, a minor, to Richland, apprentice.

9/28/1821 Rachel Snow to North West Fork.

11/2/1821 Elizabeth Downing to Bradford.

11/2/1821 Mary Downing and her son Richard Thomas Downing to Bradford.

1/4/1822 Hannah Jackson to Phila for the Northern District.

5/3/1822 Reuben Webb, wife Sarah and two minor children John Jones Webb and
Elizabeth Webb, to Phila for the Northern District.

5/3/1822 John Banes Jr. to Frankford.

5/2/1822 John Beeson Baynes, wife Miriam and their five minor children
Thomas, Fanny, John, James and Joseph Priestman Baynes to Concord.

6/28/1822 Jesse P. Richards to Phila.

8/30/1822 Hannah Stapler to Baltimore.

10/4/1822 Thomas Curle to Birmingham.

10/4/1822 James S. Peters. Mary D. his wife and minor children Dell P. Peters
and Hannah P. to Concord.

10/4/1822 Edward Needles to Baltimore.

11/29/1822 Thomazin Downing to Uwchlan.

11/29/1822 Anne Embree to Phila for the Western District.

1/3/1823 William Gilpin to Phila for the Southern District.

1/31/1823 Rachel Battin, removed to reside with her husband, to Moncey
Monthly Meeting.

1/31/1823 Osborn Reynolds (a minor) to Phila.

4/4/1823 Thomas Lea Jr. and Elizabeth his wife, with their seven children,
George, Edward, James, Sarah, Martha, Thomas and Mary to Sandy Spring,
Maryland.

5/30/1823 Adrianna Physick to Monthly Meeting of Carmarthenshire and
Glamorganshire, South Wales Great Britain.

7/4/1823 Mary Wilson (having removed to reside with her husband) to Duck
Creek.

7/4/1823 Daniel Byrnes, Esther his wife and three minor children Jonathan,
Elenor and Jacob F. Brynes to Nottingham.

8/29/1823 Lydia Way to Kennett.

8/29/1823 Isaac Pennock, wife Martha and children Sarah L, Martha W, Ann
Elizabeth, Mary Ann and George W. Pennock to Fallowfield.

8/29/1823 Jemima Morton Walters (a minor) to Green St. Phila.

8/29/1823 James Bringhurst to Phila for the Northern District.

10/3/1823 Samuel Richards, wife Ann and minor son Frederick Burge Richards,
to Bristol England.

10/3/1823 John Yarnall to Phila.

10/3/1823 James Baynes, wife Elizabeth and nine minor children Hannah, John,

Fanny, Thomas Priestman, Elizabeth, Mary, Miriam, Beeson and Alice Baynes, to Concord.

10/31/1823 Margaret Ellison to Phila.

10/31/1823 Thomas Hoopes to Phila.

11/28/1823 Isaac Warner to Green Plain, Ohio. Removed long since.

11/28/1823 Kirkbride Eastborn to Chesterfield New Jersey.

11/28/1823 Mary Hanson, (having moved with her husband) for herself and three minor children. Ann Poltney, John Poltney and Elizabeth .Hanson to Baltimore.

11/28/1823 Caleb Pusey wife Susanna and their son Joshua W Pusey to Phila.

1/2/1824 Sarah Bonsall to Darby.

1/30/1824 James Mitchell (a minor) to London Grove.

1/30/1824 Samuel Eastburn, wife Huldah and three minor children Lewis, Ellwood S. and Maria Ann Eastburn, to Falls, Bucks County.

1/30/1824 Sarah Stapler (widow of Stephen) and minor child Rebecca to Nottingham. A daughter Mary came with her parents to Wilmington some years ago.

2/27/1824 Joseph Breare (a minor) to London Grove.

2/27/1824 Howard Mitchell (a minor) to Wrightstown Bucks County, PA.

4/2/1824 Robert Hains to Nottingham.

4/2/1824 Robert Hurnard, wife Hannah and three minor children William Clark, Ann and James Hurnard to Coggeshall or any other meeting of friends in Great Britain. (61 signers).

4/30/1824 James Robinson (a minor) to Nottingham.

4/30/1824 Joseph Paxson (being about to proceed in marriage) to Horsham.

4/30/1824 Marshall Lowns Pennock to London Grove.

4/30/1824 Evan Lewis, wife Sidney Ann and three minor children James, Edward and Enoch to Nottingham.

4/30/1824 Joseph Seal (a minor) to Phila.

4/30/1824 Alice Pennock (wife of John) to London Grove.

4/30/1824 Walter Mitchell a minor to London Grove.

4/30/1824 Deborah Marot (having removed to reside with her husband) to Phila for the Northern District.

4/30/1824 David Eastborn to Falls, Bucks Co.

4/30/1824 Mahlon Eastborn to Falls, Bucks Co.

4/30/1824 Hannah Eastborn to Falls, Bucks Co.

4/30/1824 Macre Eastborn, to Falls, Bucks Co PA.

4/30/1824 Ruth Eastborn, to Falls, Bucks Co PA, a minor,

Jonathan Eastborn, and two minor sons William and Josiah, to Falls, Bucks Co.

4/30/1824 Louisa Webster, to Center.

4/30/1824 Ruth M Pennock, to London Grove.

7/2/1824 Julian Price (a minor) to New Garden.

7/30/1824 Benjamin Curle (a minor) to Birmingham.

7/30/1824 Achsah Walton, to Middleton Ohio.

9/3/1824 Alexander Dirkin to London Grove.

10/1/1824 Isaac Potts Rowland and Joseph Rowland (minors) to Radnor.

10/29/1824 Ellen Rowland to Radnor.

10/29/1824 Ruth Rowland to Radnor.

10/29/1824 Ann Rowland to Radnor.

10/29/1824 Joanna Rowland to Radnor.

12/31/1824 John Mitchell to Darby.

12/31/1824 Mary L Ballance, (having removed to reside with her husband) to Little Britain.

2/4/1825 Sally Canby to Nottingham.

2/4/1825 Beulah Bassett to Duck Creek.

3/4/1825 Joseph Wetherald (a minor) to Muncy.

3/4/1825 Joseph Plumly, to New Garden.

3/4/1825 Lemuel D Hull to Baltimore.

3/4/1825 Lydia S Richards to New Garden to reside with her husband.

3/4/1825 George Buck to Byberry.

3/4/1825 Henry D Gilpin to Phila for the Southern District.

3/4/1825 Edward T Warner (a minor) to Phila Western District.

3/4/1825 George, Charles, Benjamin and Mary Buck, minor children of George Buck, to Darby.

3/4/1825 George W Carpenter to Bradford.

4/1/1825 Thomas Bonsall, Susan his wife and their infant son Caleb J Bonsall to Sadsbury.

6/3/1825 George Buck to Radnor.

7/1/1825 Hannah Gilpin to Phila for the Western District.

7/1/1825 Elizabeth Poultney to Baltimore.

12/2/1825 Thomas L Bonsall to Phila.

3/3/1826 James Robinson (a minor) to Frankford.

2/3/1826 Jefferson Hough to Baltimore for Western District.

2/3/1826 Josiah Bassett to Egg Harbor.

3/3/1826 Mira Haines to Nottingham.

3/3/1826 James Cox to Abington.

3/3/1826 James Pancoast to Green Street Phila.

3/31/1826 Charles Denny to Duck Creek.

4/28/1826 Joseph Atherton to Green Street Phila.

6/2/1826 Grace S Mitchell to Darby.

6/30/1826 Amy Baily to Birmingham

8/4/1826 Rebecca Russel to Indian Spring

8/4/1826 Samuel Canby Norton (minor) to Phila. for Southern District

9/1/1826 Jerimiah Hartley (minor) to Phila.

11/3/1826 Samuel Bancroft to Chester

11/3/1826 John Bancroft and Elizabeth his wife, with their eight minor children,

Margaret, Sarah, Thomas, William, Edward, Esther, Martha, and Harvey to Chester.

11/3/1826 Amy Reynolds to Nottingham

11/3/1826 Rebecca Bancroft to Chester

12/1/1826 Joseph R Eastburn to Phila for Northern District

12/1/1826 Mary Eastburn to New Garden

2/2/1827 Mary Phillips to Center

3/2/1827 Sarah Ann Mitchell (minor) to Abington

3/2/1827 Philena P Swayne (minor) to Birmingham

3/2/1827 David Tatum (minor) to Phila.

3/2/1827 John Burne to Nottingham

3/30/1827 Enoch and Lydia Lewis to Phila for S District with five minor ch William, Alice, Charles, John, and Henry

3/30/1827 Hannah Lewis to Philadelphia S. Dist

5/4/1827 Samuel C Betts and wife Grace and four minor children Richard Kinsey, Alice Eliza, William C, and Sarah H Betts to Phila

5/4/1827 Hannah K Betts to Phila

6/29/1827 Calib Stroud, wife Esther, and seven minor children Margaret, Joshua, Martha, Elizabeth, William A, Mary, and Sarah, to Uwchlan

6/29/1827 Joseph Thomas and wife Adriana to Little Britain

6/29/1827 Mary, wife of Joel Fisher, to Chester

8/3/1827 Hannah Saunders, (resides with her husband) to New York Monthly Meeting

8/3/1827 Elizabeth Clark Saunders, to New York Monthly Meeting

8/3/1827 Mary Ann Saunders to New York Monthly Meeting

2/29/1828 Samuel S Griscom to Green St Philadelphia

4/4/1828 Elizabeth Jones to Phila

4/4/1828 Jonathan Lamborn, wife Martha, and children Miriam C, Ruth, Rest, Jonathan, Lewis, Rachel, Rebecca S, and Henry to New Garden

5/2/1828 Thomas and Deborah Spackman and son Chalkley (minor) to Phila, Deborah being a minister

5/2/1828 Anna Spackman, (removed with her parents) to Phila Monthly Meeting

8/29/1828 Mary B Thomas to Phila Monthly Meeting held at Cherry St

8/1/1828 William Robinson to Green St Phila

8/29/1828 Catherine Robinson to Phila held at Cherry St

11/28/1828 Hannah Quimby to Green St Phila & ch Josiah & Latitia (minors)

11/27/1828 Ellen Quimby to Green St Monthly Meeting

11/27/1828 Jane Quimby to Green St Monthly Meeting

1/2/1829 Mary Ferris to Baltimore Monthly Meeting

1/30/1829 John Farris & wife Anna and son Joseph (minor) to Milford Monthly Meeting held at Milton, Indiana

1/30/1829 Edith Ferris, to Milford Monthly Meeting held at Milton, Indiana

1/30/1829 Matthew Ferris, to Milford Monthly Meeting held at Milton, Indiana

1/30/1829 William Ferris, to Milford Monthly Meeting held at Milton, Indiana

2/27/1829 William Lea to Phila Monthly Meeting held at Cherry St

4/3/1829 Mark Kirby, wife Mary and five minor children Ann H, William, Mary, Hanson, Edward, and Elizabeth P to Whitewater Monthly Meeting Indiana

4/3/1829 Joseph Wetherald, wife Mary and seven minor ch Sarah, Haworth, Elizabeth, William, Jonathan H, Mary, and Susanna H, to Cincinnati

5/1/1829 Samuel Fisher to York Monthly Meeting held at York

5/1/1829 Joel Fisher and wife Mary to York Monthly Meeting

7/3/1829 Sarah A Dunn to Nottingham

7/31/1829 Charles Reynolds to Rose St Monthly Meeting held in New York

5/29/1829 Lydia Irwin to White Water, Indiana

5/29/1829 Elizabeth Irwin Jr to White Water, Indiana

9/4/1829 Elizabeth Irwin, wife of John, and her five minor children George W, Alice P, Susan B, Samuel, and Edwin to White Water Monthly Meeting Indiana

1/1/1830 John Irwin to White Water Monthly Meeting, Indiana

2/26/1830 Margaret Mitchell to Buckingham

4/2/1830 Margaret Bane to Phila held at Cherry St

4/2/1830 Margaret Bane Jr to Phila held at Cherry St

4/2/1830 Mary W Bane to Phila held at Cherry St

4/2/1830 Sarah Saunders to Radnor

4/30/1830 Ruth Bonsall to Sadsbury

11/4/1830 Sarah D Davis to Phila Monthly Meeting held at Cherry St

5/4/1830 William Thistlethwait and Elizabeth, his wife to White Water Monthly Meeting held at Richmond, Indiana, and their six minor children Eleanor, John, George, Timothy, Thomas, and Mary Bane.

7/2/1830 Francis Henry Reynolds (minor) to New York

7/2/1830 Thomas Jewett to New York Monthly Meeting

9/3/1830 George Kay and Cela his wife to New Garden

10/29/1830 Mercy L. Peirce, (having removed to reside with her husband) to New York Monthly Meeting

10/29/1830 Sarah Peirce to New York Monthly Meeting

12/31/1830 Hannah M Parker to Goshen, held at Willistown

3/4/1831 William Coarse to Baltimore for Western District

3/10/1831 Anna Poole to Darby

4/1/1831 Lewis Mason (minor) to London Grove (note under date: adj on 7th of 4 mo)

4/29/1831 Thomas Conard to Green St, Phila

7/1/1831 Elizabeth Robinson to Green, Phila

7/1/1831 Rebecca Stapler (minor) to Nottingham

9/2/1831 James S Gibbons to Phila Monthly Meeting held at Cherry St

9/2/1831 Francis and Hanson Robinson, minor sons of Elizabeth Robinson to Green St Monthly Meeting, Phila

9/2/1831 Alfred Pierce, a minor, to New York Monthly Meeting

12/30/1831 Margaret Kinsey, (having removed to reside with her husband) and five minor children, Nathaniel F, Samuel, Elizabeth, John W, and Margaret Ann Kinsey to Goshen Monthly Meeting held at Willistown

2/3/1832 Edward Squibb (minor) to Darby

3/2/1832 Ezra Hoopes, wife Ann, and infant son William Warner Hoopes to Phila Monthly Meeting held at Cherry St

3/2/1832 Franklin W Clement to Phila Monthly Meeting held at Cherry St

3/2/1832 Josiah Bassett (minor) to Phila Monthly Meeting held at Cherry St

3/2/1832 John Warner to Phila Monthly Meeting held at Cherry St

3/2/1832 Ann Wetherald to Phila Monthly Meeting held at Cherry St

3/2/1832 Mary Breaer to Phila Monthly Meeting held at Green St

3/2/1832 Joseph Breaer to Phila Monthly Meeting held at Green St

3/2/1832 James Corse to New York

3/2/1832 William Corse to New York

3/30/1832 Benjamin Hartley to Center Monthly Meeting

3/30/1832 James Cook to London Grove

3/30/1832 William Bassett to Phila held at Cherry St

3/30/1832 Henry Hoopes to Uwchlan

5/4/1832 Eli Heald to Phila held at Cherry St

5/4/1832 Thomas J. Squibb to Phila held at Cherry St

6/1/1832 Margaret Johnson to Waynesville, Ohio

6/1/1832 Ann Johnson to Waynesville, Ohio

6/1/1832 Robert Johnson to Waynesville, Ohio

6/1/1832 Joseph Johnson to Waynesville, Ohio

6/1/1832 Israel Saunders to New York

6/29/1832 Nathaniel T.[or F.] Kinsey (a minor) to Richland Bucks Co.

6/29/1832 William Robinson to Phila Monthly Mtg held at Green St

8/3/1832 Susanna Robinson to Phila Monthly Mtg held at Green St

8/31/1832 Elizabeth Martin to Phila Monthly Mtg held at Green St

8/31/1832 Rebecca Russell to Sandy Spring Maryland

11/2/1832 Thomas J Megear to Phila Monthly Mtg held at Cherry St

11/2/1832 Elihu Pedrick (a minor)

11/2/1832 Elizabeth Jefferis to Phila Monthly Mtg held at Cherry St

11/30/1832 Enoch Passmore to Kennett

1/4/1833 James Coarse to Deer Creek

3/1/1833 Albanus R Swayne (a minor) to Birmingham

3/1/1833 Lindley Smith (a minor) to Phila held at Cherry St

3/1/1833 Charles Gilpin to Phila Monthly Mtg held at Cherry St

3/1/1833 Oliver Canby to Sadsbury Monthly Mtg

3/1/1833 Benjamin Betts (a minor) to Londongrove

3/1/1833 John Robinson (a minor) to Kennett

3/1/1833 William P Swayne (a minor) to Londongrove

3/1/1833 Mary Wood to Gwynedd

3/1/1833 Mary Saunders to Radnor

1/3/1833 William P Gibbons to Phila Monthly Mtg held at Cherry St

3/29/1833 William Mason (a minor) to Woodbury

3/29/1833 Mary R Mason (a minor) to Woodbury

5/31/1833 Mary Williamson to Concord

5/31/1833 Rachel Wilkinson Jr to Darby

5/31/1833 Daniel Byrnes, wife Esther, and minor son Jacob F. to Buckingham

5/31/1833 Eleanor Byrnes to Buckingham

6/28/1833 Hannah George to Radnor to reside with husband

2/28/1834 Joseph Preston to Sadsbury

4/4/1834 Huson Swayne to Phila held at Spruce St

5/2/1834 Elizabeth Ann Adams to Kennett

5/2/1834 Elias H. Hayhurst to Makefield (a minor)

7/4/1834 Lewis G. Mason to Salem (a minor)

8/29/1834 Eliza Taylor to Phila Monthly Meeting held at Cherry Street.

10/3/1834 William Marshall wife Margaret and two minor children William and Susan Jane to Kennett

10/3/1834 Elizabeth Messek (a minor) to Cecil Monthly Mtg

10/31/1834 Sarah Bonsal to Darby

1/30/1835 Martha Lukens to Phila held at Cherry St

1/30/1835 Elizabeth Trump and minor children Judith B and Elias H. Trump to Phila held at Spruce St

5/1/1835 Joseph Priestman Baynes to Concord

5/1/1835 Lydia Seal to Kennett

5/1/1835 Ann Denny to Camden

5/1/1835 Sarah Denny to Camden

5/29/1835 Mary W. Chalfant (removed to settle with her husband) for self and minor child Sarah K.Betts to Kennett

5/29/1835 Mary White to Green St Monthly Mtg Phila

5/29/1835 Elizabeth White to Green St Monthly Mtg Phila

7/31/1835 Robert Squibb (a minor) to Darby

10/2/1835 Hannah Price to Phila held at Cherry St

10/30/1835 Isaac Jackson to Green St Monthly Mtg Phila

10/30/1835 Joseph B. Sheppard to Green St. Monthly Mtg Phila (a minor)

12/4/1835 Joseph G. Rowland to Spruce St. Monthly Mtg Phila also his four minor children Ann Johns, Charles, Sarah and Joseph G Rowland

1/1/1836 Charles Gibbons to Spruce St. Monthly Mtg Phila. [This was directed to the wrong mtg and was returned and another directed to Cherry St.]

4/1/1836 Hannah Baker (having removed to reside with her husband) to Fallowfield

6/3/1836 George Burge and wife Sarah to Bristol Monthly Meeting or any other in Great Britain, being about to remove from amongst us and return to their native land.

6/3/1836 Elizabeth Burge, (proposing to remove from amongst us and to return with her parents to England), to Bristol Monthly Meeting or any other Monthly Meeting of Friends in Great Britain.

7/29/1836 Samuel J Rowland, Mary L his wife and their two minor children Rebecca Mifflin and Thomas Fisher Rowland, to Cherry St Phila

7/29/1836 Rachel Squibb to Chester

9/2/1836 Elizabeth Jones to Cherry St Phila

9/2/1836 Elizabeth Hartley to Cherry St Phila (to reside with her husband.)

11/4/1836 Lewis Bonsal (minor) to Spruce St Phila

12/2/1836 Martha Bartram Bonsal to Darby

[no day or month given]/1836 Mary Bonsal and 5 minor children Mary L, Eleanor Harrison, Hannah Bunting, Vincent Philip, and John L Bonsal, to Darby

12/30/1836 Edward T Richardson to New Garden

2/3/1837 Jonathan Pennel to Concord

6/2/1837 Mary Squibb to Green St Monthly Meeting Phila

6/2/1837 Joseph C Grubb to Phila Monthly Meeting held at Cherry St

6/30/1837 George Grubb (minor) to New Garden

8/4/1837 William Cranston, wife Mary, and six minor children, Ann Pennock, Philina, Mary Marshall, Hannah Cope, Simon Sherlock, and Sarah Elizabeth Cranston to Londongrove.

9/1/1837 Joseph Pedrick to Phila Monthly Meeting held at Cherry St

9/29/1837 George Bush Jr (minor) to Concord

12/1/1837 Lydia W Gilpin to Phila Monthly Meeting Spruce St (having removed with her husband.)

12/29/1837 Jacob Carpenter to Cincinnati, Ohio

2/2/1838 Hannah McAlister, (having removed with her husband) to New Garden

3/2/1838 Joshua Barker and wife Phebe to Phila Spruce St

3/2/1838 Mary Barker (having removed to reside with her parents) to Monthly Meeting held at Spruce St Phila

3/30/1838 Mary Platt Jr to Monthly Meeting held at Spruce St Phila

5/4/1838 Hannah Woodward to Londongrove

5/4/1838 Hannah Woodward Jr to Londongrove

5/4/1838 Hester Woodward to Londongrove

5/4/1838 Lydia Woodward to Londongrove

8/3/1838 John Morton Poole, to Darby

8/9/1838 Ann Denny's ("requests for her" crossed out) daughter, Elizabeth Collins Denny to Green St Monthly Meeting.

8/9/1838 Ann Denny's ("requests for her" crossed out) Mary Sinclair Denny, to Green St Monthly Meeting (a minor)

8/9/1838 Elizabeth Osborn Reynolds, to Phila Monthly Meeting, Cherry St

9/9/1838 Isaac Dixon (minor) to Phila Monthly Meeting Spruce St

8/9/1838 Asenath Wilson, and minor children Susanna C, and Lydia T Wilson to

Kennett

8/3/1838 Ezer Lamborn to Center

8/9/1838 Hannah Gause, to Bradford

8/28/1838 Samuel Cranston, to Center

11/13/1838 Sarah Sharon, to Salem (removed to reside with her husband.)

1/4/1839 Richard Kirby, wife Mary and minor son Henry, to Pilesgrove Monthly Meeting

1/4/1839 John Elliott's minor children Rebecca M, Sarah, Wm Edwin, and Esterina Elliot to Waynesville, Ohio

2/1/1839 Elizabeth Eastburn for herself and four minor children Samuel, Sarah, Margaret, and Oliver Eastburn to New Garden.

2/1/1839 Rebecca Lloyd to New Garden

2/1/1839 Elizabeth Eastburn Jr to New Garden

2/1/1839 Isaac Eastburn to New Garden

2/1/1839 David Eastburn to New Garden

3/29/1839 William P Gibbons, wife Mary and minor son Robinson Gibbons to Oswego New York.

3/29/1839 Catharine, Anna, Elizabeth, and Susanna Robinson to Oswego, N. Y.

4/26/1839 Mary E Buckingham to New Garden, to reside with husband

7/26/1839 Edward Ferris, a minor, to Cherry St Monthly Meeting Phila

7/26/1839 Martha T Wright removed with husband to Cherry St Monthly Meeting Phila

9/27/1839 Samuel Smith, wife Sarah and seven minor children, Levi Watson, Rebecca E, Gulielma Maria, Abigail H, Percival Roscoe, Samuel Dillwyn, and Sarah Cornelia to Oswego.

9/27/1839 Harriet Amelia Gause to Kennet

10/25/1839 William P Megear to Camden, Delaware

12/27/1839 John Bancroft Jr, Susanna his wife and four minor children Napoleon, Margaret, Joseph W, Thomas B, to Cherry St, Phila

1/24/1840 Rachel W Oakford (who has removed to reside with her husband) to Darby

3/27/1840 Joseph Lukins to Chester

4/24/1840 Elizabeth Ferris Smyth to Spruce St Monthly Meeting Phila having removed to reside with her husband

5/29/1840 William Johnson to London Grove

7/24/1840 Esther Brown to Nottingham

8/28/1840 William Gilpin to Cherry St Monthly Meeting Phila

8/28/1840 James Green to Bradford

8/28/1840 Rebecca Jane Lamborn to Kennett

8/28/1840 Susannah Hayhurst to Birmingham

8/28/1840 Adrianna Physic to Nottingham

9/25/1840 Martha Hayhurst (having removed to reside with her husband) and three minor children Warner Mifflin, Samuel, and Elizabeth to Birmingham.

10/23/1840 Thomas Hayhurst Jr. (minor) to Buckingham

10/23/1840 William Johnson's ("requests for his" crossed out) daughter Sarah T (minor) to London Grove

11/27/1840 William Swayne (minor) to Londongrove

2/26/1841 Priscilla Jeanes to New Garden

4/23/1841 Hannah Grubb to Spruce St Monthly Meeting Phila

4/23/1841 Elizabeth Grubb to Spruce St Monthly Meeting Phila

6/25/1841 Mary Anna Paschal to Darby (removed to reside with her husband.)

6/25/1841 Rachel Clendenin to Muncy

6/25/1841 Eleanor Jeffries to Little Britain

11/26/1841 Edwin Hayhurst (minor) to Kennett

11/26/1841 Thomas Hayhurst Jr (minor) to Buckingham

11/26/1841 Jerimiah Hayhurst to Oswego

12/24/1841 Martha, (wife of James Baynes) and their five minor children Mary, John Beeson, George Burge, Sarah C, and James P Baynes to Baltimore

2/25/1842 Anna Smith to Green St. Monthly Meeting

3/25/1842 Hannah E Bonsall, (minor) to Darby

3/25/1842 Mary W Bonsall to Makefield

4/22/1842 James A Bonsall, a minor to Darby

4/22/1842 David Ferris to Little Falls

4/22/1842 William and Edward Ferris, minors to Little Falls.

5/27/1842 Jonathan Bartram to Bradford

6/24/1842 Henry Garrett (minor) to Darby

6/24/1842 Elizabeth C Tatum to Cherry St Monthly Meeting Phila

7/29/1842 John Woodward to Baltimore

7/29/1842 Owen D Gause (minor) to Marlborough

7/29/1842 Thomas C Hollingsworth to Cherry St Monthly Meeting

8/26/1842 Woolman J Shepherd (minor) to Spruce St

9/23/1842 Samuel Marshall to Spruce St Monthly Meeting

11/25/1842 Sarah H Way to Green St Monthly Meeting

11/25/1842 Elwood Garrett for self, Catharine W, his wife and their two minor children Charles Alfred and Howard Garrett to Little Falls Monthly Meeting

6/23/1843 Ann Pusey to Oxford

6/23/1843 Mary J Pusey to Oxford

8/25/1843 Benjamin Ferris, wife Hannah to Little Falls Harford Co Maryland

8/25/1843 Deborah Ferris to Little Falls

8/25/1843 Anna M Ferris to Little Falls

8/25/1843 Martha Ferris to Little Falls

8/25/1843 Margaret Ann Brinton, (having removed to reside with her husband Moses Brinton) to Pennsgrove

9/22/1843 Ann Armstrong to Makefield

9/22/1843 William H Sheward to Centre

9/22/1843 Sarah W Baynes for self and four minor children Miriam P, John

Haworth, Mary W, and William W to Baltimore

9/22/1843 Henry Gibbons for self, wife Martha P, and their four minor children Emelie, Rebecca D, Henry, and William Poole Gibbons to Spruce St Monthly Meeting Phila

10/27/1843 Jane G Moore to Kennett

10/27/1843 Charlotte Atkinson and her minor son Francis Fenelow Atkinson, to Cecil, Maryland (misdirected)

2/23/1844 Charlotte Atkinson (wife of Samuel C Atkinson,) with their minor son Francis Fenelow Atkinson to Baltimore Western District.

4/26/1844 Mary Woodward to Baltimore for Western District

5/24/1844 William P Hollingsworth to Spruce St Phila

6/28/1844 Samuel S Dixon to Darby

8/23/1844 Sarah Buckman to Green St Phila (having removed with her husband)

1/24/1845 Mary D Hollingsworth to Spruce St. Monthly Meeting

2/21/1845 Rebecca Matson to Spruce St. Phila

3/28/1845 Mary W Ferris (who has removed to reside with her husband) to Little Falls Md

4/25/1845 William S Poole for himself and children Sarah and Mary to Concord

10/25/1845 Rodman Gibbons (minor) to Spruce St Phila

10/24/1845 Thomas Hopkins, wife Martha M, and six minor children William T, Elizabeth E, Charles E, Martha V, Hetty A, and Edward E to Makefield, Bucks Co.

10/24/1845 Eliza Ann Henderson, having removed to reside with her husband, Joseph Henderson, to Birmingham Monthly Mtg

11/28/1845 Sarah R Wilkinson, (having removed to reside with her husband) to London Grove

1/23/1846 Margaret Bane, to New Garden

1/23/1846 Mary W Wilkinson (who has removed to reside with her husband Nathaniel Wilkinson) to New Garden

4/24/1846 Abraham Lawton, wife Sarah, and four minor children, Elizabeth, Esther B, John and Naomi to Green St Phila

5/29/1846 Rachel Forward to Concord

5/29/1846 William M Thomas to Green St Phila

6/26/1846 Daniel C Denny to Nottingham

5/29/1846 Francis Robinson to Baltimore

5/29/1846 Lea Pusey to Centre

10/23/1846 Alfred Thomas to Bybory

2/26/1847 Susanna N Wetherald to Little Falls Monthly Mtg

7/28/1848 John Kendall to Milford Monthly Mtg held at Milton Ind[iana]

6/25/1847 Jesse Kendall wife Maria G and two minor children Mary and James Kendall to Milford Monthly Mtg

6/25/1847 Eliza Kendall (having removed with her parents) to Milford Monthly Mtg

10/29/1847 Evans I [or J.?] Pusey to Londongrove

4/28/1848 Selah Kay for self and two minor children, Thomas and Selah Ann Kay to New Garden

5/26/1848 Elizabeth Ann Kirby to Pilesgrove

5/26/1848 Martha Kirby to Pilesgrove

11/24/1848 Elizabeth M Davis, (having removed to reside with her husband) for herself and two minor children Mary and Rebecca Peart to Radnor.

11/24/1848 Susan P Malin to Kennett

12/29/1848 Thomas Wollaston to New Garden

1/26/1849 Lydia B Paxson to Cherry St Phila

1/26/1849 Leah L Magilligan (residing with her husband) to Kennett

6/22/1849 Mary E Hood (having removed to reside with her husband) to Pennsgrove

7/27/1849 Eliza Taylor to Spruce St Phila

10/26/1849 William Sellers and wife Mary F to Green St Phila

10/26/1849 Jacob F Byrnes to Cherry St Phila

10/26/1849 Eliza Armstrong to Londongrove

10/26/1849 Martha Gause to Chester

10/26/1849 Francis Gibbons (minor) to Spruce St Phila

10/26/1849 Mary Wetherald and dau Anna (minor) to Little Falls

11/23/1849 Hibbert Garrett (minor) to Goshen

11/23/1849 Isaac Wollaston to New Garden

11/23/1849 Isaac Quimby to New Garden

2/22/1850 Sarah Lovering to Spruce St Phila

8/23/1850 Hannah Oakford to Green St Phila

8/23/1850 Elizabeth P Grubb for herself and minor children Samuel S and Anna E Grubb to Cherry St Phila

10/25/1850 Thomas M Ferris, a minor to Spruce St Phila

10/25/1850 John Betts, wife Phebe and three minor children Ephraim W, Mary Dorothea, and Charles W Betts, to Green St, Phila

12/27/1850 Elizabeth C Lippincott (having removed to reside with her husband) Joseph Z Lippincott) to Woodbury

Church Records of
Pencader Presbyterian Church
1718-1825

List of Elders
Mar. 13, 1717 Justice David Evans May 8, 1718 William Williams
May 11, 1726 David Howel Sept. 17, 1735 Samuel James
May 9, 1746 Simon James May 27, 1747 Thomas James
May 25, 1748 Nath'l Williams Aug. 2, 1796 John Vail*
Oct. 3, 1797 James Porter 1807 David Smith
1807 Peter Williams 1807 Henry Robinson
1807 Alex. Canvender 1807 Samuel Murphy
July 14, 1816 William Watson July 14, 1816 Seth Stewart
July 14, 1816 Thomas J Clark Nov. 3, 1823 Frisby Henderson
Nov.3, 1823 James McCollough 1833 Jacob Faris
May 2, 1835 Robert Cann
*Possibly an elder of Middletown

Marriage Records
Nov. 8, 1796 Stuart, Benjamin and Biddle, Mary
Dec. 22, 1796 Higgins, David and Wallace, Rachel
Dec. 29, 1796 Johnson, Wm. and Martin, Alice
Feb. 2, 1797 Faris, Wm. and Huckel, Elana
Feb. 2, 1797 Bradey, Samuel and Warnock, Elenor
March 13, 1797 Price, John and Bouldin, Ann of Back Cr., Cecil Co.
March 13, 1797 Bensance, Phillip and Andras, Mary of St. Georges Hd.
March 29, 1797 Murphy, Thomas and Christfield, Eliz. of Kent Co.
April 20, 1797 McHannan, Bejm. and Skeggs, Hetty of Warwick, Kent Co.

Abstracts of selected tombstones of
Welsh Tract Baptist Meeting

Tombstone inscriptions Welsh Tract Baptist Meeting Houses at the foot of Iron
Hill near Newark by Miss Winny Jones. From Records of the Welsh Tract
Baptist Meeting, Pencader Hundred, New Castle County, Delaware,
1701-1828. Published 1904. [Only those prior to 1850 are listed here.]

Fowler, Benjamin P, son of Henry and Susan, d 2/3/1836 in the 31st year of his age

Hugg, Henry, husband of Maria Hugg, d 1841, age 46 years

Hugg, Benjamin, d 11/21/1800

Maxwell, Solomon, Esqr, d 4/19/1798 aged 56 years

Maxwell, Elizabeth d 12/21/1848 aged 85 years

James, Sara wife of James James d Aprel ye 10 1721, aged 56 years.

Price, David d 1722

Price, Eliz d 1712

Adams, James son of Ann Adams b 4/8/1780, d 3/22/1850

Gottier, John d 10/6/1822 in his 49th year of age

Gottier, Elizabeth, wife of John Gottier d 9/1/1804 aged 24 years

Booth, Ebenezer d 2/20/1804 aged 72 years

Adams, Mary A d 1830, aged 25 years

Adams, John W d 1828, aged 27 years

Adams, Levi d 7/31/1819 in the 24th year of his age

Adams, Huntington Aydelott, son of James and Ann Adams d 8/17/1815 aged 3
years, 2 mos and 8 days

John, Thomas d 12/20/1720

Thomas, Mary relict of John Thomas, afterwards of David Clark, d 7/14/1775

Thomas, Thomas d4/9/1781 aged 43 years

Griffith, John d 4/12/1720 aged 23 years

Griffith, Catherine d 2/20/1755

Davis, Esther, wife of Samuel Davis of Philadelphia d 9/17/1795

Shakespeare, David d 9/29/1800 aged 68 years

Gilbert, Mary Ann daughter of Joseph L Gilbert d 3/27/1846

Gilbert, Jesse d 7/26/1844 aged 41 years

Goudy, Mary daughter of Samuel and Susan Shakespear d 4/16/1843 aged 70
years

Clendenin, Maria, wife of Samuel H Clendenin d 3/21/1843 aged 35 years

Griffith, Rebecca b 1810 d 1842

Griffith, John b 1765 d 1837

Hersey, Rachel b 1765 d 1806

McCullough, Rebecca wife of Alexander McCullough d 5/27/1842 aged 41 years

Griffith, John d 1/23/1837 aged 72 years

Griffith, Samuel son of John and Margaret Griffith d 10/30/1833 aged 24 years

Jones, Joanna d 12/15/1795 aged 65 years

Thomas, Sarah wife of Captain Benjamin Thomas d 1/16/1794 aged 51 years

Jones, Elizabeth daughter of Joshua Jones and Rachel his wife d 5/14/1763 aged 5 mos

Jones, John d 3/19/1763 aged 36 years

Delap, Ann d 3/21/1762 aged 36 years

Passmore, Jane daughter of David and Esther Jones d 7/20/1761 aged 44 years

Jones, Eleanor d 9/7/1759 aged 59 years

Jones, Morgan d 6/4/1760 aged 63 years

Jones, David Jun d 12/2/1758 aged 42 years

Jones, Esther d 10/2/1754 aged 76 years

Jones David d 8 /20/1748 aged 80 years

Jones, Esther d 1/10/1800 aged 48 years

James, John d 1/19/1811 aged 59 years

James, Susanna, wife of John James (dec'd) d 3/8/1812 aged 60 years

James, James d 3/8/1755 aged 36 years

Jones, Sarah wife of James Jones d 5/4/1827 aged 37 years

Jones, Morgan d 8/25/1820 aged 62 years 1 mo and 18 days

Jones, Zachariah d 11/1/1834 aged 66 years 1 mo and 16 days

James, Elisha son of Daniel James d 11/23/1728 aged 3

James, Daniel d 1735

James, Sarah daughter of John and Susanna James d 2/17/1819 aged 41 years

James, James d 12/11/1829 aged 42 years

James, Deborah d 12/1/1731 grandfather Daniel James aged 4

Thomas, Reverand M E. d 11/7/1730 aged 56 years

James, Susanna daughter of John and Susanna James and Relict of Benjamin B Bouldin b 4/5/1780 d 10/17/1849 aged 70 years

Davis, Rev'd David d 8/18/1769 aged 62 years

Booth, Margaret Relict of Major Thomas Booth of St. George's Hundred and youngest daughter of the Rev. David Davis. B 6/28/1743 d 12/2/1820 aged 77 years 5 mos and 4 days

Davis, Rees d 11/7/1756 aged 24 years

Miles, James b 3/13/1746 d 6/14/1797 aged 51 years

Miles, Rachel wife of James Miles b 1/7/1755 d 9/1797 aged 42 years and eight months

Glenn, Mary daughter of Thomas and Elizabeth Glenn d 11/1/ 1807 aged 22 years and 6 mos

Booth, Ebenezer d 2/20/1804 aged 72 years

Gottier, Elizabeth wife of John Gottier d 9/1/1804 aged 24 years

Drake, Ann d 8/13/1803 aged 67 years

Wattson, Thomas d 5/9/1730 aged 59 years

Wattson, David d 8/21/1739 aged 5 years

Wattson, John d 11/12/1755 aged 45 years

John, Mary d 12/2/1794 aged 78 years
John, Thomas d 6/27/1720
Wattson, Joseph d2/28/1790 aged 36 years
Watson, Benjamin d 9/18/1830 aged 47 years 4 mos and 14 days
Miles, Margaret wife of Edward Miles d 9/22/1756 aged 45 years
Evans, Mary W wife of Major John R Evans d 3/18/1843 aged 75 years and 5 mos
Stockton, Sarah d 10/26/1838 aged 77 years
Simonton, John d 4/4/1810 aged 34 years
Middleton, Robert d 1/2/1805 aged 12 years and 2 mos
Middleton, Mary wife of Robert Middleton d 8/30/1801 aged 45 years
Wattson, Thomas Esqr d 12/16/1792 aged 55 years
Wattson, Susanna wife of Thomas Wattson Esqr d 1/19/1804 aged 69 years
Wattson, Lewis son of Thomas and Susanna d 3/4/1805 aged 40 years
Wattson, John son of Thomas and Susanna d 10/24/1824 in his 57 year
Lewis, Robert M d 7/19/1790 aged 4 mos
Lewis, Philip d 5/1/1804 aged 57 years and 7 mos
Simonton, John d 7/11/1791 aged 57 years
Simonton, Frances Elizabeth d 10/16/1784 aged 50 years
Lewis, Franklin d 2/22/1814 aged 12 years 5 mos and 13 days
Boggs, Rev'd John d 12/9/1802 in the 63rd year of his age
Edmund, Thomas 7/18/1758 aged 74 years
Price, David 9/20/1736 aged 50 years
Wood, George H d 11/15/1813
Tubbs, Mary Alice d 1/19/1836 aged 48 years
Tubbs, Martha Shields d 1/19/1836 aged 20 years
Tubbs, child of Captain Calvin and Mary Tubbs
Tubbs, Captain Calvin C. J. d 9/7/1838 aged 28 years
Tubbs, Gideon Ferrell d 5/7/1839 aged 20 years 11 mos
Ferrell, Rev'd Gideon d 8/21/1820 in his 58th year of age
Ferrell, Mary Relict of the Rev'd Gideon Ferrell d 1/22/1833 in her 89th year
Jones, Rees Jun d 9/27/1757 aged 25 years
Jones, Sara wife of Reece Jones d 8/11/1747 aged 68 years
Jones, Rees d 11/23/1739 aged 4__ years
Jones, twin sisters Sara and Susanna d 10/7/1730 or 1737 aged 6 mos
Morgan, Rev'd Enoch b. of Mr Abel Morgan Jun S. Wales d 3/25/1740
Eaton, Kezia wife of Isaac Eaton d 5/9/1796 aged 33 years
Thomas, David d 9/29/1748 aged 32 years
Thomas, Richard d 11/20/1753 aged 75 years
Thomas, Catherine wife of Richard Thomas Sein d 1/16/1760
Thomas, Cap't Lewis d 5/10/1761 aged 40 years
Thomas, Mary relict of Cap't Lewis Thomas d 9/9/1774 51 years
Thomas, Richard Junr d 1/15/1762 aged 37 years
Thomas, Mary d 1/20/1762 aged 45 years

Eccles, Samuel d 9/18/1800 aged 51 years

Bouldin, Hannah wife of Benjamin Bouldin and daughter of Robert and Hannah
Shields d 1/22/1801 aged 23 years and 5 mos

Shields, Martha youngest daughter of Robert and Hannah Shields d 10/29/1842

Shields, Susannah daughter of Robert and Hannah Shields d 12/15/1854

Criest, Samuel d 9/29/1764 aged 4 years

Jones, Thomas d 7/19/1764 aged 24 years

Underwood, Ann d 7/30/1845 aged 75 years

McConaughey, William d 6/9/1842 aged 59 years

Law, Elizabeth d 11/10/1837 aged 46 years

Tyson, Mathias Jr d 6/25/1849 in his 54th year

Tyson, Mathias Sen d 3/25/1829 aged 75 years

Tyson, Jane wife of Mathias Tyson d 10/10/1811

Jones, Margaret wife of Isaac Menough d 7/16/1826 aged 66 years

Menough, Isaac d 12/9/1826 aged 79 years

Adair, Robert d 3/24/1843 aged 37 years and 3 mos

Adair, Gilbert Beebee b 6/10/1839 d 6/27/1840

Gottier, Margaret wife of Francis Gottier d 8/30/1820 in Elkton, Maryland aged
73 years

Gottier, Francis d 12/11/1826 aged 79 years

Frances, wife of John Kean, d. 11 Sep 1821, aged 59 years

Newton Kean McCord, son of John and Susan F. McCord, d. 4 Oct 1832, aged 5
years, 1 month, 19 days.

John Kean, d. 31 Aug 1834, aged 60 years

Mary, dau. of John and Mary Green, d. 15 Jan 1826, aged 26 years

Benjamin, son of John and Mary Green, d. 1 Oct 1825, aged 18 years

John Green, d. 22 June 1825, in 55th year of his age

Patrick Coulter, d. 9 June 1848 in 84th year of his age

Martha, wife of Patrick Coulter, b. 9 June 1769, d. 21 Feb 1861

Our father, Alexander Coulter d. 9 June 1883, in 83rd year of his age

Our mother, Ann M. Coulter d. 29 Jan 1896, aged 83 years.

Jane McCullough b. 1829, d. 1852

A. D. W. McCullough b. 1837, d. 1851

James Griffin b. 1808, d. 1866

Samuel Greist d. 29 Sep 1766, aged 4 years

Thomas Jones d. 19 July 1764, aged 24 years

Our father. J. G. Underwood b. 14 Feb 1810, d. 22 Sep 1891

Jane, wife of John Price, Sen., d. 22 May 1866, aged 71 years, 14 days

Ann Underwood d. 30 July 1845, aged 75 years

Sarah Patterson d. 20 Aug 1814, aged 25 years

Sarah Underwood, wife of Solomon Underwood, d. 29 Aug 1814, aged 69 years

Solomon Underwood d. 28 April 1815, aged 70 years

Lewis Underwood, son of Solomon and Sarah Underwood d. 25 April 1821, aged

40 years

Amos B. Cann, b. 16 Jan 1837, d. 10 April 1884

Mary Austin, wife of Edward Collings, b. 3 Jan 1802, d. 21 March 1883

Father, Zebulon G. Austin, b. 9 March 1794, d. 7 March 1849

Susan Austin, Vernon, b. 31 Jan 1808, d. 4 March 1879

James and Susan Austin, his wife, d. 17 and 18 Sep 1826, in 56th year of his age.

Mahala P., dau. of John and Sarah Wingate, d. 28 May 1864

Hance Miller d. 17 May 1809, aged 64 yers

Mary, wife of Hance, d. 21 March 1779, aged 58 years

John Egnor d. 18 Aug 1817, aged 43 years

Charles C. Johnson d. 6 July 1821, aged 35 years, 4 months, 24 days

Elizabeth T. Johnson, wife of Samuel Johnson, d. 2 Oct 1821, aged 23 years, 2 months, 14 days.

Ellen Aliza Johnson, d. 21 Oct 1824, aged 7 years, 11 months

Camilla Williamina L. Johnson, d. 5 March 1829, aged 5 months, 3 days

William M. Campbell b. 5 Sep 1830, d. 13 June 1889

Julia B. Campbell, b. 13 Jan 1835, d. 5 Aug 1903

Elizabeth, wife of Louis E. Pennington, d. 11 July 1840, aged 23 years

Samuel McMullen d. 27 Aug 1845, aged 51 years

Mary, wife of Samuel McMullen, d. 20 Nov 1866, aged 64 years

Ann Alice Underwood, dau. of William and Elizabeth Cowan, d. 21 Nov 1845, aged 12 years, 1 month, 10 days

Samuel Rambo Jr., son of Samuel and Margaret Rambo, b. 16 Feb 1824, d. 5 May 1855

James Jones d. 2 March 1852, in 66th year of his age

Jane, wife of James Jones, d. 4 March 1844 in 41st year of her age

Jane G., wife of Thomas Benneson, b. 14 April 1777, d. 18 June 1851

Thomas Benneson, b. 10 May 1774, d. 21 Oct 1849

Margaret A. Benneson, b. 9 March 1803, d. 12 Oct 1867

Maria M. Bennison, b. 2 Jan 1800, d. 7 Nov 1872

Joseph T., youngest son of Joseph and Agnes Griffith, d. 18 March 1866, aged 28 years, 10 months, 13 days

Agnes Irvin, wife of Joseph Griffith, d. 3 Oct 1876, aged 81 years, 10 months

Joseph Griffith, b. 20 April 1793, d. 25 Aug 1879

John I., eldest son of Caleb and Mary E. Griffith, b. 22 May 1847, d. 11 June 1870

Jane M., wife of William J. Griffith, b. 6 Oct 1822, d. 7 Aug 1887

William J., son of Joseph and Agnes Griffith, d. 16 March 1872 in 29th year of his age

Caleb, son of Joseph and Agnes Griffith, b. 14 Feb 1821, d. 18 April 1855

John Irwin, son of Joseph and Agnes Griffith, d. 24 Jan 1828, aged 9 years, 2 months

William J. Patton, b. 22 Jan 1825, d. 28 Aug 1852

Francina B., wife of James Lindsey, d. 12 April 1882, in the 82nd year of her age

James Livingston d. 17 Feb 1852, aged 67 years, 20 days

Joseph F., son of William and Mary J. Slack, b. 1 Jan 1836, d. 30 Oct 1867

Uriah Slack d. 10 Sep 1835, in 75th year of his age

Hetty, wife of Enos Slack, b. 20 Dec 1790, d. 6 Oct 1858

Enos Slack d. 14 June 1853, aged 67 years

George E., son of Enos and Hetty Slack, b. 24 Oct 1811, d. 19 March 1840

Amos Slack d. 30 Nov 1836, in 57th year of his age

Ann, wife of George Slack, b. 22 Aug 1811, d. 30 July 1892

Tamar Cooch b. 24 Nov 1787, d. 15 Jan 1871

William Cooch b. 20 Sep 1796, d. 31 May 1869

Margaret Cooch, wife of William Cooch, d. 19 Sep 1833, in 67th year of her age

William Cooch d. 24 Sep 1837, aged 75 years

Levi G. Cooch b. 17 Feb 1808, d. 7 Feb 1859

Sarah C. Wilkins, wife of Levi G. Cooch, b. 17 Sep 1812, d. 8 May 1900

Our brothers, John J., son of John & E. J. Herdman [*inscription obliterated*]

James B., son of John & E. J. Herdman, b. 7 July 1848, d. 7 April 1876

Rebecca Thomas d. 12 Nov 1822 in 80th year of her age

Susan Thomas d. 20 Jan 1852, aged 75 years

Jesse Thomas d. 4 Aug 1854, aged 68 years

Edmund Bacheluer of Vermont d. 12 Feb 1835, aged 21 years

Father. William Miggett d. 11 June 1882 in the 87th year of his age

Mother. Agnes, wife of William Miggett, d. 6 Oct 1876, in 84th year of her age

Our beloved boy, William, d. 10 Feb 1865, aged 3 years, 13 days and Robert d. 19
    Feb 1865, aged 17 months, 19 days

Peter Miggett b. in Barrhead, Scotland, 15 April 1821, d. 28 Jan 1893

Amy Roberson, wife of Francis Bryson, d. 21 Oct 1843, aged 23 years, 4 months,
    21 days

Margaret Adair, b. 9 Nov 1810, d. 27 March 1883

Mother. Sarah, wife of James Nicholson, b. 12 Jan 1808, d. 30 Nov 1880

James, b. 6 Feb 1814, d. 18 Nov 1886

Mother. Father. L.V.N. & M.J.H.

Nathan Thomas Boulden, b. 27 Dec 1819, d. 3 April 1868

Sarah A. McCullough, wife of Nathan F. Boulden, b. 12 May 1828, d. 3 June
    1863

Samuel H. Campbell, 12 April 1841, 2 April 1898

Mary, wife of Adair Kincaid d. 19 Nov 1834 in 36th year of her age

J. Thomas Fisher, son of Levi B. and Martha J. Fisher, d. 16 March 1853, aged 8
    years, 2 months, 16 days. Also William H. Fisher d. 10 May 1812, aged 11
    years, 10 months, 13 days

Robinson Davis b. 30 July 1795, d. 24 Dec 1863

Our father. John Campbell, b. 16 July 1804, d. 11 Oct 1881

Our dear mother, Ann Jane, wife of John Campbell, d. 1 May 1874, aged 66 years

Job M. Frazier b. 25 Aug 1829, d. 24 July 1899

Catharine A. Campbell, wife of Job M. Frazier, b. 23 Dec 1828, d. 12 Aug 1897

David McConaughey b. 17 July 1822, d. 20 Nov 1879

Rebecca Sutton b. 15 Dec 1814, d. 14 Aug 1901

William McConaughey b. 6 June 1831, d. 24 Dec 1887

Father. William Slack b. 23 June 1804, d. 15 Nov 1882

Mother. Mary Ann, wife of William Slack, d. 25 July 1879, aged 68 years

Father. James Miggett b. 28 June 1828, d. 6 Dec 1879

Mother. Sarah Jane, wife of James Miggett, b. 22 Oct 1837, d. 31 July 1884

Ida R. Miggett b. 3 June 1867, d. 21 July 1889. Lizzie S. Miggett b. 27 Nov 1869,
    d. 31 Dec 1887. Daus. of James & Sarah J. Miggett

Mother. Catherine A. Hill b. 15 Aug 1813, d. 15 Jan 1892

Father. John R. Hill b. 22 Sep 1814, d. 5 Jan 1892

Mary J. Legates b. 23 June 1847, d. 31 Jan 1899

Father. Alexander Wilson d. 16 Jan 1896, aged 66 years

William R. Rees d. 5 Oct 1903, aged 59 years

Col. Thomas Cooch d. 16 Nov 1888

Sarah Lowen, wife of Col. Thomas Cooch, d. Oct 1784

Thomas Cooch Jr. D. Feb 1785

Sarah Griffith, wife of Thomas Cooch Jr.

William Cooch Sr. b. 5 June 1762, d. 25 Sep 1837

Margaret Hollingsworth, wife of William Cooch Sr., 7 Dec 1766, d. 4 Sep 1833

Elder Wm. K. Roberson, late pastor of the Baptist Church of Bryn Zion, d. 17 July
    1845, in the 55th year of his age

Rebecca, wife of William Gray, b. 20 March 1824, d. 23 March 1897

Jeremiah Taylor d. 7 May 1825, aged 48 years, 8 months, 14 days

Mary, wife of Jeremiah Taylor, d. 25 March 1825, aged 76 years, 1 month, 5 days

Gideon Taylor b. 20 Aug 1814, d. 23 Nov 1872

John Gooding, d. 4 March 1832, in 38th year of his age

Eliza, wife of John Gooding, d. 11 Jan 1848 in the 48th year of her age

Elizabeth, dau. of John and Eliza Gooding, d. 15 April 1832, in 11th year of her
    age

Sarah S. Taylor, wife of William Taylor, and dau. of Jesse & Hannah Boulden, d.
    16 July 1851, aged 20 years, 4 months, 14 days

Charles, son of William & Sarah S. Taylor, d. 3 Oct 1830, aged 1 year, 11 months
    and Sarah Ann, their dau. d. 10 Aug 1831, aged 1 month, 8 days

Levi Boulden d. 8 Sep 1822, aged 9 years

John, son of Jesse & Hannah Boulden, d. 28 April 1831 in 24th year of his age

Jesse Boulden d. 28 May 1855 in 81st year of his age

Hannah, wife of Jesse Boulden, d. 27 Sep 1842, in 60th year of her age

Harriet, wife of George W. Boulden and dau. of Jesse & Hannah Boulden, d. 19
    Dec 1843, in 27th year of her age

James Lewis, son of James and Sarah Nicholson, b. 18 July 1844, d. 4 Sep 1865

Anna M., wife of Edward F. Boulden, d. 9 Jan 1864, in 23rd year of her age

Mrs. Catherine Ash d. 30 Jan 1838, at age 84

Joseph Ash b. 21 Feb 1791, d. 4 Dec 1829

Ann Ash, consort of Joseph Ash, d. 12 Sep 1824, in 26th year of her age

Sarah Ash d. 24 July 1822, aged 24 years, 8 days

William Hutchinson d. 21 Feb 1865, aged 32 years

Amelia A., wife of the late John T. Ross, and dau. of the late William & Elizabeth
Gowan, d. 27 July 1879, aged 39 years

Head of Christiana Presbyterian Church

McCrery, Rev John, A. M., who died Jan 18, 1800, in the 68th year of his age & 34 of his ministry.

Wallace, Andrew d. 3 Mar 1775, 79 years

Wallace, Fanny d. 12/1753, 73 years

Phillips, John, son of Joseph and Elizabeth Phillips, 10/7/1809, 4th year of his age

Scott, Hannah, d. 2/27 1845 in the 67th year of her life.

Bryan, Martha, d. 10/25/1772 aged 65 years

Garrett, Sarah, d. 10/4/1830, 61 years, 2 mos & 9 days

Barr, David, d 4/25/1772, aged 20 years

Barr, Eliz wife of Dav'd Barr, d 7/27/1774, aged 51 years.

Crozier, Adam, d 7/20/1810 aged 29 years

Whann, John d 7/14/1858, aged 60 years

Huggins, Robert d 8/20/1836 aged 67 years & 7 mos

Price, Mary P relict of the late Wm Price d 3/5/1849, aged 75 years

Garrett, James d 1/19/1803, aged 50 years and 2 mos and 19 days

Garrett, Harriet, b. 9/7/1833, d 2/22/1853

Wallace, Joseph d 5/28/1776, aged 63

Wallace, Mary d 1/1/1794 aged 73 years

Garrett, David d 9/22/1828

Garrett, Rebecca b 7/15/1832, d 7/27/1832

Garrett, Willie b 1/1/1837, d 7/16/1839

Barr, David d 7/2/1787 aged 82 years

Stewart, Jane wife of William Stewart daughter of David and Elizabeth Barr d 12/23/1775 aged 16 years 9 mos.

Wallage, Dr. George d 5/17/ 1796

Garrett, Mary b 11/11/1829, d 4/27/1847

Fulton, Hugh b 10/4/1777, d 3/24/1842

Fulton, Ann wife of Hugh Fulton, d 10/141863 aged 84 years

Davis, Levi, d 1/31/1816 & 55 years of age

Graham, Mary d 9/28/1734

Bennett, Major Richard of Washington City who died October 8, 1845. "Blessed are the pure in heart for they shall see God"

Whiteley, Col Henry who died in October 2nd, 1811 in 57th year of his age

Whitel(e)y, Ann d aged 30 in 1830

Gordon, John d 7/10/1811 aged 70

Griffith, Sinay d 9/7/1824

Howard, Wm d 4/13/1827 aged 57 years

Wilkinson, Sarah A b 2/26/1843, d 5/28/1854

Garrett, Rebecca W b 4/16/1843, d 9/8/1856

Anderson, Elizabeth daughter of Thomas and Elvira Whann d 5/14/1857 aged 9 years & 2 mos & 7 days

Richey, John d 1748 aged 60 years
Richey, Isabel d 10/7/1746 aged 30 years
Huggins, Mary d 4/20/1853 aged 73 years
Alexander, Mary A wife of Moses d 10/25/1738 aged 58 years
Berry, Richard, d 5/1/1828 aged 68 years
Howard, Rebecca, d 10/28/1812 aged 49 years 8 mos 16 days
Ridgly, Benjamin, son of John and Elvira Jane Johnson b 12/17/1850 d 7/29/1852
McCoy, Lew. Henry d 1761 aged 24 years
Rambo, John b 7/28/1819 d 9/25/1855
Mathias, Susan Jane, daughter of Jones and Hettie Ann b 12/9/1844 d 8/21/1852
Fobes, Ann consort of Daniel Fobes d 10/2/1800 in 29 years of her age
Scott, Alexander d 3/16/1832 aged 66 years
Scott, John H d 3/5/1832 aged 23 years
Alexander, Amos d 1780, aged 51 years
Alexander, Walter d 1780 in the 27th year of his age
Alexander, Mark son of Amos and Sarah Alexander b 11/13/1771 d 10/1/1802
Scott, Rachel d 11/9/1805 in the 2nd year of her age
Scott, Ann d 10/11/1804

Holy Trinity Church Records
(Old Swedes)
1800-1850

Register of Marriages

1800
March 27 Lyman, Joseph and Stamcast, Ann
Nov 19 Sroder (?), Amos and Stilly, Kitty

1801
Jan'y 29 Springer, Joseph and Hendrickson, Polly
Feb'y 12 Askew, Samuel and Hedges, Hannah
        Poulson, Jacob and Sinex, Susanna
March 5 Cannon, Thomas and Henry, Susanna
April 6 Liston, Edmond and Pluright, Ann
        20   Johnston, Simon and Poulson, Elizabeth
        22   Torbert, John and Warner, Elizabeth
        27   Roberson, Jacob and McDaniel, Hannah
June 21 Gillespie, Major and Hannah, Katherine
        27 Sowings, Samuel and Norton, Elizabeth
        McGoney, Henry and Woods, Elizabeth
August 13 Anderson, William and Robinson, Margaret
        13 Davis, Amos and Seville, Elizabeth
        30 Hanna, John, Jun and Davis, Amy
        Rumford, Samuel and Cox, Margarett
Sept 12 Peterson, Andrew and
Oct 27 Wonderly, John and Mahon, Jane
Nov 1 Hemphill, John and Stilly, Elizabeth
Wolf, Michael and Carson, Ann
Dec 19 Bayley, James and Bradford, Rachel
        Wood, William and Robinson, Margaret
        Bratton, Jno and Nixon, Mary
        24 Burns, Nicholas and Bruce, Charlotte
        _____, ? and Reynolds, Rachel
Sayers, Jonathan and Syng, Susanna

1802
Jan'y 1 Allison, Jno and Ferriss, Elizabeth
        7 Foot, Geo and Evans, Sarah
        8 Springer, Thomas and Faulk, Sarah
Feb'y 4 Plantern, John and Savoy, Sarah
March 8 Cummings, Jno and O'Brian, Ann

22 Taylor, William and Beeson, Elizabeth
April 5 Hendrickson, Joseph and Henderson, Elinor
7 Robinson, Alvin and Smith, Katherine
23 Milligan, Wm and Fife, Rebecca
Smidner, Wm and Savoy, Anna
May 27 McCowin, James and Byas, Martha
29 Mathews, Saml and Jaquett, Hanna
Andrews, Benjamin and Elbeson, Eliza
31 Rambo, Daniel and Brown, Elizabeth
June 3 Derickson, Joseph and Derickson, Sarah
Masters, David and Newlin, Phebe
Sep 9 Clark, Thos and Bowman, Elizabeth
Dec 2 _____, Jno. (?) and McMastney, Mary

1803
Feb 3 Derrickson, Zachariah and Alexander, Sarah
Jan 8 Mercer, Hugh and Peterson, Catherine
May 27 Gulbands, Adolphus and Ford, Mary
July 7 Shmitt, Robert and Holley, Sarah
9 Dellano, Thomas and Smith, Jane
Aug 11 Wells, Zenos and Harris, Sidney
19 Bowden, John and Springer, Elizabeth
23 Wilson, Joshua and Harlin, Susanna
25 Johnson, Joshua and Stidham, Sarah
Smith, Thomas and Bullock, Margery
Sept 15 Sherry, Henry D and Smith, Mariah
Nov 2 McGee, Alexr and Morrow, Jane
8 Corsons, Matthew and Cowan, Rachel
Souter, Jno and Moore, Ann
22 Conner, Solomon and Mays, Hannah
April 20 Robinson, Aquilla and Sheward, Sarah

1804
Jany 25 Whitelock, Geo and Sheward, Sarah *****
Feb 2 Rice, Thomas and Rice, Ann
15 Oldham, Edwd and Oldham, Ann
Ap'l 14 Reynolds, Alexr and Flinn, Elizabeth
June 14 Brooks, Benjamin and Derrickson, Elizabeth
July 18 Meece, Thos. and Hill, Hester
24 Hamilton, Joshua(?) and Hunter, Jane
25 Kasey, Michael and Stevenson, Rebecca
Aug 4 Connway, Jno and Ford, Ann
Sept 27 Perkins, Jos and Grubb, Hanna

28 Wilson, Joshua and Sum____, Hannah
Wood, Geo and Stuart, Mary
Nov 20 Minghon(?), Patrick and Kerr(?), Elenor
22 Enoch, Gregg and Crips, Elizabeth
28 McCabe, Jas and Johnson, Elizabeth
Dec 5 Sharpley, Jacob and Eliott, Elizabeth
12 Campbel, Alexr and McConnell, Lydia
20 Gordon, Jno and Sharp, Ann C
Justice, Jos and Sroud, Jane

1805

Jan 3 Ewing, Saml and Jones, Mary
5 Stidham, John and Owens, Rachel
31 Ross, Jas and Harden, Elenor
Feb 9 Talley, Thos and Welden, Mary
Mar 26 Mercer, Hugh and Stewert, Rachel
Ap'l 4 Robinson, Jacob and White, Elizabeth
11 Johnson, Jas and Moore, Margaret
May 8 Branford, Th and Miller, Liza
June 29 Pouge, Jno and Pierce Phebe
July 16 Cox, Esau and McKean, Eliza
25 Baldin (Bardin?), William and Ash, Esther
Sept 3 McGordon, Jas and Brian, Ann
29 Vanlmace, Henry and Kirkpatrick, Elizabeth
Oct 29 Armstrong, Wm and Armstrong, Ann
Dec 3 Rumford, Th and Cox, Catherine
13 Davis, Rich and Wynhoop, Mary
22 Rice, Washington and White, Ann

1806

Jan'y 11 Spatts, Geo and Croxall, Sarah
25 Chapman, Luke and Stilly, Mary
Feb'y 27 Driver, Matt'w and Alford, Charity
March 1 Stilly, Isaac and Caldwell, Leah
6 Boyer, Jesse and Reynolds, Ann
12 Talley, Harman and Talley, Mary
13 Robinson, Thomas and Naff, Catherine
April 8 Burman, Edw'd and Barnett, Leah
9 Cropper, Wm and Ritchie, Mary
13 Robinson, Jehu and Wells, Mary A.
May 22 Brown, Wade and Ford, Sarah
Aug 26 Furguson, Jno and Ball, Mary
30 Hanson, Peter and Hanson, Rebecca

Sept 18 Paulson, Saml and Foreman, Lydia
        27 Robinson, Vincent and Lyman, Hanna
Nov 22 Carter, Jno and Barnett, Ann
Dec 8 Roberts, Jas and Brinton, Sarah
        23 Wallace, Jno and Taylor, Rachel
        Conningham, Pat'k M and Hanson, Mary
        Naff, Henry and Jaquett, Mary
        Rankin, William and Crips, Priscilla

1807

Jan'y 5 Fife (File), Jno and Wells (Wills), Elizabeth
        17 Faulk, Jno and Jackson, Candie (Candice)
        22 Morris, Evan and Stone, Amilea T.
Feb'y 2 Williamson, Jno and Clouds, Orpha
Mar 12 Elliot, Wm and McVee (McKee), Esabella
Ap'l 4 Rock, Andrew B and Fletcher, Elizabeth
        11 Byles, Rob't and Taylor, Mary
May 2 Barns, Isaac and Blackford, Lydia
        6 McClusky, Jas and McBeth, Margaret
        11 Welch, Jas and Naff, Elizabeth
July 2 Lodge, Henry and Grubb, Prudence
Oct 2 Marshall, Jno. and Waggoner, Mary
        15 Hays, Jos: and Rogers, Sarah
        22 Corbitt, Pennell and Clark, Mary
        27 Raman, Jno and Woods, Jane
Nov 1 Brown, Jno and Rowen, Elizabeth
        17 Crow, Jno and Bradun, Elizabeth
Dec 19 Jones, Jos: and Rea, Sally H
        5 Woodward, Wm and Brown Hanna
        9 Simmons, Geo: and Evans, Ruth
Oct 24 Snyder, Saml and Pierce, Debora

1808

Jan 19 Griffin, Lisby and Grubb, Imus (James?)
Feb 24 Ivens, Ezekiel and McMahon, Ann
March 2 Stilly, Jno and Cartmell, Susanna
        Tally, Elihu and Twaddle, Ann
        22 Beeson, Jonathan and Kenton, Margaret
        23 Hendrickson, Abram and McConnell, Elizabeth
        26 Rigby, James and Kenedy, Rebecca
Apl 6 Bratten, Geo: and Smith, Mary
        16 Bennet, Ezekiel and Bannard, Mary
        21 Arnould, Justus and Sellars, Susanna

May 31 Hart, Oliver and Philips, Hanna
Jun 2 Parven, Daniel and Thompson, Abigail
    8 Nixon, John and Kenedy, Mary
July 23 Weldon, Richd and Pierce, Lydia
August 3 German, Jas and Waggoner, Elizabeth
    31 Abrams, Benjamin and Sinex, Ann
Sep 1 Gourdan, Jas and Evans, Nancy
Oct 11 Gregg, Saml and Walraven, Ann C.
    12 Cling, Jacob H. and Armstrong, Elizabeth
Nov 3 Pyle, Jos and Steele, Mary
    10 Hays, Israel and Whiteman, Sarah
Dec 20 Tally, Peter and Wilson, Anna
    24 Sterrett, Thomas and Bing, Sarah
    31 Louge, Major and Carlisle, B.

1809
Feby 16 Eves, Jno. D. and Crow, Mary
Mar 23 Dill, Francis and Thomson, Mary
Mar 28 McMullen, Wm and Pennington, Mary
Apl 20 Griffith, William and Allender, Phebe
Apl 15 Brown, Thomas and Wade, Mary
May 11 Todd, William and Twaddle, Rebecca
    16 Ward, William and Reading, Maria
    23 Scott, Robt and Spots (Spats), Ann
    25 Baker, George and Boder (Bodle), Charlotte
June 17 Sinex, Wm and Seville, Charlotte
    21 Beeson, Archd and Sweeny, Berthia
July 24 Stille, Thomas and Wethy, Sarah C.
Sept 4 Divenny, Geo. and Walters, Maria
Sept 7 Moor, Samuel and Bean, Elizabeth,
Sept 26 Reece, John and McMichael, Margaret
Oct 12 Frazier, Jno: and Austin (Ausin), Mary
    24 Garesche, Vital M. and Bauduy, Mimika Louisa
    26 Watson, Wm and Manuel, Mary
Nov 15 Steelman, Isaac and Clark, Polly
    8 Jackson, Wm and Hendrickson, Jane
    2 Smith, Jno M. and Bullock, Hanna
    28 Cling, Geo. and Twaddle, Sarah
    20 (28?) Trueman, Amos and Clinton, Hanna
Dec 16 Hickman, Wm and Cartmell, Elizabeth
    Day, Jno and Cling, Sarah
    19 Robinson, Jos: and Carter, Amelia
    23 Pierce, Isaac and Pierce, Rebecca

30 French, William and Justice, Eliza

1810

Jany 18 Paulson, Peter and Robenson, Mary
    23 Taylor, James and Murphy, Ann
March 8 Ring, William and Raney, Jane
    15 Paterson, Wm and Henry, Jane
    27 Bratten, Wm and Smith, Sarah
Apl 20 Rawlins, Thos and Derickson, Rachel
    26 Jones, Edwd and Delcart, Susanna
May 9 Stedham Jr, Isaac and Lafever, Ingebar
    25 Bole, Benjn and Gardner, Anna
July 31 Switzer, Christian and Conklin, Jane
August 27 Roberts, Thomas and Broom, Levenia
    29 Walker, William P. and McGee, Eliza
Oct 18 Seville, Levi and Farren, Margaret
    27 Senex, John and Stidham, Susan
Nov 15 Larkin, Isaac and Grubb, Sarah
    22 Friese, Daniel and Rice, Nancy
Dec 29 White, John and Vandeveer, Keziah
    31 Justis, Justa and Bracken, Ann

1811

Ireland, Shadrack and Coudratt, Hester
Feby 28 Foot, Lewis and Foulk, Esther
March 5 Philips, Calvin and Springer, Cathrine
Apl 3 Nelson, Hugh B. and Davis, Elizabeth
May 29 Shaw, Joshua and Shetterly, Cathrine
June 29 White, William and Glacker (Glarken, Clacken)
July 13 Buck, Isaac and Grimes, Hanna
Oct 15 Oldham, Edward and Ogle, Mary A.
Nov 5 Winterbottom, Thos and McBride, Cathrine
    23 Wilson, Saml and Grubb, Clariss
Dec 24 Williams, John and Stedham, Rebecca

1812

Feby 5 Pierce, Amos and Jackson, Mary

Register of marriages celebrated by Wm Wickes, Rector of Trinity Church

December 25 Wigdon (Wigton), Andrew and Taylor, Isabella, both of Christiana
    Hundred, N.C. County
March 16 Wright, Saml Queen Ann's County Md. and Warner. Eliza L. M. of

Wilmington, Del.

March 28 Watson, John M. of Elkton Md. and O'Daniel, Mary of Wilmington, Del

June 20 Springer, Benjamin A. and McGee, Ann, both of Wilmington, Del

July 6 Jones, Thomas and Byrnes, Jane, both of Wilmington, Delaware

Oct 10 Johnson, William and Barratt, Ann, both of N.C. County, Del

January 17 Clungeun(?), William and Byrnes, Mary, both of Wilmington, Del.

February 19 Springer, John Jnr. and Elliott, Ann, both of Wilmington, Del

February 22 Collins, Daniel and Stedham, Kitty, both of N.C. County, Del

March 21 Justis, Justa and Phillips, Cathrine, both of N.C. County, Del

May 2 Derickson, Jacob and Ruther, Isabella, both of N.C. County, Del

Register of Marriages celebrated by Levi Bull, Rector of Trinity Church

1818

April 22 Alexander Willson to Ann Rice, both of Wilmington, Del

July 12? Joseph Hendrickson to Mary White of N. Castle County, Del

1819

Jany 19 Erby Piner to Margaret Cooper, both of Wilmington, Del

Feby 25 Robert Robinson to Lydia Brignbury (Brynberg) of New Castle Co, Del

March 11 Robert Richie to Maria Pierce of Wilmington, Del

Feby 18 John Boys to Mary Stidham of N. Castle County, Del

Register of marriages celebrated by the Rev. Richard Drasen Hall, Rector
    of Trinity Church borough of Wilmington Delaware

1819

June 3 Robert Armstrong to Elizabeth McHaffy, both of New Castle Co.
    Same day John King to Elizabeth Hayes, both of New Castle Co.

June 24 Thos Seal to Maria R. Justis of Newport, N.C. Co.

Aug 6 John Sharp to Sarah Miller, both of Chester Co Newgarden

Oct 7 Thos Freese and Sarah Ann Miller, both of N.C. Co.

Oct 21 Alexr S Van Pelt to Mary Ashmead, both of Phila

Oct 26 Andrew Peterson Reading to Lydia McDonough Foard, both of Cecil Co. Md.

Nov 11 John Foulk Talley to Hannah Paulson, both of New Castle, Del

Nov 18 Married in Phila Isaac G. Elliott to Eliza Thomas, both of Phila

Dec 14 Wm George Winslow to Elizabeth C. Welsh, the former of the District of Maine

Dec 16 Thomas Powell and Catharine Wright, both of New London Church

1820

Jany 13 Joshua Bunting and Elizabeth Wright, both of Bucks Co. Penna.

Jany 28 Jesse Klair to Ann Stidham, both of New Castle Co.

Feb 10 Lewis Foulk to Eliza Shephard, both of N. Castle C.

Feb 24 Married Joseph Springer to [blank]

March 2 Buffum, Daniel to Sarah Landers

March 4 Moor, Jeremiah. to Sarah Harvey - Colored

Thursday 23 March Eli Evans to Ann Paulson, both of Christiana Hundred N.C.
    Co

Thursday 6 April, Joseph Shipley and Sarah Bird, daughter of Thos Bird of
    Brandywine H.

Tuesday 12 Sep Robert Aikin to Elizabeth Hudley, both of Wilmington

Nov 3 John D. Vaughan to Lydia G. Gilpin

Nov 5 Jacob Stevenson to Keziah Davis

    9 Robert Sargent to Rachel Faris

    Do Aquilla Thomas to Eliza Faris

    10 Andrew Armstrong to Rebecca Thompson

Dec 14 Thomas Searles to Hannah Cripps

1821

Feb 8 Thomas Sinex to Elizabeth Foulk

    Do Henry Bracken to Susan Yarnall

    20 Married in Georgetown, Kent, Md., the Rev. Purnell Fletcher Smith
    Rector of Shrewsbury Parrish, to Mary Everitt

7 March James Smith to Sarah Reynolds

    8 Do William Smith of Del. Co., [PA] to Rebecca C. (L.?) Bird

    15 Stephen Foulk to Priscilla Cloud

    Do John Foulk to Elizabeth Storey

12 April Joseph Hanson to Eliza Flintham

    20 April Henry Moore Hayes to Eliza Brooks

5 Oct Elie Rinear to Mary Toy of Mt. Holly

6 Nov James Green to Christiana McCauley of Wil.

    24 William Armstrong to Rebecca Pearson of N.C. Co.

    29 Elisha Huxley(?) to Elizabeth Derrickson of Brandywine

Dec 13 William R. Welden to Sarah Sterne

    Do Joseph Gill to Rebecca Springer

    Do David T. Jones to Hannah Giffing

1822

Jan 3 1822 John Robb to Nancy Keen

Same night as above William Rossell to Sarah Friese, both of the borough of
    Wilmington

10 James Jeffries to Parthena Vandever, daughter of Thomas

Marriages by Rev. R. Williston
1822
29 April Daniel Husted to Rebeckah Vandever
23 May Samuel Smith to Rebeckah Malone
16 Oct Mr. John Hayes to Eve Roatman (Boatman?)
18 Dec Mr. James Ritchie to Catherine Bannard
21 Dec Mr. Jefferson B. Williamson to Jane Jeffries

1823
15 Jan Richard Woodward to Lydia Welch
13 March Jacob Foulks to Edith Garnell
21 April Jacob Starr to Sarah Ann Hutton
12 May Charles Forwood to Dianna Talley
11 June Isaac Anderson to Ann Hall
21 July Jonathan W. Mifflin to Mary H. Wilson
16 Aug James Siddall to Hannah Wagstaff
21 Oct Mr. Samuell Battersby to Jane McIntire
11 Dec Isaac Spear to Mary Ann Hendrickson

1824
4 Feb Joseph B.(L?) Stidham to Elizabeth Reynolds
8 May 8 May Francis A. Whitaker to Leah Evans

1827
May 31 Francis (Franck?) DeSanque to Ann Porter Lockerman
Aug 3 Solomon Huff and Phoebe Ann Mason
Oct 24 John Ormand Monges? and Sedney Ann Cecilia Gordon
Nov 21 George Lockyear and Lydia Faring, widow
Nov 22 John Simmons and Margaret Talley

1828
Jan 24 William Sharpley and Jane Forwood
March 4 John Lynam and Lydia Brembers? Stidham
July 24 Harry Connelly and Eliza Andrews

Marriages by Isaac Pardee minister of Trinity Church

December 18 1828 Isaac Houston and Rebecca Vandever
January 13 1829 David (Daniel?) Cross to Aceniah Sharp
Feb 13 John Irving and Mary Ann Cleny

March 12 Ellen Cox and Charles Bush
April 9 1829 James G? Todd and Ellen Vain?
    Do William Still and Eliza Ritchie
May 6 George M. Rogers and Ann Maud Sharp
June — — [line unreadable] ---
Oct 16 1829 Mr. George Jones to Miss Leanah Hoff
March 27 1830 Caleb G. Kirk to Hannah Peach
April 13 1830 Mr. Edward Williams to Miss Maria Johnson
April 20 1830 Mr. Zebulon Lusbey to Mrs. Ann Elizabeth Rice
April 22 1830 William Pogue to Sarah Ann Smith
May 23 1830 Enock Knight to Margarett Smith
Oct 14 Thomas McClure and Martha Russell
Dec 1 1831 Clement Palmer and Elizabeth Anderson
Dec 19 1831 Zenas B. Glazier to Mary Ann McGill
Feb 22 1832 Amos Perkins to Keranhappenck Sharpley
Feb 27 1832 Jabez Maul Fisher to Nancy Andrews
March 17 1832 Joseph C. Gregg and Ann Wilson
April 29 John Watson to Mary Boyes
Sept 12 1832 James Mullen to Mary Green
Sept 12 1832 William Wallace Whitney to Myra Elizabeth (Davis) Clarke
Jan 31 1833 Henry W. Bartram and Hannah Maria Vandiver
March 14 1833 William Taylor and Mary McDaughle
June 27 1833 Samuel F. Dupont to Sophia M. Dupont
Aug 29 1833 David H. Hoops to Mary W. Painter
Aug 29 1832 Nathan Kirk to Catharine White
Nov 6 1833 James E. Rice to Catharine Gadon
Jan 21 1834 Lydia Gilpin Hirons to George Clinton Veasey
Feb 16 1834 Peter Storey to Elizabeth Russell
April 1 1834 Amon (Amor) Harvey to Martha Derrickson
April 17 1834 Peter Ramo (Rambo?) to Hannah Roberts
April 21 1834 John Williams to Mary Fleming
June 5 1834 Cyrus Kennard to Eliza. Stephenson
June 19 1834 John Moore and Esther Cooper - Colored
July 7 James Fad and Ellen Kane
July 16 Henry Lucas and Julianna Williams (colored)
Aug 27 1834 William Lard (Lord?) and Sharloote Lisbie (coloured)

<u>Rev. Hiram Adams Mar 31 1835-Feb 22 1838</u>

Mr. Henry D. Gilpin to Mrs. Eliza Johnston, Wilmington Sep 15 1835
William Forrest to Margaret Parvis, Wilmington Oct 29 1835
Marcillus Price to Mary Ann Richardson Wilmington Feb 25 1836
John Elliott 3d to Sarah Hollingsworth Wilmington March 23 1836

George Sayres to Nancy King, Trinity Church May 22 1836
Joseph Dewitt to Cath. Carnahan, Wilmington July 9 1835
William Buck to Gabriella Josephine Dupont, Wilmington Oct 1836
James Kid to Elizabeth Kellam, Wilmington 1836
Henry M. Bayard to Emma Dixon, Trinity Chapel Dec 22 1836
Geo. R. Baker M.D. to Elizabeth Gordon March 7 1737
Edward Manning Roach to Hannah H. Conneway, Wilmington Oct 5 1837
Mr. Chas Springer to Elizabeth Ford, Wilmington, Oct 7 1837
Michael McLaughlin to Hannah Holland, Brandywine Dec 7 1837
Mr. John Monagle to Jane Graham, Wilmington Dec 21 1837
Robert Baxter to Margaret Donaldson, Wilmington Jan 11 1838
Albert Lyman to Mary Jane Stidham, Wilmington March 1 1838

Marriages by Rev. John W. McCullough, Rector of Trinity Ch Wilmington Del

David Medill(?), N.C. Co. and Ann Morison (Monson?), N.C. Co., at Wilmington
    Oct 1 1838
Thomas V. Ward, Cecil Co. Md., and Mary T. McLane, Wilmington, at
    Wilmington Dec 18 1838
William Galagher to Francine Schrader, both of N.C. Co., at New Castle Jan 1839
John Lawyers(?) to Elizabeth King, both of N.C. Co., at Wilmington Feb 10 1839
James W. Bracken to Miss Eleanor A. Lynam, both of N.C. Co., at Thos Lynam's
    – Feb 14 1839
Levi H. (N?) Clark to Susan Elliott, both of N.C. Co., at Mrs. Elliotts, Brandywine
    May 2 1839
Benjamin Bartram and Elizabeth Vandever, both of N.C. Co. Feb 16 1839,
    Brandywine —?
Menden Wall and Miss Lovell?, both of N.C. Co. Feb 18 1839
Thomas Dixon of Dauphin Co., (PA) to Elizabeth Ann Baker July 1 1839 in
    Wilmington
Isaac [Helmes?] and Rebecca Robinson, both of Philadelphia, June 23 1839 at
    Phila.
John Sayers and Sarah Read (Reid?), both of N.C. Co. July 1839
William Dever and Sarah McCluskey, both of N.C. Co. July 18 1839
Thomas Johnson of Delaware Co. and Jane Conelly of N.C. Co. Aug 28 (20?)
    1839
Andrew Dever to Jane Forrest, both of N.C. Co. Oct 31 1839
Joseph Hann (Hawn?) to Frecerica Schrader, both of Wilmington, Del, Jan 7 1840
William Ritchie to Henaretta Green, both of N.C. Co. April 9 1840
John Hanna to Miss Esebella (Isabella) Reynolds, both of N.C. Co. June 25 1840
William Flemming and Miss Mary Dunnard, both of N.C. Co. Oct 20 1840
Dr. John Alex. Lockwood and Miss Julia McLane, both of N. C. Co., Dec 9 1840
Morris Spackman to Lydia Yearsley, Chester Co., Penna, Feb 4 1841

James Armor Jr. to Ann Hendrickson, both of N. C. Co. March 11 1841

James Grubb Jr to Eleanor Nivins, both of N.C. Co., April 1 1841

George Springer to Rebecca Graves, N.C. Co. April 27 1841

Matthew Maury of New York City to Miss Elizabeth Gilpin of Kentmere near Wilmington, June 9 1841

George Russell to Mary Forrest, N.C. Co. Sep 5 1841

Rev. J. W. McCullough (Rector) to Miss Catharine Roberts Canby (By the Rt. Rev. Alfred —?, both of Wilmington, Oct 26 1841

John Henman (Freeman?) of Phila., Pa., to Mary Cronsberry of N.C. Co., Del., March 21 1842

Alexander Byrns and Sidney Talley, both of N.C. Co., July 1842

Edward E. Blackford (Bradford?) and Mary Alicia Raymond (Hayward?), both of Wilmington, Del., Dec 1842

Rev. Corry Chambers to Miss Mary Anna Williamson, both of Wilmington, Dec 26 1842

John Justis to Lavinia Armstrong Jan 1742 (1743?)

Hugh Read to Jane Coyle April 1843

Edward L. Bailey to Margt. Griffin May 1843.

John Sharpley and Mary Jane Springer, both of N.C. Co. Feb 1843

Thomas R. Smith and Emma Simmons, both of Wilmington, Del. May 1843

William L. Derickson to Sarah K. Linam, both of N. C. Co., Feb 1844

P. Brynley Forman of N.C. Co., Del., and Margaret Ross of Chester Co., Pa., Feb 1844

Samuel Sears to Elizabeth McDougal, both of N.C. Co., Del., Aug 1844

John Merrick (Minick?) to Sarah Stevens, both of Wilmington, Del., Dec 1844

William McLaughlin and Frances Ruth (Reed?), both of N. C. Co., Del., May 1845

John Wier and Sarah G. Galagher, N.C. Co., Del., Aug 1845

Geo. M. Bramble (Bramole?) and Eliza. B. Moody, both of N.C. Co., Jan 1846

Robert Beatty and Faith Little, both of N.C. Co., Del., Aug 1846

Nathaniel Brown and Sarah Little, both of N.C. Co., Del., Nov 1846

John B. Stokes and Eliza. Ann Grimes. Both of Wilmington, Del., Jan 1847

Baring Powell of Phila., Pa., and Caroline Bayard, of Wilmington, Del., Feb 22 (28?) 1847

James Fisher and Margaret Peterson, both of N.C. Co., Del., March 21 1847

Marriages by Rev. E. M. Van Deusen Rector

Henry Prizchner(?) and Margaretta Hacker, both of Wilmington, Del., June 29 1848

James Tilton and Isabella H. Adams, both of Wilmington, Del., Sep 20 1848

William H. Fleming of Hudson, NY, and Caroline B. Lisle of Wilmington, Del. Nov 20 1848

John Fleming Smith and Martha Huxley, both of Wilmington, Del., by Rev. A. Prior minister, Feb 20 1849

Samuel Fisher and Mary Russel, both of N.C. Co., Feb 24 1849

Thomas Crosier and Henretta A. Giffing, both of Wilmington, Del., by Rev. A Prior Minister, Feb 25 1849

Geo. A. Armstrong of Wilmington Del. and Eliza Jane Elliot of N.C. Co., April 4 (16?) 1849

Springer Spear of Chester Co., Pa., and Amy Greenholgh (?) of N.C. Co., July 4 1849

Thomas Allen and Mary D. Woodall, both of Wilmington, Del., July 12 1849

Richard T.(S?) Wainwright of Phila., Pa., and Margaret Elizabeth Lysle of Wilmington, Del., Aug 2 1849

Lewis Runyan (Ringan?) of Phila., Pa. and Jane Baxter of N.C. Co., Del., Jan 3 1850-

Wm Sayres and Margaret McLaughlin, both of N.C. Co., Del. March 7 (17?) 1850

Joseph Guly (Galy?) and Criscens? Stokely, both of N.C. Co., Del., Dec 30 1850

Register of Baptisms solemnized by William Pryce

NAMES	BIRTHS	PARENTS	DATE BAPTIZED
John	3/26/1800	Levi and Breata Springer	June 1800
Mary	6/30/1794	Michael and Elizabeth Key	1/4/1801
William	3/22/1797	"	"
Richard	7/26/1799	"	"
George	1784	Jacob and Susanna Cling	
Sarah	1787	"	
John	12/21/1800	William and Rebecca Seal	2/20/1801
Henry Heath	3/18/1801	Hance Naff and Mary	
Eliabeth	4/23/1799	John and Mary Peach 3/22/1802	
William	10/26/1800	"	"
Foxon	4/28/1800	Benjamin and Ann Holmes	4/5/1801
Charles Ridgely	9/14/1798	John and Mary Vining	5/3/1801
Isabella Jane	9/18/1799	John William and Elizabeth Erwin	5/7/1801
Linsey William	7/11/1801	"	
Elizabeth	5/26/1796	John and Elizabeth Hadley	5/18/1801
Ann	8/5/1798	"	"
John	7/24/1801	Andrew and Elizabeth Moris	9/6/1801
David	8/11/1793	Ebenezer and Rebecca Jones	12/29/1801
Thomas	-----?	Elijah and Sarah Skillington	3/7/1802
Thomas	3/6/1802	Jacob and Hannah Robinson	5/-/1802
John Pennington	9/27/1800	Richard and Margarett Price	-/20/1802
Hester	1/0/1802	Peter Walraven and Hester	9/22/1802
Jeremiah Wilts?		An adult	"

Rebecca 8/24/1803   Argergraves? Macklin and Margery 10/9?/1803
Catharine 3/27/1792?   John -ockshot and Mary   4/16/1792?
Levi   11/24/1802   Levi and Beata Springer   9/22/1802
Beata   1/1/1805   Levi and Beata Springer   3/1/1805
William Henry 12/31/1806 Thomas Robinson and Catherine 1/1/1805
Margaret   2/10/1808   Levi and Beata Springer   1/20/1808
Emmet Madison 1/14/1807 Thomas Robinson and Cathrine   2/10/1808
Rebecca   10/5/1810   Levi and Beata Springer   11/20/1810
Lewis (daughter) 12/3/1812 Levi and Beata Springer   7/20/1813
Susanna Naff 5/2/1813   Thomas Robinson and Cathrine
Sarah Maria 4/26/1810   Isaac and Sarah Hendrickson   10/30/1813
Sidney Jane 2/1/1812   Isaac and Sarah Hendrickson   10/30/1813
William Robeson 8/8/1801 Aaron and Margaret Paulson   1/-/1813
Charles   9/14/1803   Aaron and Margaret Paulson   1/-/1813
Alexander 3/24/1906   Aaron and Margaret Paulson   1/-/1813
Jane Ann   11/30/1809   Aaron and Margaret Paulson   1/-/1813
Sarah Geddes 8/20/1814   Aaron and Margaret Paulson   5/14/1815
James Hamilton   Daniel and Catharine Norrett
Mary Ann 7/26?/1807   John and Mary Gaut (recorded 9/1/1821)
Emelia   5/11/1797 at Pultah Factorie J. J. Ullman and Perrine Jeane
Jeane   1/14/1799 at the same place J. J. Ullman and Perrine Jeane
Rose   9/6/1800 at the Danish residence at Patica? J. J. Ullman and Perrine
    Jeane
Sophia   3/21/1802 at Pultah Factorie J. J. Ullman and Perrine Jeane
Eliza   8/24/1805 at the same place   J. J. Ullman and Perrine Jeane
John Janus 1/10/1808 at this place   J. J. Ullman and Perrine Jeane
Daniel   4/28/1810 at this place   J. J. Ullman and Perrine Jeane
Elizabeth Vaudever 2/1/1815 Jacob B. and Rebecca Vandever 6/10/1815
Peter   2/19/1816   Jacob B. and Rebecca Vandever 6/9/1816
John Rawselt   An adult of Brandywine
William   8/25/1797   John and Rebecca Rawselt   in his 6th month
John James Ullman 8 175- at Strasburg in France, d. in Wil. Del. 1811
John   9/18/1798   Francis and Isabella Daniel   9/5/1814
Eliz.? Ann 8/14/1800   Francis and Isabella Daniel   9/5/1814
Thomas   12/9/1804   Francis and Isabella Daniel   9/5/1814
William   5/8/1807   Francis and Isabella Daniel   9/5/1814
David   8/25/1810   Francis and Isabella Daniel   9/5/1814
Mary Ann 7/19/1811   Saml and Mary Harris   Not recollected
Maria Matilda 12/21/1804 John and Martha Wormsdorff   11/6/1814
Carolina Johnson 6/6/1806 John and Martha Wormsdorff   11/6/1814
Henrieitta 1/19/1809   John and Martha Wormsdorff   11/6/1814
Elizabeth 11/19/1814   John and Martha Wormsdordf   11/6/1814
Magdelin? 2/1/1812   Hannah Wilson   11/6/1814

Charlotte	6/7/1815	John and Sarah Smith	11/12/1815
Elizabeth	2/1/1815	Jacob and Rebecca Vandever	6/10/1815
Peter	2/19/1816	Jacob and Rebecca Vandever	6/9/1816
Sarah	1/31/1799	David and Catherine Stidham	10/1/1815
Rachel	5/27/1795	[blank] Stidham	10/1/1815
Jno Crafford	1/26/1796	John and Elizabeth Brinkle	4/14/1815
Wm. Draper	2/9/1798	John and Elizabeth Brinkle	4/14/1815

Baptisms by Levi Bull, Recter of Trinity Church 1818

Ann Bayliss	5/31/1813	An adult	
David	1818	[blank] Kellum	7/21/1818
Mary Sophia	5/13/1818	John and Maria Laura Shenove	8/3/1818
...uttrud?	8/17/1818	Abraham and Ann Shroeder	9/11/1818

William Pierce and Lydia his wife adults

Eliza	5/29/1818	John W. and Hester Laten	9/13/1818
Johanna	5/20/1818	Morgan and Sarah Mason	10/1/1818
John	11/30/1816	John and Anna Springer	11/24/1818
Susanna	7/13/1818	John and Anna Springer	11/24/1818
– Miller	2/1/1817	Aaron and Margaret Paulson	11/24/1818
Elizabeth	11/21/1817	William and Margaret Forster	12/8/1818
Isaac Stidham 12/20/1816		Benjamin and Mary Elliott	1/191819
Anna Mary Bird 12/24/1818		Benjamin and Mary Elliott	1/19/1819
Susan Margaretta 8/23/1817		Cloud and Eliza Elliott	1/19/1819

Patrick? McCurdy, John Mason, Ann Thompson, Susan Rogers, Ann Bainburg
   -Warrington and Sarah Tompkins Physick and adult all baptized 12/24/1819

Joseph Hedges Stidham, adult, bapt. 7 Feb 1819 - all of Wilmington

Dell Noblet, William Simington Middleton, Albert Willson, John Mastin, John
   Foreman, Eliza W. Hendrickson, Ann Hendrickson and Mary Stidham, all
   adults and all bapt. 2/28/1819

Sarah P. Fairlamb daughter of Jonas P. Fairham and Sarah his wife, b. 24 Dec
   1818, bapt 22 Mar. 1819

Michael Reign and John Lewis adults bapt. 3/21/1819

Joseph son of James and Ann Davis b. 3/9/1817, bapt. 3/27/1819

Sarah Jane dau. of the same b. 9/9/1818, bapt. 3/27/1819

James, son of Evan and Elizabeth Cox, b. 8/24/1808 - Edward son of same b.
   11/13/1810, Martha Ann daughter of ditto, b. 10/3/1812, Esau Lyon, son of
   do b. 1012/1818 - all bapt. 3/27/1819

Mary Collins daughter of Thos and Mary McDowell, b. 8/28/1816, bapt.
   3/27/1819

Loisa Edmondson, daughter of John and Ann Catharine Gordon b. 9/23/1812 -
   Sally Matilda daughter of the same b. 11/22/1814 - Elizabeth b. 2/18/1818 -
   bapt. 3/27

Thomas son of Wm and Ruth Pogue - Joseph son of the same - both bapt.
   3/28/1819
Elizabeth Physick an adult bapt. 3/28/1819
Resigned in Apl 1819

Register of Baptisms not before recorded but now registered by Rev. Rd. D. Hall

Marietta Manning, dau. of Edward and Eliza Roche, b. 4 May 1791 and bapt. By
   Rev. Simon Wilmer in Trinity Church 2 Oct 1814
Manning Brinckle, son of Edward and Eliza Roche b. 5 Dec 1796, bapt. By Rev.
   William Wickes
Jonas Preston Fairlamb, b. 22 May 1785. Susan Boggs, Jonas Preston Junr., Ann
   Richards, Hannah Preston, children of Jonas Preston and Sarah P. Fairlamb.
   Susan Boggs was b. 5 Ap. 1810. Jonas Preston b. 27 Oct 1812. Ann Richards
   b. 9 Sep 1814. Hannah Preston b. 7 Sep 1816. These children with their father
   were all bapt. By Rev. Wm Wickes at the house in Wilmington on 5 June
   1817.
Asbury b. 25 March 1811. Mary b. 25 Feb 1814. Joseph b. 29 Feb 1816 - children
   of John and Dorcas Baley and bapt. By Rev. Wm Wickes 2 July 1816
Anna Mary, dau. of Cloud and Eliza Elliott b. 16 March 1814 and bapt. 2 Nov
   1815. Susanna Cloud, dau. of Benjamin and Mary Elliott b. 14 Dec 1813 and
   bapt. 2 nov 1815. Benjamin, son of Benjamin and Mary Elliott, b. 4 Sep and
   bapt. 2 Nov 1815 - all by the Rev. Wm Wickes.
John Vandever, son of Peter and Eleanor, b. 12 Feb 1803 and bapt. The year
   following, the day of mo. Forgotten. Thos. son of the same, b. 25 Sep 1804,
   bapt. 9th month of his age.
Mary, b. 13 March 1812. Rachel b. 23 March 1814. Hannah, b. 18 April 1816.
   Children of Jacob and Barbara Welsh, bapt. 1817 by Rev. John Armstrong.
Elizabeth, dau. of Peter and Mary Bedford, b. 23 Feb 1808, bapt. By Rev. Wm
   Pryce when between 2 and 3 years old.
John, son of Wm and Ruth Pogue, b. 30 Dec 1814.

The following were bapt. By the Rev. Wm Wickes and now recorded. Abigail, b.
   13 June 1810 Jacob b. 17 Nov 1811. Hannah b. 6 Oct 1813. Lydia b. 8 Feb
   1816. Children of William and Elizabeth Hampton and grandchildren of Mr.
   Bailey Wil? At the same time - Charles b. 24 Sep 1812, son of John and
   Catharine Johns. Albert b. 26 Dec 1810 son of George and Nancy Asby.

Register of Baptisms administered by Rev. Richard D. Trail Rector of
Trinity Church, borough of Wilmington Del.

Sunday 2 May 1819. Bapt. In the church, Mary, dau. of William and Mary Ann
Reese?, b. 29 April 1818.

Sunday 9 May 1819. Bapt. At the Lecture Room Rebecca Midlen, dau. of William
and Mary Clungon, b. 23 Sep 1817. Mary Clungon's mother standing
sponsor.

Allen ... son of Allen and Eliza Mills b. at Brandywine mills 23 Sep 1817 and
bapt. 23 May 1819 in the church

Eliza Maria, Junr., dau. of Edward B. and Maria Roche b. at Petersburgh,
Huntington Co., Pa, 22 Feb 1814 and bapt. At the house of her grandfather
(he and Eliza Maria Roche his dau. Standing for said child) on Tuesday 15
June 1819.

Sunday 25 July 1819 bapt. in the church, Sarah Ann, an adult. Mrs. Jane Bannard
standing for her.

Friday 30 July 1819, bapt. in Spring Garden, suburbs of Phila., Joseph Samuel,
son of George and Catharine Cline, b. [blank] The grandparent Joseph Graff
and his wife standing for said child.

Henry McGee, son of Benjamin Horner and Anna Springer his wife, bapt. 7 Nov
1816 and b. 23 June —Tuesday 3 Aug 1819 bapt. At the house John, son of
Benjamin and Anna Springer b. 1 Ocvt 1818. Mrs. Ann Cannors? Standing as
sponsor

Tuesday night Aug 1819, bapt. At Wm Gasby's house, Mary Ann, dau. of Daniel
and Catharine Norrett

Friday night, 27 Aug 1819, bapt. At the house on account of extreme illness, John,
son of John and Ann Catharine Gordon and d. the next day, b. 15 instant.

Friday night 27 Aug 1819, bapt. At the house on account of extreme illness,
Mortimer Richard, son of Nicholas N. and Sarah H. Robinson, b. 4 Aug 1817
and died 2 Sep 1819.

Sunday 29 Aug 1819, bapt. John Wilkins, an adult, son of Jno and Catharine —
Thomas Cole and Michael Reign being sponsors, b. 20 May 1801

Sunday 24 Aug 1819, bapt. At St. Anne's Church, Middletown, Del., Sarah
Jemima, dau. of James and Jemima May, b. 20 Nov 1818. At the same time
and place, Benjamin Flintham, son of Peter and Christiana Hanson?, b. 30
May 1818

Tuesday night 14 Sep 1819, bapt. At Wm Gailely's? John Weldon of Jacob and
Lydia Pierce, Wm Gailey and his wife being sponsors

Tuesday night, 14 Sep 1819, bapt. At the house being near death, Sarah, dau. of
George Golts (Holts?) and Sarah his wife, b. 5 Sep 1819 and died the night
above.

Sunday 19 Sep 1819 Bapt. In the church, Rachel Ann Dingey, dau. of Daniel and
Mary Dingey, b. 8 June 1802 - an adult. At the same time, Jane Mason, dau.
of Benj. — an adult.

At night in the Lecture room, Ann, infant dau. of John and Ann Thornly

St. Johns Church, New London Cross Roads, Tuesday 28 Sep 1819, bapt. In the
Church P.M., Alexander, son of Alexander and Margaret Harper, b. 2 March
1819. Also same time and place, Margaret Jane, dau. of James and Catharine
Cane, b. 16 April 1816 (1818?). Also same time and place: Charles Gakeen,
son of John and Lydia Nail, b. 16 Jan 1817.

Sarah Clements, bapt. In the church on Sunday 3 Oct 1819, an adult.

Joseph Abraham, son of George and Elizabeth Witsil, b. 14 July 1819 and bapt. at
the house in Wm? [*abbreviation for Wilmington?*] on account of extreme
illness, and died same week.

The following adults were bapt. on Saturday night 9 Oct 1819 in the Church to
wit, Jacob Justis Robinson, son of Joseph and Mary, b. 31 March 1791 near
Miltown, Del. Charles Barnett Peterson, son of John and Sarah Peterson, b.
20 March 1804. Adriana, dau. of Henry and [blank]

Maria, dau. of [blank]

Lydia, dau. of Lawrence and Lydia Greatrake, aged 16 years, 9 mos.

Sarah, dau of do, aged 12 years, 3 mos.

Sarah Ann, dau. of Jacob and [blank]

Mary Pierce

Bapt. In the Church, Sunday 17 Oct 1819, Margaret, aged 20 mos. and 15 days,
dau. of John and Martha Ritchey.

Bapt. The following at the house Oct 1819.

Phebe Dunn, wife of Benjn. and dau. of Obadiah and Jane Dingee, b. 16 Jan 1786.

Isaac, son of Benjamin and Phebe Dunn, b. 27 Jan 1808

Charles, son of Benjamin and Phebe Dunn, b. 28 Oct 1810

Lavinia, son [*sic*] of Benjamin and Phebe Dunn, b. 14 Feb 1816

Henry, son of Benjamin and Phebe Dunn, b. 10 April 1818

Bapt. 19 Oct 1819 at the house in Phila. Elizabeth, dau. of Wm and Elizabeth
Jones, b. 18 Dec 1819. Mary Elizabeth, dau. of Jacob and Catharine Wagner,
b. 17 Oct 1819.

Bapt. In Phila. 19 Nov at the house because of illness, Joseph Edmund, b. 14 Oct
1815 and Hannah Eliza, b. 27 Sep 1818, children of John Joseph and
Margaret Ann Norman.

Bapt. At the parsonage 11 Dec John Torbett, son of John and Mary Wilgus, b. 28
Sep 1819. Sponsors with the Mother John Hammers and Nancy,
grandparents.

Bapt. At the house, 18 Dec, Sarah Foulke, wife of John, in the 84th year of her age.

Bapt. The following in Trinity Church 20 Dec, the 4th Sunday in Advent, Thomas
Strode and Prudence his wife and their five children, Mary Ann, b. 5 Feb

1809; Levi, b. 17 Feb 1811; Isaac Shallcross, b. 24 Nov 1813; Thomas, b. 1 Aug 1816; Elizabeth Robinson, b. 3 July 1819.

Sarah Derrickson, aged 51 years, dau. of the late Wm. and Rachel Reynolds. Mary Campeson, aged 45 years, dau. of Thos. and Sarah Hampton. Lydia Campeson, dau. of Joseph and Mary, b. 17 — 1798 and bapt. By the Revd. Wm Wickes June 1816 and now recorded at the request of the parents - Sarah Anderson Haslett, aged 24 years., dau. of Thomas and Jane Smith, Brandywine. Abigail Sharp, aged 23 years. John and Henry, twins, b. 24 Nov 1810 - Hannah, b. 17 Dec 1818 - children of Andrew and Elizabeth Peterson. Also Sarah Ann, b. 20 Aug 1802. Elizabeth do 28 Dec 1803 - Samuel do 28 Oct 1805 - Mary do 6 March 1808 - Margaret do. 19 Feb 1810 - George do 24 Aug 1812 - Rebecca do 3 Sep 1813 - Susan do 3 Oct 1815 decd. 17 Jan 1816 - children of A & E Peterson, bapt. In infancy.

Bapt. 26 Dec in Trinity Church, Sarah Freese, dau. of [blank] Witnesses Rebecca Rozell and Betsy Naff

Bapt. At the house 4 Jan 1820, Isaac Stidham, son of Cloud and Eliza Elliott, b. 6 May 1819

Bapt. At their house, near Newark, 6 Jan, being Epiphany, Maria Louisa, b. 10 June 1817. Also same day Margaret Caroline, b. 10 June 1819 - children of Francis and Rachel O'Daniel, being his second wife.

Bapt. The following in Smyrna 18 Jan Ann Webb in her 17th year.

Richard, son of Richard and Sarah Keyes, b. 27 July 1810

Elizabeth, dau. of George and Ellen Jennings, b. 25 March 1814

Eliza Jane, dau. of Matthew and Sarah McGar, b. 18 Aug 1818.

These families are attached to St. Peter's Church in Smyrna.

Bapt. In the church, Sunday 5 March, Perthina, b. [blank] and Mary Ann, daus. of Thomas and [blank] Vandever. Also same time, Rachel Rossell, adult,

Bapt. At the house, 6 March, Margaret, b. 19 Jan 1820, dau. of Hugh and Jane Press - Also Elizabeth, b. 4 Oct 1818, bapt. 12th is here recorded, dau. of the same.

Elizabeth Carter, b. 27 Feb 1805, at Brandywine, Thomas, b. 7 Dec 1806, and bapt. When they were about 6 months old. John, b. 26 July 1809 at Burne?, Ann Charlotte, b. 8 March 1812. Eliza Carter, b. 21 Jan 1815, in Phila., and all three bapt. In infancy. - Catharine and Joseph, twins, b. Sunday morning 26 March 1820 and bapt. At the house by me R.D.H. on Thursday the 30th March 1820. Hugh Brady, sponsor with the parents, viz. Allen and Elizabeth Mills.

Bapt. Sunday 9 April 1820, John, son of William and Elizabeth Gibbs, English people - b. 23 Feb 1820

Bapt. In trinity Ch. Sunday 16 April the following. John Mullica and his wife Margaret Mullica, and their son William Halt, b. [blank}, Samuel, son of Jos. and Mary Campison(?), b. 4 Jan 1801 and Margaret McBeath, in her 20th year.

Bapt at the house, 21 April 1820, Thomas, son of Thomas and Martha Elliott, b.
  28 Jan 1803. Mary Anderson, dau. of the same, b. 29 Aug 1811. Same time,
  Isabella, dau. of William and Isabella Eliott, b. 1 Sep 1811. James McKee,
  son of the same, b. 15 Sep 1819
John, b. 1 April 1810, bapt. In his third year. William Auwl, b. 11 Oct 1812, bapt.
  in infancy, children of William and Isabella Elliott.
Samuel, b. 12 March 1813. Allen, b. 29 May 1814, bapt. In infancy - Mary
  Thompson, b. 29 May 1815. Juliana, b. 25 Feb 1818. George Reed, b. 20 Dec
  1819. These last three children were bapt. By me at the house, on 29 April
  1820. The parents Dr. Allen and Catharine Ann McLane.
25 April? 1820, bapt. At the house, Eleanor Brynberg, b. 26 Jan 1815. John
  Brumberg, b. 9 March 1816 - children of Charles and Rebecca Justis. At the
  same time, Peter Brynberg, b. 3 Aug 1818, son of John and Ann Foreman.
18 June 1820, bapt. In Trinity Church on 3rd Sunday in Trinity the following, Mrs.
  Hannah Smith, wife of Thomas, and their four children, Juliann Davis, b. 12
  April 1810, Charles Bunnor, b. 1 Feb 1812, Hetty Bunnor, b. 19 Feb 1814.
  Eliza Davis, b. 2 Feb 1816.
Mrs. Maple Thatcher, widow of [blank] and her 5 children, viz., Hannah, b. 12
  Oct 1806, Mary, b. 11 Dec 1809, William, b. 3 July 1811, Albert, b. 16 June
  1813, Lewis, b. 10 Sep 1815. and the following adults, Abraham Smith, aged
  23; Samuel Duncan, aged 21; Joseph Seeds, aged 19; Rebecca Hale; Louisa
  Smith; Maria Foulke; Mary Ann Welsh Hawkins; Elizabeth Storey.
7 June bapt. at the house, Edward Bodle and George Baker, twins, b. 12 May
  1820, children of Alexr. Hall and Mary Hall. Bapt. In the house, John, b. 20
  April 1818; Sarah, b. 18 March 1825 - children of Hugh and Ellen Welsh.
  Margaret Jane, b. 4 Oct 1818; Charlotte, b. 23 April 1820 - children of John
  and Elizabeth Bodle. Edward, b. 12 June 1817 of the same parents, bapt. By
  Rev. Wm Wickes. John Frederic, b. 29 Oct 1819, son of John Frederic and
  Marce? Martin?
15 July 1820, bapt. At their house, Thomas William, b. 6 June 1819, son of John
  and Elizabeth Sinex, being sick.
23 Sunday, bapt. In Trinity Church, Charles Minor, an adult – Hannah, b. [blank]
  dau. of John and Elizabeth Fisher.
24 Monday, bapt. In St. John's, New London Crossroads, Chester Co., Thomas
  Strawbridge Dickey, b. 27 April 1820, son of John and Lydia Neal of said
  congregation.
Bapt. Abner, son of Wesley and Ann Bayly, b. 15 Feb 1818. Same day, Martha,
  dau. of Wesly and Ann Bayley, b. 15 Oct 1819. Died.
Same day, Tabitha, dau. of William and Elizabeth Hampton, b. 15 April 1820,
  died 13 Aug.
6 Aug, bapt. Adults - Allen Jack, John Taylor, Thomas Jeffries, Keziah Smith.
27 Aug, bapt. Hester Yarnall Warner, dau. of John and Eliza Ann Brobston of
  James - Eliza Garretson of Elizabeth Phillips, wife of [blank] - Adults

18 Sep bapt. In St. Johns, N.L., Eliza Ann, b. 1 Aug 1817, James, b. 2 April 1820, children of Thomas and Maria Lindew.

22 Sep, bapt. Marce Martin, wife of John Frederic.

29 Nov Bapt. 29 Nov 1820, the following children of John and Hannah Ritchie, Rachel, b. 11 Feb 1811; Ann Jane, b. 14 May 1815; William, b. 7 Dec 1817; Sarah, b. 1 April 1820. The following baptized by Rev. Wm Pryce - Mary Baldwin, dau. of the above Hannah Ritchie by Antony Baldwin, a former husband, b. 17 Nov 1806, bapt. In her 2nd year. Elizabeth, dau. of Jno V. and Hannah Ritchie, b. 13 May 1809, bapt. In the 5th month. Lydia, dau. of John and Hannah Welsh, b. 20 Jan 1798 and bapt. By the same in the 9th year.

The following bapt. By the Rev. Wm. Wickes, Mary Ann, b. 13 March 1810; Thomas, b. 26 June 1812, children of Valentine and Ann Beason. Lydia, b. 18 Sep 1816 of Anthony and Ann Christy, formerly Beason. Bapt. by me R. D. H. 29 Nov 1820, James, b. 23 Sep 1820 and John Vertue, twins, sons of Anthony and Ann Christy. By Rev. S. C. Brinckle, Peter and Isabella, twin children of the same, b. 26 Feb 1818, bapt. 7 May 1819. Peter died soon after baptism.

Catharine Ann, b. 9 April 1809 - John Henry, b. 8 Oct 1807, children of James and Elizabeth Welsh, both bapt.

19 Nov, bapt. In Trinity Church, Rachel Ann Hillman, an adult; also Cornelius Stedham, son of Joseph and Ann.

24 Bapt. At his dwelling, John Simmons, b. 10 July 1765 and his six children, to wit, they answering for themselves, William, b. 3 April 1795; George, b. 31 Jan 1797; Mary, b. 3 Dec 1798; John, b. 2 May 1801; Hannah, 26 Dec 1802; Bauduy, 24 June 1805.

10 Dec Bapt. In St. Martin's, Marcus Hook, Mary Gray, an adult, dau. of Thomas Gray.

17 Bapt. In Trinity, Rosanna Freese, dau. of [blank]. Also same time, Frederica, b. 26 Aug 1820, dau. of Abraham and Ann Schrader.

24 Bapt. In Trinity, Elizabeth Brinton, dau. of Cap. Jacob Brinton and Sarah, now Roberts.

26 Bapt., Elizabeth McGee, dau of Benjamin H. and Ann Springer, b. 2 July 1820.

January 1821

21 Jan, bapt. In Trinity Ch. Ann Dorothy, dau. of Wm and Catharine Hall, b. 16 June 1820.

22 Jan Bapt. In Phila. Elizabeth, dau. of William and Elizabeth Jones

25 Bapt. Samuel, b. 4 April 1817. Robert, aged 4 mos and 20 day. Children of Joseph Grimes

14 Bapt. In St. Martins, Marcus Hook, the following adults [*sic*] Ann Entricken.

18 Feb Bapt. in Trinity Church (Sunday), John Bradford, 29 years, Jefferson Burr Williamson; and Sarah Margaretta, dau. of John and Margaretta Bradford, b. 9 March 1818.

11 March. Sunday, in Trinity, Benjamin Pert, and — Williams - Adults

16 March Bapt. In the house - Deborah, b. 29 Aug 1820, dau. of William and Ruth Pogue. Same Time - Thomas, b. 8 Nov 1820, son of John and Rebecca Stevens.

30 March Bapt. in Phila. Margaret Perroteau dau. of Joseph and Margaret Brognard, b. 6 Sep 1820. Same time Betsy Ann, dau. of John and Maria Dunphy and b. 3 Feb 1820. Sponsor Mrs. Hannah Perroteau

12 April Bapt. on the Levels at Mr. Flintham's - Joseph, son of Peter and Christiana Hanson, b. 3 Oct 1820. Same time - Henry, b. 22 July 1819, son of Charles and Sarah Johnson, coloured persons.

June 1821

Bapt. at Dover June Nicholas, b. Dover on the morning of Monday 18 Dec 1820 at 5 o'clock, the 10th child of H. M. Ridgely and Sarah his wife.

Bapt. at Smyrna 5 June 1821, Matthias, b. 18 Sep 1820, son of Matthew and Sarah McGar. Also at Smyrna the 6th - Susan Holliday, b. 4 Nov 1807 - George Wilson, b. 18 Jan 1809 - John Hollady, b. 19 July 1810 - Alphonia, b. 13 Aug 1812, William, b. 21 June 1814 - Martha Ann, b. 22 April 1817 - Mary, b. 5 Sep 1818 - Daniel, b. 12 April 1820 - all children of John and Susan Cummins his wife- also at the same time, bapt. The mother, Susan Cummins, b. 29 June 1788. All of St. Peter's, Smyrna.

Bapt. In Trinity Church, wile on Whitsunday, 1– June the following adults - John Malone, Sarah Malone, Maria Malone, Rebecca Malone - Jesse Taylor - P. Malone b. 23 Aug 1793. J. Malone 7 Feb 1798, M. Malone 13 May 1802, R. Malone 26 Feb 1804 - children of Jno Malone aged 45 years and Rebecca Malone aged 4-?

Bapt. The following on Cape May, 6 Aug 1821, Rachel, b. 4 Feb 1820, dau. of James and Weighty Dempsey of Goshen - Jane, b. 28 Dec 1821, 12 Aug, dau of John and Mary Rutherford.

1 Sep John, b. 26 —, son of John and Mary Weaver, at the house in Wil. on account of sickness.

2 — Bapt. In Trinity on Sunday the following adults - Sarah, dau of Jacob and Elizabeth Matthews in the 18th year of her age.

Susanna, dau. of Leonard and Elizabeth Seal, in the 16th year of her age - Sarah, dau. of Patty Bluit and [blank] in the 22nd year of her age.

27 Nov Bapt. At the house at Dupont's factory - on account of illness, Mary Ann infant child of Andrew and Rebecca Armstrong.

23 Dec Bapt. In the Church, Mary Ann Freese, an adult. Witness Margaret Johnson.

January the 17th 1822

Bapt. At the house on account of illness - Charles Henry, son of John and Ann Catharine Gordon, b. 19 Feb 1821. Also I here word the name of William

Hemphill, b. 21 Oct 1805 and bapt. By the Revd. William Pryce in his 3rd year - also Sidney Ann Cucha(?), b. 7 Nov 1807 and bapt. By the same in her 1st year - also Catharine Sharp, b. 5 June 1810 and bapt. By the same in her 1st year - all children of Jno. and Ann Catharine Gordon.

Bapt. 16th inst. George Washington, son of Jonas P– and Sarah P. Fairlamb.

Baptisms by the Rev. Ralph Willison. At Dover, June 9th 1822, Eugene, son of Harry and Sarah Ridgely, b. 4 May 1822. Bapt. In Trinity Church, June 1822, William Gustavus, son of R. Williston and Ann M., b. 18 Oct 1821. Bapt. At the same time William Henry, son of William D. and Sarah T. Brinkle. Bapt. 30 July, Jane, dau. of Allen and Elizabeth Mills, b. 12 Aug 1821. Bapt. 22 Aug 1822, Elizabeth, dau. of John and Mary Weaver, b. 25 Oct 1821. Bapt. At the same time, Margaret, dau. of John and Ann Springer, b. 2 Nov 1821. Bapt. 9 March 1823, Mrs. Hariot Saville, Miss Sally Ann Warner, and Miss Mary day, adults. Also, Mrs. Catherine Bryan.

June 1823. Bapt. At Smyrna, George Washington, son of James and Susan Webb, b. 11 Sep 1822.

Also Rachel Wilson, dau. of John and Susan Wilson Cummins, b. 8 May 1822.

Bapt. In Trinity Church, Deborah, dau. of John and Mary Lynam, b. 19 Aug 1821.

Bapt. Aug 1823, James Fountain, son of Andrew and Rebecka Armstrong, b. 25 March 1823.

Bapt. 28 Oct 1823, Mary Ann Rose, dau. of Nathaniel and Anna Maria Forbes, b. in New York 8 May 1819. Also Augustus Davis?, son of the same, b. 1821. Saml. B. and Mary Ann Rose Davis, sponsors.

Bapt. 7 March 1824, Mary Ellenor Townsend, an adult.

Bapt. on Easter Sunday, 18 April, Mrs. Ann Stidham and Hannah Weldin, adults.

Bapt. 12 Dec 1825 by Rev. R. Willison, Rector of Trinity, George, son of John L. and Martha M. A. Milligan, comitted by Mrs. Williston aged — 4 months.

<u>1827-1828 Pierce Connelly Minister of Trinity</u>

William, Kesiah and John White children of Isaac and Ann Anderson 5 Aug

William Gustavus, son of Josiah and Martha Moffet Gilpin 8 Aug

Mary Jane, dau. of John and Elizabeth Aiken, 28 Oct

Ann Eliza, dau. of Cloud (decd) and Eliza Elliott 8 April

Eliza Margaretta, dau. of Benjamin and Ann Elliott 8 Aug

Edward Callender, son of Robert and Margaretta Andrews 24 July 1828

Mary, dau. of John and [blank] Gordon

John, son of John and [blank] Gordon

Katharine, dau. of John J. and Martha M. A. Milligan, Sunday 19 Oct 1828, aged 13 months and 13 days

Baptisms by Isaac Pardee Minister of Trinity Church

28 Dec 1828 Mary, dau. of Cornelius and Elizabeth Stidham

26 March 1829 Ann Jane, dau. of James and Elenor Hannah Fleming

26 March 1829 James, son of Jane and Robert Hinnah [Hannah]

29 March 1829 Henrietta Colesberg, Mary Ann Elenor Linam, dau. of Ann Davis.

20 April 1829 Victorina?, dau. of — Christ–. At the same time Jea–? son of ----
    Shake–? 20 May 1829 -----?

13 June Ann, dau. of Ormand and Sidney Ann Monges

20 June 1829 Julius, son of Phoebe(?) and John (?) Bradford

23 June 1829 Sarah Elizabeth, dau. of John and Mary Linam

18 Oct 1829 Mrs. Ellen Tood

23 Feb 1830 Miss Joana Pierce

28 March 1830 Rebecca Coxe b. 28 May 1821. Louis Henry Coxe, b. 18 April
    1824. Elizabeth McKane Coxe, b. 12 Nov 1826. Albert Fisher Coxe, b. 4 Nov
    1828. At the same time Sarah Vandever, b. 12 May 1817, Ingeber Robinsor
    Vandever, b. 20 May 1818, Emmit Vandever, b. 24 March 1820, Peter
    Vandever, b. 27 Sep 1822, Catharine Vandever, b. 24 April 1824 - at the
    same time Sarah D Huxley, Elizabeth Rebecca Huxley, Martha Ann Huxley,
    Catharine Jane Huxley. At the same time Sally Ballach Smith 23 May.
    Thomas Smith 27 May 1830. Mrs. Vandever, wife of Thomas Vandever 30
    May 1830. Miss Peach

Bapt. 5 July 1830 John Shecker Richelson

21 July Jane Macomb

11 Sep 1830 Cora Monges, b. 22 Aug 1830

12 Sep Margaret Jane Stidham, aged 7 months and 3 days.

Bapt. 18 Oct 1830 James -aufax? Smith

John Leonard Riley - Henry Reed Waples

Thomas Peterson Waples - Sarah Elizabeth Still

Sarah Ann Stokes

1831

Bapt.. 15 Feb Joseph Pogue infant son of William and Sarah Ann Pogue

Bapt. 5 April 1831 Rodney Esthentberge, son of Eliza (Rodney) and John
    Ethenberge

Bapt. 21 April 1831 Rebecca Stephens, Elizabeth Stephens and Mary Ann
    Stepens [*sic*]

Bapt. 29 May 1831 Mary Hannah and Mary Jane Reed

Bapt. 3 June 1831 James Cragg McComb

Bapt. 25 Sep 1831 Edmund Right (Wright)

Bapt. 5 Feb 1832 Adaline Saville and Eliza Savill

At the same time Hellen Mar Gadon and George Clinton Gadon

Bapt. 13 May 1832 Hugh Percy Redfpath Blandy, son of Thomas and Frances

Paca Smith Blandy, b. 31 Jan 1831

Bapt. 9 July 1832 Gadon Monges, son of Armond and Sidney Ann Monges.

Bapt. 11 Aug 1832 Arther McAllester, aged 22 months.

Bapt. 30 Aug 1832 Sarah Abel Christie, aged 7 months - at the same time William Henry Riley aged 11 months.

Sunday 2 Sep 1832 Caroline Sophia Armstrong, b. 14 June 1827 and Maria Armstrong, b. 4 Dec 1829.

Bapt. 26 Nov James Thomas, Henry, Fanny Eliza, Mary Ann, John Alexander, and Julia Sophia McRay(?)

At the same day bapt. William Fleming, Margarett Jane and Geage Martha

Bapt. James P. Pogue

1833, Bapt. 12 Feb 1833, Francis Lawdon, b. 30 Aug 1827, James Robeson Lawdon, b. 25 Aug 1830 - children of Francis and Isabella Lawdon.

At the same time William Gilbert Henderson, b. 9 Oct 1830 and James Wood Henderson, b. 21 Dec 1832 - children of James and Hannah Henderson. At the same time Joseph Carr, b. 14 March 1829 and Mary Shepherdson Carr, b. 13 Nov 1831 - children of Joseph and Barbara Carr.

Bapt. In Trinity Chapel 7 April 1833

John Poulson Armstrong, William Armstrong, James Armstrong, Ann Armstrong and Rachael Armstrong. At the same George and Adam Turnbull. At the same time Miss ... Peach and Ann Eliza Jane Hays, b. 21 Jan 1821. All adults.

At the same time Joseph Stidham Farman, Robert Robison Farman and Ellen Brynbergh Farman, children of John and Ann Brynbergh Farman.

Bapt. 15 Sep 1833 Catharine Thompson.

At the same time Lydia Yeasley.

Bapt. 18 Sep 1833 Olivia McDowell.

Bapt. 17 Oct William Hannah.

Bapt. ... George Bates and Martha Bates

Bapt. — John Frederic Blandey, b. 24 April 1833. At the same time Joseph Dixon Armstrong, 29 Dec 1832 - James ... H— and Mary Ann Stokes

17 Feb 1834 Bapt. Emanuel Valentine Souville?

28 March 1834 bapt. James Conly

23 May 1834 bapt. John Smith

12 July bapt. John Watson

20 July 1834 Bapt. William Henry Jendell

16 Sep 1834 Bapt. Mrs. Sarah Beak. At the same time Mary Landne– Beak

16 Sep 1834 William H. Henry Todd

Bapt. 21 Dec 1834

George Bush Magens and William Solomon Magens

John Lewis

Elizabeth Washington
George Francis
Mary Ann Smith children of Mrs. Gouley - Mother and Ann(?) Washington
    sponsors. Wilmington 28 May 1833
Hannah, dau. of Mary and Anthony Chrigstee (Christee?) Privately Wilton
    [*Wilmington*]. June 1835
Robert, son of John and Mary Andrews. Sponsors: Parents, Mrs. Newman.
Robert Andrews, Myers, Morton Coats sons of Jabes and Nancy Fisher. Mother
    sponsor. Wiltn.[*Wilmington*] 24 Sep 1835
Sally Ann McDaniel witness Mrs. Gordon. Wilt [*Wilmington*] 11 Sep 1835
Agnes Camell, dau. of John Hyland and Margaretta Price - The mother and Miss
    Agnes Stedham [*sponsors*] Wilmington 29 Sep 1835
Thomas, Sarah, Robert, children of William and Sarah Holland.
Samuel, son of John and Margaret King.
Ann, dau. of John and Margaret Leuia. Bapt. At Mr. Bandway Sunday School
    room Aug 1835
Matilda, dau. of John Armstrong, Trinity Chapel 11 Oct 1835.
Sarah, dau of – Hanna. Private 21 Oct 1835
Sarah Ann dau. of Wm and Eliz Wilson.
Mary Ann and Samuel, children of John and Mary Coil
Mary, dau. of Geo and Susanna Lamar All on the Brandywine Banks 29 Oct 1835.
Mary Anna, dau. of — Riley
William Francis, son of — Lagan (Sagan?), Trinity 5 Nov 1835.
Mary Hovten?, adult, 25 Dec 1835. Mrs. Harvey witness.
Sarah Jane Riddle, dau. of Collins and Eliza Stevenson, Parents sponsors 13 Jan
    1836
Geo. son of Mr. and Mrs. White. Brandywine 17 dec 1836.
Harriet Elizabeth, dau. of the Rev. H. Adams and Mrs. H. E. Adams. Sponsors
    Rev. Wm Russel. Mrs. Adams, Mrs. Weyward, Mr. Adam Priest
Ann, dau. of Mr. and Mrs. Archy Watson. Parents sponsors. Wilmington 15 May
    1836.
Ellen, dau. of Mr. Fleming. Privately 11 Jan 1836.
Ann, dau. of Wm. and Mary Porter 17 July 1836.
Rosanna, dau. of Saml and Isabella Foster. Parents sponsors 21 July 1836.
Sophia and [blank] Lewis, children of Jacob and Sophia Topman. Wilmington 14
    Aug 1836.
Robert, son of John and Margaret King. Brandywine 28 Aug 1836.
Franklin DuPont, son of John and Mary Jack. Private. Brandywine 31 Aug 1836
John Robert and William Henry, children of Robert and Ann Evans.
Susan, dau. of N [*Neal*] and Fanny Conelly. 31 Aug 1836
Mary Elizabeth, dau. of Sebastian and Maria Planck - Brandywine 18 Oct 1836.
Barbara, dau. of William and Margaret Foster. Brandywine 22 Nov 1830.
Issabella, dau. of Eleanor Young. 22 Nov 1836.

Henry, son of John and Sarah Smith. Parents sponsors 29 Dec 1836.

Maryan Mathison. - Margaret Mathison [*sponsor*] 29 Dec 1836

St. Julian, infant son of John Armand and Sidney Ann Monges 4 Jan 1837.

Sarah Ellen, dau. of Elizabeth and Samuel Thompson 19 March 1837. Parents sponsors.

Sidney Louisa, child of Mr. and Sidney Ann Monges - Parents sponsors and Mrs. Gordon. 6 April 1837. Wilmington

Ann and Margarett Tatnall, children of James and Cath?. Grandmother and Mrs. Gordon sponsors. Wilmington 11 April 1837.

James, son of Mrs. Euphala Gore (Gove?)

Andrew, son of Mr. Wm. and Elizabeth Wilson. Brandywine 16 April 1837.

Miss Sarah Elizabeth Colwell. Trinity Chapel 16 April 1837.

Nathaniel Platt, son of Nat and Mary Platt. Parents and Mary Platt.

Jas Platt, son of Nat and Mary Platt. Sponsors Jas Platt - Archy — and Ann Platt.

Joseph Platt, son of Ditto Samuel and Joseph Platt and Gaston (?), sponsors. Wilmington 13 May 1837.

Anna Longester, dau. of Mr. and Mrs. White. Brandywine - Wilmington 11 Jan 1837.

Sarah Redwood, dau. of Mr. Jabes and Ann Fisher. Mother spon. Wilmington 21 Jan 1837.

George Lardner, son of Wm. and Gabiella Josephine Breck. Wilmington. 14 Oct 1837.

Mary Ann ------ Tailor. 15 Oct 1837.

Samuel Johnson, son of Mr. and Mrs. Davis. 22 Oct 1837.

Hester Fountain?, dau. John [blank] Armstrong. 19 Nov 1837.

Martha Elizabeth, dau. of John and Martha Milligan. Parents and Miss Guston(?) [*sponsors*]. 26 Nov 1837.

George Bush, son of Anthony and Ann Chester. 29 Nov 1837.

Sabilla, child of Mr. and Mrs. Porter. Parents spon. 21 Jan 1838.

George Washington, son of Joseph and Mary Ann Riley

Hannan? Jane, dau. of Wm. and Eliza.

John, son of Wm. and Ann Willis, 8 Feb 1838.

Elenor, dau. of John and Mary Coyle. By Mrs. Dowdsly? 31 March 1838.

Sarah Martha, Ann McKim, Allan Thompson, children of James and Jane Perry?. Parents sponsors 13 April 1838.

Baptisms during the Rectorship of Rev. John W. McCullough (which comenced 11 Sep 1838).

1. Ellen, aged 9 weeks, dau. of Robt. and Jane Hannah 16 Sep 1838. Bapt. At the Hannah's.
2. Charles William, son of Mr. and Mrs. Thompson. Bapt. In Trinity Chapel 28 Oct 1838.

3. Sarah Jane, dau. of Mr. and Mrs. Forrest10 Dec, aged 1 month - At home

4. 28 Dec 1838 in Trinity Ch Chapel, Mrs. Rebecca Hootin (adult). Sponsor Miss Wooten.

5. Miss Ann Eliza Roche (adult) sponsor the mother Mrs. Roche. 5 Jan 1839 at the Kings

6. Elizabeth, dau. of William and Elizabeth King, b. 18 Oct 1838.

7. Joseph Alexander, son of Gilbert and Margaret Matheson, b. 10 March 1838.

8. [blank] Thurlow Sanders, dau. of [blank]

9. 25 Jan 1839 Anna Mary Louell, b. 14 July 1836.

10. William Radcliffe, son of Radcliffe and Mary Chadwick, b. 22 Dec 1838, bapt. 19 May 1839.

11. Edmund Jeffries, son of Mr. and Mrs. Jeffries (now Chandler), b. 1830, bapt. 19 May 1839. Sponsor - Mrs. R. Hootin.

Sarah Jane, b. 29(24?) June? 1839, dau. of George and Nancy Sayers. Parents sponsors.

Elizabeth, b. 10 March 1839, dau. of Neal Conelly and Fanny Conelly. Parents sponsors.

John Newman, son of John W. and Mary Andrews. Parents sponsors July 1839.

Mary Elizabeth Hedges, b. 7 Aug 1837, dau. of Joseph and Mary Jane Hedges. - Mrs. Hedges —?, A— Hedges - —? 4 Aug 1839, bapt.

James, son of James and Eleanor Bovard, b. 10 July 1839. Sponsors parents.

John Weright, son of John and Margaret King, b. 27 July 1839.

Margaret, dau. of Robert and Margaret Baxter, b. 5 Nov 1838. Sponsors parents. 25 Aug 1839 at the home of Mr. Greens?—?

Charles Ambrose, son of Sebastian and Mariah Planck, b. 18 Dec 1837.

Charles, James, Maria, Margaret and William, ages 14, 12, 6, 4 and two years respectively and children of [blank] Green.

William (Smith) b. 21 Aug 1839, son of John Hunter Smith and Sally Green Smith 31 Aug 1839 at the church.

Adalein, b. 26 June 1832, Charles, b. 1 Oct 1834, children of Joseph and Mary Jane Hedges. 1 Sep 1839 in the church.

Mary Jane Hedges (adult) b. 23 Sep 1810.

Sarah Ann Magers (adult), b. 2 Aug 1839.

Henrietta, b. 9 July 1839, dau. of William and Isabella Sparks. Sponsor Mary Weaver

Baptisms by Rev. J. W. McCullough 3 Sep 1839.

Lydia, b. 17 Oct 1835, Caroline, b. 11 Sep 1838, children of Abel and Mary Ann Stokes.

Elizabeth, b. 25 July 1839, dau. of Henry and Sarah Hamilton.

John Henry, b. 4 June 1839, son of John and Eda Davis.

Catharine [blank] (adult), dau.of James and —? Canby.

Emeline of Joseph and Mary Ann Riley, b. 24 Sep 1838, bapt. 22 Sep 1839.

Martha Jane of William and Ann Jane Willis, b. 31 Dec 1838.

Archibald, b. 19 Sep 1839, son of Archibald and Margaret Watson, 22 Sep 1839.

William Gordon, b. 2 May 1838, son of James E. and Catharine Hope (Rose?) Price, 5 Jan 1840.

Isabella Hart. Sponsors Fanny Hacket

Elizabeth Hootin. Frances —? Hootin. 26 Jan 1840.

Elizabeth Moore (adult) 25 Jan 1840.

Sarah, b. 11 Jan 1840, dau. of John and Mary Coyle - Sponsors.

Hannah Elizabeth, b. 18 Dec 1828 and Jacob, b. 3 April 1831, children of Jacob and Isabella Hart.

Sydney Lane [blank] dau. of [blank]

Margaret, b. 18 May 1840, John and ... Sayers. Parents sponsors, bapt. 12 June 1840.

Margretta Ann Gamble, b. 6 April 1840. William and Mary Stevenson. Parents sponsors.

Margaret, b. 12 Jan 1835

John, b. 22 Sep 1839. Edward and Elza Gowans. Parents sponsors.

Robert, b. 30 July 1840, Robert and Margaret Baxter. Parents sponsors.

James, son of William and Isabella White, b. 29 Feb 1839, bapt. 19 Sep 1840.

1811 Feb 25 - buried Madam Mary Dee-? decd 24th inst [or Decr 24th inst.?]

Baptisms by Rev. J. W. McCullough, Rector of Trinity Church

Elizabeth, b. 11 Sep 1840, of Andrew & Jane Forrest. Sponsor: Samuel Forrest and Mary Forrest.

William Henry, b. Jan 1840 of Henry and Jane Masterson? Sponsors: Jane Masterson and Fanny Smith?

Mary Sophia Gilpin, adult, dau. of Joshua Gilpin. Sponsors: Martha Milligan, Sarah Gilpin, bapt. 3 Oct 1840.

...? Irene duPont, b. 18 May 1840, of –Etta Buck? Sponsors: parents.

Elizabeth Tatnall Brobson, adult. Sponsor: Mrs. Margaretta –. 18 Jan 1841.

Orpho Hall, adult.20? Jan 1841.

Miss Rebecca Springer Derickson, adult, 20 Jan 1841.

Samuel, b. 2 Jan 1841, of William Forrest and Margaret Forrest. Sponsors: parents. 5 Jan 1841.

Sarah Ann, b. 28 Jan 1841, of Moses Journey and Margaret Linsey?. Sponsors: William Forrest, Margaret Watson. 5 Jan 1841.

William John, b. 29 Jan 1841, of Wm and Elizabeth King. Sponsors: parents. 24 Jan 1841.

John, b. 5 March 1841 of Samuel and Sarah McCollam. Sponsors: parents. 27 March 1841.

Benjamin, b. 10 March 1841, of William and Jane Willis.

John Harmon, b. 18 Oct 1833, Ann Eliza, b. 19 Jan 1836, James Evans, b. 30 May 1838, Caroline, b. 18 Aug 1840 - children of James Evans and Rachel Savill

Sophia, b. 31 Dec 1840, of John and Lydia Davis. Sponsors: parents. 5 June 1841.

Mary Elizabeth, b. 6 March 1841, of James and Rebecca —?. Sponsors: parents. 5 June 1841.

Ann Jane, b. 19 April 1840, of Ezekiel and Elizabeth Aikins. 5 June 1841.

Elizabeth, b. 31 July 1841, of John and Sarah Sayers. Sponsors: parents. 5 June 1841

Jane, b. 15 May 1841, of John and Margaret King. Sponsors: parents

Mary Jane, b. 10 Aug 1840, of William and Elizabeth. 31 July 1841.

Hannah Elizabeth, b. Feb 1841, of Wm and Henrietta Ritchie

Joseph, b. 14 Dec 1840, of Joseph and Mary Ann Riley. 2 Aug 1841.

Samuel, b. 26 Oct 1841, of Wm and Mary Porter

Mary Ann, b. 13 Nov 1839 and James, b. 14 Sep 1841, of Wm and Catharine Thomas (Thorn?)

Smiley, b. 16 Feb 1842, of Geo. and Nancy Sayres. Sponsors: parents. 1 March 1842.

Eleanor, b. 20 Feb 1842, of John and Elizabeth Sayres. Sponsors: parents. 1 March 1842

Matheas? of [blank] Baxter. Sponsors: parents. 6 March 1842.

Hannah Maria?, b. 22 Nov 1830 of [blank] M–?. 11 March 1842.

Eliza Ann File (adult). Sponsors: C. R. Th—? and Mary McDavid?. March 1842.

Rosalie, b. 16 Nov 1840, of James Ferguson. Sponsors: parents. March 1842.

Joseph Smith, b. 18 May 1835, Elizabeth Jackson, b. 21 Nov 1837, Margaret, b. 21 March 1841, children of Joseph Smith Davis and Jane Sharp his wife. Sponsors: Mrs. Davis. 8 April 1842.

Mary, b. 14 Sep 184-, of Dr. and Julia Lockwood

George, b. 1 April 1842, of Thomas and Mary Little Whalin. Sponsor: parents.

Isabella, b. 24 Aug 1841, of Edward and Rebecca Hurst. Sponsors: Rebecca Hurst, John McGiniss, Robt Beattee(?). 9 April 1842

Emily, b. 7 Feb 1835, Martin, b. 25 May 1837, Algernon Cecil, b. 18 Jan 1840, Elizabeth Shoals, b. 19 Feb 1842, children of John A. and Lydia R. Willard

Matthew, b. 31 May 1842, son of Geo. and Mary Russell. Sponsors: parents. 21 June 1842.

Mary Ann, b. 29 Sep 1841, of Neal and Fanny R. Conelly. Sponsors: parents. 21 June 1842.

William, b. 20 April, 1833, John, b. 12 Aug 1835, Sarah Brouster, b. 17 Jan 1842, of Saml and Elizabeth Brown. Sponsors: parents.

Mary Elizabeth, b. 24 Dec Ezekiel and Elizabeth Aikins. Sponsors: parents.

Mrs. Rachel Smith, an adult. 20 Nov 1840.

Rebecca Ann, b. 7 Sep 1837, of James and Charlotte Coxe. 27 - 1840.

Mary Kirby of Capt Nones (Mones?).

William James, b. 27 Nov 1842, of William and Margaret Forrest. Sponsors: parents. 18 [16?] March 1840.

William, b. 16 Feb 1843, of Wm and Catherine Morin. Sponsors: parents.

Smiley Wright, b. 7 March 1840, of Wm and Elizabeth Ling. Sponsors: parents. 26 March 1840.

Lewis Gibbons, adult, of Witney? W. F. –?. 12 Feb 1843.

Mary —, — Dauphin

Elmira Lucretia, b. 1 July 1837, Leonzo Griffin, b. 27 Nov 1842, of James E. and Eliza Ann File. Sponsors: parents.

Margaret White Hendrickson, Mary Elizabeth Armstrong, Ann Armstrong - adults. 9 April 1843.

Isaac Pardu, b. 11 April 1838, of A. Forman, mother. Sponsor: Mother.

George Robert, b. 19 Oct 1841, of Hugh and Rebeca Wright. Sponsors: parents. [blank] Macomb and Catherine Baxter.

Mrs. Charlotte Coxe, adult. Sponsors Miss E. Montgomery. 9 April 1843.

Margaret Jane, b. 13 Jan 1843, of John and Catharine Russel. Sponsors: parents. 12 May 1843.

Evan Henry Thomas, adult; John Hollingsworth, adult; Mary Ann Melson, adult; Rachel Armstrong, adult. 7 May 1843.

Richard Springer, b. 26 Aug 1840, Anne Eliott, b. 2 Nov 1841, Mary Jane, b. 3 April 1843 - of Wm and Susana Lovell. Sponsors: parents. 19 May 1743.

[blank] of Mary Ann Watson?. Sponsor: Mother. - May? 1843.

Isabella, b. 4 June 1843, John, b. 13 Oct 1839, Mary Elizabeth, 3 Nov 1842, of Nathaniel Chadwick. Sponsors: Mother and Mrs. Platt, 4 June 1843.

John, b. 16 May 1843, Benj. and Sarah Lenderman. Sponsors: parents. 16 June 1843.

Elizabeth Canby, b. 19 April 1843, of Rev. J. W. and E. R. McCullough. Sponsors: parents. 31 July 1843.

Margaret, b. 31 Aug 1842, of Francis and Elizabeth Bell. Sponsors: parents. 3 Aug 1843.

Williamina Donovan, b. 27 Aug 1843, of Wikison? S. and Mary Clem— ? Fleming. Sponsors: parents. 27 Aug 1843.

Sarah Frances, b. 16 Feb 1842, of ditto, ditto, ditto.

James Holmes, b. 3 March 1843, of Alex. and Mary Bratton. Sponsors: parents. 10 Aug 1843.

John Peoples, b. 12 July 1843, of James and Rebecca Dean(?). Sponsors: parents. 10 Aug 1843.

Margaret, b. 8 Oct 1743, of John and Sarah Sayres. Sponsors: parents. Oct 1843.

Dr.? Gideon Jaques - At his house, very ill, son of Capt. & Mary Riley. 23 Oct 1843.

Emma Eleonora, b. 2 Sep 1843, Lars (Sam?) and Ida Christiana Wilbye (Welby?) (Davis). Sponsors: parents. 19 Nov 1843.

Margaretta Harker (adult)

James, b. 17 Nov 1841, of John and Sary Smith. Sponsors: parents.

Catharine Read, b. 1 Oct 1843, of Dr. and Julia Lockwood. Sponsors: W. L. Readley and C.?? 1 Jan 1844.

William P. Bisterson?, adult, July 1844.

Abel, b. 13 March 1841, of Capt. Abel P. Stokes. Sponsor: —?

Alfred, b. 1 July 1843, of Capt. and S. Stokes. Sponsors: Mother and Miss Mary —?

Thomas Jefferis, adult, bapt. 2 Jan 1844.

Amon (Amos?) Harvey, adult, bapt. 2 Jan 1844.

Margaret D.? Hedges, adult, bapt. 2 Jan 1844.

George D. Armstrong, adult, bapt. 10 March 1844

Mary Timmons, adult, bapt. 10 March 1844.

Sidney Burns, adult, bapt. 10 March 1844

Samuel of George and [blank] Russell

Septima Serina, b. 5 March 1844, of Edward and Rebecca Hurst. Sponsors: parents.

Faithy Littell, of Robt. and Margaret Burns. Sponsors: parents.

Elizabeth, of same. Sponsors: same

George Peterson, b. 6 Dec 1841 and Eliza Ann Peterson, children of W. S. and Sarah O'Daniel. Sponsors: The father and Maria Louisa O'Daniel and P(O?) Petersson, bapt. 9 April 1844.

Thomas Mackie Smith, b. 19 March 1844, of John and Sally Smith. Sponsors: parents. Bapt. 19 May 1844.

Jane Miller, b. 3 Sep 1843, of Saml. and Isabella Browne. Sponsors: parents. Bapt. 19 May 1844.

Isabella of John and [blank] Sayres. Bapt. 24 May 1844.

Elizabeth, b. 29 1844, of Wm and Mary Watsons? Porter. Sponsors: parents.

Mary Elizabeth, b. 7 July 1843, of John and Margaret King. Sponsors: parents. Bapt. 29 Aug 1844.

John, b. 18 May 1844, of Thomas and Mary L. Whiton(?) Sponsors: Parents. Bapt. 2 June 1844.

Lucy Emily, b. 1 July 1842. Bapt. 14 June 1844.

Ellen Reynolds, b. 26 May 1846 and Joseph Hazlitt, b. 18 July 1844, children of John and Isabella Hannah. Sponsor: Miss Reynolds, grandmother. Bapt. 14 June 1844.

Amelia Elizabeth, b. 28 Nov 1844, of Wm. and E—ella Bush. Sponsors: parents. Bapt. 19 Dec 1844.

Horatio Nelson, b. 17 May 1840.

Charles, b. 20 Sep 1844, of Francis and Ann Perry. Sponsors: parents. Bapt. 20 Oct 1844.

Elizabeth, b. 10 Jan 1844, of Wm. and Catharine Morin. Sponsors: parents. Bapt. April 1844.

Sarah, b. 2 April 1844, of Alex. and [blank] Burns. Sponsors: parents. Bapt. July

1844.

Lucy Emily, b. 1 July 1842. Bapt. 14 June 1844.

Sophia Magdelan, b. 9 Nov 1843, of John and Lydia Davis. Sponsors: Mother and Mrs. Logan. Bapt. 31 Oct 1844.

Isabella, b. 7 March 1844, of Geo. and Elizabeth Sayres. Sponsors: parents. Bapt. 24 May 1844.

John of William and Margt. Forrest. Sponsors: parents. Bapt. July 1844.

John, b. 29 Wep 1844, of John and Margt Forrist. Sponsors: parents. Bapt. 15 Nov 1844.

Mary, b. 3? Nov 1844, of Hugh and Jane Reed. Sponsors: parents. Bapt. 15 Nov 1844.

Mary, b. 6 Oct 1844, of Rev. Corry and Mary Ann Chambers. Sponsors: parents. Bapt. 10 Nov 1844.

Charity Ann, b. 30 March, of James and Susannah Vaneman. Sponsors: parents. Bapt. 16 March 1845.

Neal, b. 27 Aug 1845, of James and Jane Conelly. Sponsors: parents.

Fanny, b. 20 March 1845, of Neal and Fanny Conelly. Sponsors: parents and Geo. Davenport. Bapt. May 1845.

Ellen, b. 12 March 1843?, of Geo. and Catharine Russell. Sponsors: parents. Bapt. 1845.

Elizabeth Frances, b. 2 May 1845, of Saml. and Isabella Brown. Sponsors: parents. Bapt. 1845.

Jacob [blank]

Byron, b. 1 March 1845, of Stephen and Sarah Boddy. Sponsors: parents. Bapt. 1 May 1845.

Isabella, b. 10 June 1845, of John and Lydia Davis. Sponsors: parents. Bapt. 5 Aug 1845.

Frances, b. 30 Nov 1844, of Wm and Susannah Lovell. Sponsors: parents. Bapt. 30 Aug 1845.

Mary Elizabeth, b. 2 Aug 1839, John, b. 5 Sep, 1842? and Sarah Ann, b. 3 Sep 1843, of Wm. and Esther Washington. Sponsor: Parents and Mary Gordy?. Bapt. 6 Aug 1845.

Clara Forrester, b. 3 April 1845, of Dr. Geo Read and Mary McLane. Sponsors: parents. Bapt. 4 Sep 1845.

Catharine, b. 16 Sep 1845, of James and Rebecca David (?) Sponsors: parents. Bapt. 16 Nov 1845.

Dorothia Eleanor, b. 22 Nov 1844, of Wm S. and Mary C. Flemming (dau. of John and — Sayres. Sponsors: parents.

Malchomb, b. 10? May 1845, of Malcomb(?) and Cath. Baxter. Sponsors: parents. Bapt. 19 April 1846.

James, b. 29 March 1846, of William and Grace Edwards. Sponsors: Father and Mrs. Porter and Elizabeth Little

James Henry, b. 28 Feb 1846, of Wm and Ann Payne. Sponsors: parents. Bapt. 27

March 1846.

Samuel Ross, of Brinley Forman and his wife. Sponsors: parents. Bapt. 10 April 1846.

Mary, b. 28 Dec 1845, of Robt and Margaret Baxter. Sponsors: parents. Bapt. 19 April 1846.

Margaret, b. 2 June 1846, of Wm and Margaret Forrest. Sponsors: parents. Bapt. 9 Aug 1846.

Sarah Ann, b. 4 July 1846, of John and Sarah Sayres. Sponsors: parents. Bapt. 9 Aug 1846.

William, b. 9 May 1846, of Alex. and Sidney Burns. Sponsors: parents. Bapt. 9 Aug 1846.

James, b. 10 Sep 1846, of Thomas and Jane Johnson. Sponsors: parents. Bapt. 18 Sep 1846.

Sarah Derickson, of Amos and Martha Haney. Sponsors: parents. Bapt. 2 Oct 1846.

James Hayward, b. 13 Oct 1844, of E. G. and Mary Bradford. Sponsors: parents. Bapt. 2 Oct 1846.

Cornelia, b. 28 May 1846, of E. G. and Mary Bradford. Sponsors: parents. Bapt. 2 Oct 1846.

James, b. 3(2?) May 1846, of John and Sarah Obier. Sponsors: parents. Bapt. 31 May 1846.

Moses, b. 15 July 1846, of Moses and Margaret Journer. Sponsors: parents. Bapt. 31 May 1846.

William, b. 9 May 1846, of Alex. and Sidney Burns. Sponsors: parents. Bapt. 9 Aug 1846.

Margaret, b. 2 June 1846, of Margt. and Wm Forrest. Sponsors: parents. Bapt. 9 Aug 1846.

Sarah Jane, b. 4 July 1846, of John and Sarah Sayres. Sponsors: parents. Bapt. 9 Aug 1846.

James, b. 10 Sep 1846, of Thomas and Jane Johnson. Sponsors: parents. Bapt. 15 Sep 1846.

Edward, b. 20 Sep 1846, of William and [blank] Nethon-?. Sponsors: parents. Bapt. 29 Nov 1846.

Julia, b. 8 July 1846, of Dr. Geo. R. and Mary McLane. Sponsors: parents. Bapt. Nov

William, b. 29 Dec 1846, of Hugh and Jane Reed. Sponsors: parents. Bapt. 24 Jan 1847. Rev. Bishop —.

Lewis B. Woodward, adult. Bapt. Feb 1847.

Sarah Derickson, adult. Bapt. 3 March 1847.

Carry, b. 7 Oct 1746, of Rev. Corry and Mary Ann Chambers. Sponsors: parents. Bapt. 8 March 1847.

Nancy, b. 4 June, of Wm. and Fanny Millingston. Sponsors: parents, bapt. 14 March 1847.

Levinia Justis, adult, bapt. 19 March 1847.

Robert Lewis, b. 13 Oct [blank], of [blank] Armstrong. Sponsors: Mary Elizabeth and Ann Armstrong. Bapt. 19 March 1847.

Elizabeth Armstrong, b. 29? Jan 1844 and Sarah Eleanor, b. 7 Aug 1840, of John and Lavinia Justis. Sponsors: The mother and Rebecca Justis. Bapt. 19 March 1847.

Mary Jane, b. 5 June 1842 and Henry Moore, bapt. 25 Nov 1845, of Wm and Elizabeth Isabella White. Sponsors: parents. Bapt. 19 March 1847.

William, b. 8 Feb 1847, of John and Ann Ritchie. Sponsors: parents. Bapt. 19 March 1847.

Hannah, b. 4 Oct 1846, of Wm and Ann Aveyard. Sponsors: parents. Bapt. 19 March 1847.

William Dawson, b. 26 May 1845, of James and Ann Platt. Sponsors: parents. Bapt. 19 March 1847.

James Christie? [blank]

Lucy Welsh, b. 2 Aug 1845, of Joseph and Mary Ann Riley. Sponsor: the mother. Bapt. 19 March 1847.

Eliza? Ann, b. 2 Oct 1845, of [blank] and Elizabeth Hawn. Sponsors: The mother and Eliza Reynolds. Bapt. 19 March 1847.

Emma, b. 17 July 1746, of Wm F. and Elizabeth D. O'Daniel. Sponsors: parents. Bapt. 19 March 1847.

Charles, b. 29 April 1841, of John W. and Elizabeth S. Duncan. Sponsor: the mother. Bapt. 19 March 1847.

Henry Banning, b. 25 May 1845, of same. Sponsor: same. Bapt. 19 March 1847.

James Hemphill Jones, b. 24 — 1844 and Letitia Patton, b. 1 Jan 1845, of Joseph and Jane S. Davis. Sponsor: The mother. Bapt. 19 March 1847.

Mary Ann, b. 18 Jan 1847, of John — and? and Anne his wife Christie. Sponsor: The mother. Bapt. 19 March 1847.

Amanda Eleanor Armstrong, adult. Bapt. 19 March 1847.

[blank] of William and Susanna —?. Sponsors: parents.

Baptisms by Rev. Edwin Martin Van Deusen, Rector

William Henry, b. 16 Oct 1846, of Thos. R. and Sarah L. McCallister. Bapt. 2 Aug 1847.

James, b. 15 Aug 1847, of Nathaniel and Sarah Brown. Bapt. 28 Aug 1847.

Robert, b. 17 March 1847, of Neal and Fanny Connelly. Sponsors: The Parents. Bapt. 10 Sep 1847.

Andrew, b. 13 May 1847, of John and Elizabeth McLane. Bapt. 4 Oct 1847.

Isabella, b. 14 Sep 1847, of Thomas and Mary Armstrong. Bapt. 4 Oct 1847.

Martha, b. 24 Sep 1847, of Samuel and Elizabeth Sayres. Sponsors: parents., Bapt. 31 Oct 1847.

Henry, b. 24 Aug 1847, of Moses and Margaret Journey.

Mary Ann, b. 3 Dec 1747 of John and Catharine Morrow. Sponsors: parents. Bapt. 19 Dec 1841.

Mary, b. 14 April 1842, William, b. 22 Sep 1844 and Sarah, b. 8 May 1847, of David and Sebra Hanson. Sponsors: parents. Bapt. 2 Jan 1848.

Catharine, b. 19 Dec 1847, of Francis and Anna Perry. Sponsors: parents. Bapt. 9 Jan 1848.

Alexander, b. 19 Nov 1847, of Robert and Feathy Betty. Sponsors: parents. Bapt. 9 Jan 1848.

John James of Wm and [blank] Betty. Sponsors: parents. Bapt. 16 Jan 1848.

Alexander, b. 16 April 1847 of Edward and Rebecca Hurst, bapt. Jan 1848

Thomas, b. 4 Aug 1844, Joseph b. 3 Oct 1842(?), Mary b. 14 Sep 1847 of James and Alice Ogram. Sponsors: parents. Bapt. 9 Feb 1848.

Washington Jackson, of George and Clementine Radew?. Private. Bapt. 15 Feb 1848.

Jack? Lane, of Absalom and Phebe Brown. Private, Bapt. 20 Feb 1848.

Margaret Anne, of Edward and Margaret Lewis. Private. Bapt. 20 Feb 1848.

Mary Anne Isabella of William and Martha Ragins. Sponsor: Rebecca Cox. Bapt. 27 Feb 1848.

John of Andrew and Jane Dever. Private. Bapt. 13 March 1848.

Eupenna Mansley, adult. Sponsor: Sarah Ann Moursley?. Bapt. 16 April 1848.

Isabella, [blank] Fletcher. Sponsor: Henrietta Davis. Bapt. 7 May 1848.

John, b. 27 Dec 1848 of Nathaniel and Anna Morris. Sponsors: parents. Bapt. 5 June 1848.

Elewthera Paulina of Alexr. and Joanna DuPont. Sponsor: Doctor Makie and Elenthera Smith. Bapt. 9 June 1848.

James, b. 2 May 1848 of Andrew and Jane Dever. Sick. Bapt. 12 June 1848.

Ellen Caroline, b. 10 June 1846, of Jeremiah and Elizabeth Scott. Sick. Bapt. 15 June 1848.

Louisa, b. 15 June 1848, of Isaac and Frances Strain. Sick. Bapt. 29 June 1848.

William Alexander, b. 5 July 1848, of Robert and Margaret F.? Reed. Sick. Bapt. 12 July 1848.

Daniel Alexander, b. 6 July 1848, of William and Margaret Forrest. Sponsors: parents. Bapt. 10 Sep 1848.

Mary Grimshaw, b. 20 Sep 1848, of John L. and Henrietta F. Bullom. Sick. Bapt. 23 Sep 1748.

John, b. 3 1848, of John and Isabella Chambers. Sponsors: parents. Bapt. 24 Sep 1848.

James, b. 28 Aug 1848, of Charles and Jane Morrow. Sick. Bapt. 5 Oct 1848.

Emma Elizabeth, b. 12 April 1848, of Abel and Mary Ann Stokes. Sick. Bapt. 6 Oct 1848.

Isabella and Emily, twins, b. 14 Oct 1848, of Neale and Fanny Connelly. Sponsors: parents and James Connelly. Bapt. 18 Oct 1848.

Maria Caroline of [blank] and Catharine Fletcher. Sponsor: Henrietta Javis?. Bapt. 15 Nov 1848.

Gabriella, b. Aug 1848, of William and Gabriella Breck. Sponsors: parents and

Capt. J. Shubrick, U.S.N. Bapt. 17 Nov 1848.

Mary, b. 15 Nov 1839, James Edward, b. 15 Feb 1842, Catharine Gordon, b. 20 Sep 1843, of James E. and Catharine C. Price. Sponsors: Mother and Mrs. Anne Catharine Gordon grandparents. Bapt. 6 Dec 1848.

John Peckleford, b. 24 Dec 1848?, of Joseph S. and Mary J. Hedge. Sponsors: Mother and Mr. and Mrs. John Hedge, grandparents. Bapt. 24 Dec 1848.

William, b. Aug 1848, of Arthur and [blank] Cook. Sponsors: parents. Bapt. 28 Dec 1848.

William Henry, b. November 1848, of Thomas and Catharine Walker. Sick. Bapt. 28 Jan 1849.

Elizabeth, b. 22 Dec 1839, of James and Jane Derry. Bapt. 16 Feb 1849.

Thomas, b. 14 Feb 1849, of Thomas and Anna Maria Bush. Sick. Bapt. 24 Feb 1849.

Dennis Harpwood, b. 17 Aug 1848, of William and Ann Jane Willis. Sick. Bapt. 12 March 1849.

Martha, b. 14 March 1849, of Samuel and Martha Matchet. Sponsors: parents. Bapt. 5 April 1849.

John Brynburg, b. 26 1846, of Peter Brynburg and Margaret R. Forman. Sponsors: parents. Bapt. 6 April 1849.

Margaret Booth Roberts, adult. Witness: The mother and Margaret Booth. Bapt. 10 April 1849.

Ella Olivia 11 May 1849, of Peter L. and Sarah Ann Johnson. Sick. Bapt. 9 April 1849.

Margaret Ann Gallagher child. Sponsors: Henrietta Davis, Gertrude Chraider?. Bapt. 9 April 1849.

Jeremiah Woolston Duncan, adult. Witness: The wife, Moses Bradford and William Brick. Bapt. 15 April 1849.

Elizabeth, b. 18 June 1848, of Jeremiah W. and Elizabeth Duncan. Sponsors: parents. Bapt. 29 May 1849.

A child of Mr. Waters. Bapt. 29 April 1849.

Isabella, b. 29 May 1849, of William and Mary Porter. Sponsors: parents. Bapt. 24 June 1849.

Margaret, b. 15 May? 1849 of same. Same. Same.

Rachel, b. 12 June 1849, of William and Fanny McLaughlin. Sick. Bapt. 15 July 1849.

James, b. 31 March 1849, of Joseph and Mahala Platt. Sick. Bapt. 15 July 1849.

Andrew, b. 24 Jan 1849, of Samuel and Margaret Ba—ay. Sick. Bapt. 19 July 1849.

George, b. 20 Feb 1849, of Thomas and [blank] Gallagher.. Sick. Bapt. 22 July 1849.

Emma, b. 19 April 1849?, of Alexander and Ann Hazelet. Sick. Bapt. 2 Aug 1849.

William, b. 1 Aug 1849, of James and Mary Stein. Sponsors: parents. Bapt. 2 Sep 1849.

Hannah Brinton, b. 16? July 184, of William and Sarah Ann Magens. Sponsor: Parents and Mary B. Solemon? Bapt. 25 Sep 1849.

Ann Catharine, b. 3 May 1849, Bauduy and Ann Simmons. Sponsors: Mother and Margaret Conner?. Bapt. 7 Sep 1849.

Thomas Carton (Caston?) Rea, b. 2 May 1849, of John W. and Phebe Dubree. Sponsors: parents. Bapt. 7 Sep 1849.

Edward Green, b. April 1848, of Edward G. and Mary A. Bradford. Sponsors: The father and grandmother. Bapt. 7 Sep 1849.

John Brown of John and [blank] Ritchie. Sponsors: The mother and grandmother. Bapt. 14 Sep 1849. James, b. 1 Sep 1849, of David and Sebra Hanson. Sponsors: parents. Bapt. 21 Sep 1849.

Henry, b. 7 July 1849, of Moses and Margaret Journey. Sick. Bapt. 16 Sep 1849.

James, b. 1 Sep 1849, of David and Sebra Hanson. Sponsors: parents. Bapt. 21 Sep 1849.

John Thomas, b. 13 Aug 1849, of William and Alice Balm. Sponsors: David & Selia Hanson; the parents. Bapt. 21 Sep 1849.

John, b. 5 May 1849, of John and Catharine Morrow. Sponsors: Sam-? Sayres, Martha Dean and mother. Sick. Bapt. 25? Sep 1849

Catharine Louisa, b. 2 April 1849, of William and Martha Regens. Sponsors: the mother and grandmother. Bapt. same.

Margaret Ann, b. 18 July 1849, of James and Caroline S. Dean. Sick. 25 Sep 1849.

Mary Maria, b. 10 Aug 1849, of William and Eliza New. Sick. Bapt. 15 Oct 1849.

Elizabeth Jane, b. 15 Oct 1849, of Robert and Fathy Beatty. Sponsors: parents. Bapt. 30 Nov 1849.

Jane, b. 14 Aug 1849, of William and Rachel Craig. Sponsors: parents. Bapt. 2 Dec 1849.

Anne, b. 22 Jan 1849(?), of George and Nancy Sayres. Sick. Bapt. 31 Dec 1849.

Margaret, b. 31 Aug 1849, of John and Elizabeth Payne. Sick. Bapt. 7 Jan 1850.

James? Henry, b. 11 March? 1849, of James and P— deaf and dumb. Sponsors: parents and Mr. Wm Forrest. Bapt. 15? Feb 1850.

Essex (Eper?), b. 17 Dec 1849, of Myers and Sarah Hayes. Sick. Bapt. 27 Feb 1850.

Sally Brindly, adult. Sponsor: Ann Brinckley. Bapt. 14 April 1850.

Richard Brindly, adult. Sponsor: —? Bapt. 14 April 1850.

Josephine, Seal Myers and Joseph, of Myers and Sarah Hayes. Sponsors: —? Bapt. 14 April 1850.

Elizabeth Alfred Elliot, adult. Sponsors: Mrs. Ben Elliott and Eliza M. Van Dusen?

Alexander, b. 13 March 1850, of John and Isabella Chambers. Sponsors: parents. Bapt. 9 Jan 1850.

William, of Mary Ann Jackson. Sponsors: parents. Bapt. 26 July 1850.

Rebecca Baker Brindley, adult. Sponsors: Sallie Brindley, Elizabeth Brinckle.

Bapt. 31 July 1850.

John William, b. 28 July 1850, of Daniel and Martha Bardsly. Sponsors: Sebra Hanson, the parents. Bapt. 23 Aug 1850.

Francis Philip, b. 2 Sep 1842, Mary McLane, b. 21 April 1845, Ida Carlotta, b. 25 April 1847, Ella Harlan, b. 28 – 1848, of Francis Carrolla(?)

Mary McLane, b. 21 Aug 1845, [bapt.] 11 Sep 1850, of Altamont and Sarah Ann Wittenberg.

Ida Carlotta of same, b. 25 April 1847.

Robert sick, b. 12 Sep 1850, of Wm Forrest. Bapt. 14 Sep 1850.

Franklin, b. 16 Aug 1844, George, b. 12 Nov 1847 - of George and Nancy Sayres. Sponsors: James and Isabella C. Bo..? and John and Elizabeth Sayres. Bapt. 15 1850.

Robert, b. 15(18?) May 1850, of Robert and Margaret Reed. Sick. Bapt. 25 Sep 1850.

Anne Gorden, b. 7 Jan 1844 and Rebecca George, b. 4 Sep 1846, of George W. and Elizabeth G. Baker. Sponsors: Geo. C. Gordon, Ann Gordon and the mother. Bapt. 25 Sep 1850.

Martha, b. 26? Aug 1850, of Wm and Fanny McLaughlin. Sick. Bapt. 11 Nov 1850.

James, b. 18 July 1839, George, b. 3 Jan? 1842, Margaret Jane, b. July 1844, Robert, b. 3 May 1847, Wm Henry, b. 4 Sep 1849, of [blank] McClintock. Sponsors: the mother, Mrs. James Dever. Bapt. 24 Nov 1850.

Sarah Blanch, Dunlin, b. 17 Oct 1850, of J. Dunlin and Mary An Parkinson. Sponsors: Abraham Parkinson, Sarah Cricktor. Bapt. 30 Nov 1850.

Isabella, b. 4 Oct 1850, of Lewis and Jane Runyan. Sponsors: Geo Fisher, Martha Hastings. Bapt. 15 Dec 1850.

John Franklin, b. 2 Feb 1848, of Hugh and Jane Reed. Sponsors: the mother, John? Keys? Bapt. 15 Dec 1850.

Caroline Amelia, b. 19 Sep 1850, of Samuel and Margaret Barday. Sponsors: the mother, Mary Ann Fleming. Bapt. 5 Jan 1851.

Hannah S. Vaux Chandler, adult. Sponsors: Wm. Samson Vaux, Fanny Vaux. Bapt. 28 Feb 1851.

Geo Richard Baker, adult. Sponsors: Dr. Thos Mackie Smith, Mrs. Ann Gordon. Bapt. 13 April 1851.

Levi Hendrickson Springer, adult. Sponsors: G. D. Armstrong, Richard Brindly. Bapt. 13 April 1851.

Baptisms E. M. Van Drusen Rector, [*The first date is obviously date of birth and the second date is day of baptism.*]

Mary - 3/17/1851 - Arthur and Mary Cook – Sick - 5/5/1851

Anthony Cristy - 2/20/1847 - John and Lydia Davis - The Parents - 5/11/1851

Charles ?ancy - 3/18/1848 -   "   -   "   - 5/11/1851

Mary Vandyke - 2/13/1851 -   "   -   "   5/11/1851

Rebecca Jane - 4/18/1851 - James & Rebecca Deon – Sick - 6/19/1851

Elizabeth DePug - 7/10/1848 - Wm. F. and Elizabeth – The Parents - 7/2/1851

Julia Newton - 4/4/1850 - E. O'Daniel - " - 7/2/1851

Jane - 7/10/1851 - John & Elizabeth Reed - Thos & Jane Gallagher - 7/27/1851

Elizabeth Charlotte - 11/12/1850 - Sam'l & Elizabeth Sagris – Sick – 8/7/1857

Charles Henry - 1/20/1851 - John & Catherine Morrow - The Mother - 8/8/1851

Albert Alonzo - 8/15/1838 - Matthew Mark &The Mother - 8/27/1851

Horatio Nelson - 7/9/1840 - Catherine Cook - Dau, Amelia Cook

Sydney Pearl - 8/30/1843 - " - " - 8/27/1851

Ada Burroughs - 2/14/1845 - " - " - 8/27/1851

Hiram Bust - 4/14/1847 - " - " - 8/27/1851

Walter Herbert - 4/1/1849 - " - " - 8/27/1851

Lucius Gilbert - Thos E. & Martha I Frederick, The Parents & H.L.Gilbert - 8/29/1851

Frank - 6/19/1851 - Baudey & Ann Simmons - The Mother and Mary Simmons -
    10/10/1851

Vincent Gilpin - 9/21/1851 - Jacob F. & Rebecca Robinson - The Mother & Sarah
    Robinson - 10/3/1851

Elizabeth Emily - 11/1/1847 - Poulson & Susan C. Armstrong - The Parents - 11/7/1851

Benjamin Elliot - 1/21/1849 - " -" -11/7/1851

Ellen - 11/11/1851 - John and Hannah Ash - Grandmother & Aunt - 11/16/1851

Mary Chase - 1/3/1851 - Wm. P. & Frances A. Steel - Barny and Mary C. Rogers -
    11/10/1851

Tamor Boggs - Sick Adult - Mr. & Mrs. P.B. Forman - 12/9/1851

Ogram - 1/23/1851 - John & Elizabeth Mausley - Sarah Mausely & John Trabers -
    12/25/1851

John - 9/28/1851 - Patrick & Mary McLaughlin - The Parents - 2/18/1852

Mary - 1/17/1852 - Robert & Phitha Betty - The Parents - 3/5/1852

Anna Martha Mausley - An Adult - Alice and Sarah Mausley - 3/14/1852

Thomas Cleveland - A Sick Adult - Dr. A. Grimshaw and Clement - 3/30/1852

John - 10/17/1852 - John & Sarah Weir – Sick - 3/31/1852

Henrietta Hall - A Sick Adult - The Mother & Dr. S. R. Baker - 4/2/1852

Lebra - 2/3/1852 - David and Lebra Hanson - The Parents - 4/28/1852

John Sydney - 9/30/1841 - John A. & Deborah M. Grohe - Dr. Grimshaw & L.E. Lynam -
    5/7/1852

Margaret Ann - 2/10/1852 - Robert & Mary Hardy - The Mother & E. Rupel - 5/14/1852

Caroline - 1/28/1848 - George & Rachel A. Stokis – Sick - 5/30/1852

Mary Chase - 3/27/1852 - Samuel & Mary Barne - Mary Barney & Mary C. Rogers, George
    Gordon - 7/8/1852

Sarah Jane - 2/27/1852 - Thomas & Jane Gallagher - The Parents - 7/8/1852

Lewis Martin - 1/13/1852 - Geo. & Jespeima Paynter - The Mother & M. Fleming Arthur -
    7/21/1852

Ann M. McCandlar - 8/18/1852 - John Lawrence Walter – Wm. & Eliza Ness, The Mother-
    8/20/1852

John Brown - 7/4/1852 - James and Jane Woods - The Parents - 9/3/1852

Sarah Louisa - 11/11/1851 - Wm. & Nancy R. Beatty - The Parents - 9/3/1852

Thomas Mackie - 8/20/1852 - Alexander & Joana DuPont - Wm. Brick & Elenthisa Smith
    & Wm. Passuts - 9/29/1852

Anna Rebecca - 11/10/1842 - James and Mary S. Elliot - G. D. Armstrong & - 10/6/1852

James - 2/20/1841 - Charlotte Rimshaw
Eleanor - 1/28/1845
Mary Elizabeth - 9/6/1840
Edward Gilpin - 5/20/1852 - P. Shirvard & Helen D. Johnson - Emily S. Carpenter & M.G.
     McDowell - 10/8/1852

Register of Deaths 1819

Page 77

Anthony Cristies child, decd, Saturday 8, May, interred the 9th.

John Brynberg, vestryman, aged 61 years, died 16 July interred 18th

Eleanor Lynam, wife of John, aged ....died 29th July interrred 31st in peace

Margaret L. Barker, wife of ....Barker, died Aug 2, 1819 aged 43 years, interred
     on the 3rd

John, infant son of John and Ann Catharine Gordon, interred 29th Aug.

Mortimore Steward, infant son of Nicholas H. and Sarah H. Robinson, born
     8/4/1817 died 9/2/1819, interred the 7th

Mary Derrickson, widow, aged about 96 years, born 5/18/1723 dec'd 10/19/1819

Peter B. Brynberg, aged about 61 years, died July 13, 1816 interred the 15th

Peter Derrickson died in Nov. aged about 70 years

Benjamin Elliott aged 74 years, died 12/28/1815, a vestryman and communicant,

John Husband, aged about 85 years, died Dec. 4th interred the 6th

Margaret Welsh, widow of John, decd Aug 21 aged 48 years and interred 22nd,
     1819.

1820

Mrs. Elizabeth Brown decd Feb 9th and interred the 11th the wife of William
     Brown in the 54th year of her age.

Lydia Stille, a maiden woman interred the 17th from the Kennet Road.
     Somewhere about 60 years old.

Miss Sarah Tabitha Pryer, eldest daughter and child of the late Rev. Wm. Pryer
     and [blank] his wife in the 23rd year of her age departed this life the 19th and
     interred the 21st in a ? and placed in her mother's grave...in peace.

Charles Ridgely Vining, about 21 years died on Friday the 3rd March a nd
     interred the 5th.

Sarah Jane died (20 months old) on the 6 Oct 1819 interred the 7th. Daughter of
     Thomas and Hannah Smith of ?

John File, died in June 1820 aged about 70 years and interred on Friday in the
     church yard

James Rice, a Communicant, died in May and interred in the Presbyterian yard on
     the hill.

Page 78
Register of Deaths 1820 and interments in Trinity Church Yard

George Taylor died Wednesday the 14th June, aged about ____ and interred the 15th.

Mrs. Martha Wolmesdorff, a Communicant, died the 7th of July and interred the 8th in the 42nd year of her age in peace.

Mrs. Hannah Bryan, wife of David, died the 8th in the 30th year of her age and interred the 9th.

Son of Benjamin and Mary Elliott___ Trust of Allen and Elizabeth Mills, died and buried the 18th.

Fairlands, of Jonus and Sarah P. Fairland

Margaret Springer, mother of Levi, interred the 23rd Aug. in the 79th year of her age.

Betsy Henderson, died in August aged about 26 years

Son of William and Ruth Pogue, drowned Thursday, 21 Sept interred 22nd in the 3rd year of her age.

James Brindlay, Sr. died 24th November in the 73rd year of his age and interred at McAnnan's the 26th.

Mary Ann, daughter of Thos and Prudence Stroder, died Dec 11th in the 12th year of her age and interred the 13th inst.

Isaac Bryan, son in law of Isaac Stidham, Sr. interred the 24th in the 34th of his age

1821

Sarah Springer, born January 17, 1787 died January 7, 1821 interred daughter of John and Sarah joined the hold Comm in Oct 1819 She departed in peace.

Thomas Jones, died January 18, 1821 in his 81st year and was interred the 20th he departed in peace.

152 Page 79

Register of Deaths continued 1821

Departed this life, May 14, 1817. Mr. Lawrence Greatrake, aged 56 years

Departed this life Jacob Derrickson, late Sexton of the Church

Departed this life April 6th 1821, Edward Roche, in his 68th year, a communicant of Trinity, and was interred the 8th.

Departed this life, April 17th Mary Bedford widow of Peter, in the 60th year of her age, a communicant of Trinity and was interred the 18th.

Departed this life April 20th Mary Vining, a maiden in the 65th year of her age, and was interred on the 22nd at Trinity Said M. V. was the daug. of John and Phebe V. born at Dover, the 20 August 1756.

Departed this life   Springer and was interred.

Departed this life, Mr. Couteau on Saturday the 25th August and was interred in Trinity yard the 26th

Departed this life Mrs. Eleanor Derrickson, wife of the late Jacob Derrickson, aged 74 years and a communicant of Trinity Church on the 1st October and was interred the 3rd.

Departed this life Jacob Derrickson son of Jacob a in the year of his age, and was interred the 12th October.

Departed this life October 14 Thomas Lynam, in the year of his age and was interred the 16th son of Thos. & Eleanor.

Departed this life on the 17th Oct. Isaac Stidham, Sr., of New Castle hundred, in the 59th year of his age and was interred on the 19th formerly a vestryman of Trinity.

153 Page 80

Record of Burials from March 1827 to May 1828

Pierce Connelly Minister of Trinity

April 8	Alexander McFarlinder
19	James Baltersby
20	Hannah Welsh
-	Mrs. Fairlamb
Oct 12	Mrs. Starr
13	Peter Coverly
15	Mrs. E. Hawkins
Omitted	Susanna Elliott
3	Infant Child of Jacob J. Robinson
November 10	Hugh Johnson (in the Presyterian burial ground)
13	Jeanette Boyd (child - ditto)
30	William Battersby - ditto

Omit Sept   Mrs. Poltage
1828
Jan 25   Victoire Virginie Cauchois of Havanna
Feb 11   John Sellars
   23   John Ustick
   23   Beaston Vandever
March 7   James Davis
   9   Jacob Hays
   28   John Reynolds
April 10   Priscilla Wayne
   20   William Donnan
Mr. Levi Springer at Wilmington Del April 10th 1835
Child of Mr. Willis Wilmington April 18, 1835
Child of Mrs. Logan WIlmington Del May 16th 1835
Hanah Child of Andrew and Ann Chester Wilmington July 5 1835
Mrs. Fleming Trinity Oct 2 1835
Gregg ---- - Trinity Oct 22 1835
Mrs. Coipse - Trinity Jan 11 1836
Mrs. John Elliott - Trinity Jan 18 1835
Bayard - Trinity Feb 5 1836
Mrs. Amos - April 28, 1836

154 Page 81
Mrs. Mary Elliott May 15th 1836
Mrs. Addison Jun 7th 1836
Child of Mrs. Knight July 22 1836
Mr. Hacket Aug 26 1836
Miss Beatte Springer Sept 15 1836 Trinity
Mrs. Rachel Young Sept 23 1836
Mr. Pierce Sept 24 1836 Trinity
Springer - Child- Sept 23 1836 Trinity
Miss Napf Oct 15 1836 Trinity
H. Julian son of Mr. Monges
Wm. Gordon Jan 11, 1836
Isaac Hendrickson March 12 1837
John Hemphill March 16 1837
Dr. Derickson May 17 1837
Mrs Kirk May 23 1837
Mr. [?] McAllister Trinity July 24 1837
Child of Mr. Smith Sept 12 1837
Sarak Redwood Child of Yabes Fisher Trinity Sept 20 1837
Jacob Banner Child of Banner B.W. Oct 16 1837
George Bush son of Anthony & Christy[?] Dec 13 1837

Robert Armstrong March 1838
John Poulson April 5, 1838

Burials during the Rectorship of L. U. McCullough
Nov 19 1838 Mrs. Pritchard (of St. Andrews, at St. A's)
Nov 20 1838 Mrs. Smith, at Trinity Church Cemetery
Nov 28 1838 Mrs. Ann Pearce at Trinity Church Cemetery
Dec 8 1838 Mrs. Margaret McAllister Trinity Church Cemetery

155 page 82
John Weaver Deceased April 14 1839
Laura Vandevier daughter of Jacob Vandevier deceased May 12 1839
Archibald Hamilton Cox, son of James Cox, deceased May 21 1839
Elizabeth N. Hackett - Child July 27 1839
A child of Mrs. Harri??? of Alexandria D.C.
A child from New York - John VanCleavers daughter aged 17 months Aug 26
    1839

Interments during the Rectorship of Rev. Edwin Martin Van Deusen ? to May
    1847
1847-
July 4 John Adam Grohe, who died July 2 1847 aged 41 years
11 Robert Hanna who died July 10 1847 aged 50 years
23 Sarah Elizabeth daughter of Charles and Catharine Huston aged 9 mos
23 A son of Capt. Chaytor, U.S. Volunteers aged 5 months
Aug 1 John Elliot Jr. who died July 30 1847 aged [?] years
    12 Anne Armor who died August 12 1847 aged 30 years
    13 Thomas Vandever who died August 12 1847 aged 65 years
    19 Edward Mitchel who died August 17 1847 aged 53 years
Sept 6 Catharine Dever, who died Sept 5 1847 aged 27 years
Nov 14 Susan Robinson, who died Nov. 12 1847 aged 30 years
Dec 2 Mrs. Baxter who died Dec 1 1847 aged 75 years
    25 James Stewart who died Dec 27 1847 aged 20 years
    31 Hannah Derrickson who died Dec 29 aged 30 years
January 20 John Holland who died January 18, 1848 aged 57 years
Feb 7 Andrew J. ColeMary who died Feby 5 1848 aged 19
    17 Washington Jackson Taylor died Feby 16 1848 son of George & [?]
    Rades?
Mar 29 Mrs. Platt who died Mar 28 1848 aged 80 years
Apr 5 Mary Bondford who died Apr 3 aged 28 years
    23 Benjamin son of Isaac Elliot died Apr 22 1848 aged 2 years
May 8 Sarah Francis daughter of [?] Fleming died May 3 1848

156 Page 83

Interments during the Rectorship of Rev E. M. VanDeusen 1848

May 7 Mary daughter of Giles and Sarah Broadbent of Frankford Pa. who died May 5 1848 aged 18 months

13 Benjamin Rock wo died May 11 1848 aged 14 years

22 Mrs. Nanna who died May 21 1848 aged 89 years

May 28 A child of Mr. Nae of Philadelphia, Pa aged 7 months

June 13 Susanna Jane daugher of Jeremiah and Elizabeth Scott aged 4 years 3 mos

15 William Gailey who died June 13 1848 aged 79 years

21 Mary Hannah daughter of the Rev. Jacob B. and Mary E. Smith who died June 18 1848 aged 20 mos

29 Elizabeth daughter of Wm. and Francis McLaughlin who died June 27 1848 aged 7 mos

29 Jacob Cripps who died June 28 1848 aged 64 years

July 1 Henry son of Moses and Margaret Journey who diedJune 30 1848 aged 10 mos

Aug8 Ann Gorgas wife of John Gorgas who died Aug 5 1848 aged 32 years

26 Collins Denny who died Aug 25 1848 aged 52 years

Sept 11 Mrs. Mary Springer who died Sept 10 1848

13 Dr. Wm. Colesbury who died Sept 10 1848 Phila aged ?3 years

24 Thomas Bullom who died Sept 24 1848 of small pox aged -

24 Elizabeth daughter of and Martha Bardsley aged 11 mos

Oct 27 Elizabeth daughter of Charles and Margaret Sinex who died Oct 26 1848 aged 1 year

Nov 14 Sarah Jane daughter of James and Sarah Edwards who died Nov 12 1848 aged 10 mos

Dec 2 William G??? son of Henry and Mary Morrison who died in New Castle Del Dec 1, 1848 aged 2 years.

1849

Jan 7 A Child of Mr. Vining of DuPont? Del aged 5 years

12 John H. son of Samuel and Sarah ?? who died Jan 10 1849 aged 21 mos

18 John son of Bandey and Ann Simmons who died Jan 17 1849 aged 4 years

29 Margaret Vining who died Jan 28 1849 aged 35 years

31 Mrs. Jane Hags who died Jan 28 1849 aged 90 years

Feb 20 Charles Holmes who died Feb 18 1849 aged 45 years

Mar 12 Catharine H. daughter of Jackson H. Smith who died Mar 11 1849 aged 3 mos

23 John Slater from the Alms House who died Mar 22 1849 aged 53 years

Apr 10 Ella Olivia daughter of Peter L. and Sarah Ann Johnson who died Apr 10 1849 of small pox aged 2 years 11 mos

May 4 Mrs. Ann Prestman who died May 4 1849 aged 73 years

26 Mrs. Stena Gailey who died may 24 1849 aged 82 years
June 11 Elizabeth Jane Almond who died Jun 10 1849 aged 21 years
      16 John Elliot who died Jun 14 1849 aged 81 years
      30 Jesse son of Wm. H and Mary C. ???? who died June 24 1849 aged 20 mos
July 8   John Ritchie who died July 7 1849 aged 26 years
      17 Jonathan Saville who died July 11 1849 aged 78 years
Aug 20 James son of Joseph and Mahata Platt who died Aug 18 1849
July 23 Mrs. Sonll?? who died July 22 1849 aged 37 years
Aug 28 Alexander Armstrong, who died Aug 27 1849 aged 32 years
      30 Mr. Adams
Sept 9   Noah Connelly who died Sept 7 1849 aged 40 yearears
      16 George Matthew, who died Sept 15, 1849 aged 65 years

157 page 84
Interments duirng the Rectorship of Rev. E. M. VanDusen

1849
Sept 24 Elizabeth Robinson who died Sept 22 1849 aged 71 years
Oct 14 Joseph son of Collins and Mary McCallister who died Oct 12 aged 2 years
      16 Rachel, daughter of Wm. and Nancy McLaughlin aged 5 mos.
      24 John Dauphain who died Oct 23, 1849 aged 20 years
Nov 14 Margaret Sinex who died Nov 12 1849 aged 73 years
      27 Ann Catherine daughter of Baudey and Ann Simmons who died Nov 23
      1849 aged 7 mos

1850
Jan 10 Isaac Anderson who died Jany 8 1850 aged 60 years
Feb 22 Wm. P. B??? who died FEb 19 1850 aged 64 years
Apr 11 Isaac P. Derickson who died Apr 8 1850 aged 38 years
May 19 E??? son of Myers and Sarah Hayes who died May 19 1850 aged 5 mos
Apr   John L??man who died aged 60 years
May 20 Wm. C. Daniel son of John and — Vesik who died March 18 1849 aged
      13 mos
      30 Esau Cox who died May 29 1850 aged 68 years
June 2   Dennis son of Wm. and Ann Millis who died June 1 aged 21 mos
      20 John Hall who died Jun 19 185 aged 55 years
      30 John Foulk who died June 28 1850 aged 70 years
July 3   John Fleming who died July 2 1850
Aug 6   Margaretta Price who died August 4 1850 aged 39 years
      7   Ann Cole who died Aug 5 1850 aged 80 years
      12 Euan H. Thomas who died Aug 10 1850 aged 40 years
      18 Mary Mana, infant daughter of Wm. & Eliza ??? Aug 17 1850
Sept 29 Robert, son of Wm. Foonst who died Sept 28 1850 aged 4 weeks

Oct 7   Agnes Stothart who died Oct 5 1850 aged 75 years
    12 Thomas F. Hall who died Oct 11 1850 aged 32 years
Nov 16 William son of James Stein who died Nov 13 1850 aged 15 mos
Dec 30 Mary Ann daughter of Wm. Beatty who died Dec 28 1850

1851
Jan 5   Susanna L. daughter of George & Rebecca m. B??? died Jan 2 1851 aged
    9 years
    6   Sarah Justis who died Jany 4 1851 aged 70 years
    31 Sarah Ann Pogue who died Jan 29 1851 aged 42 years
    31 Emma C. daughter of Wm. F. and Elizabeth O'Daniel who died Jany 27
    1851 aged 5 years
Feb 2   Edmond son of Wm. & Mary Dak who died Jany 30 1851 aged 7 years
    6   James Robinson who was killed Feby 4 1851 aged 35 years
Apr 3   Elizabeth Foote who died Apr 2 1851 aged 35 years
    11 Archie Reed who died Apr 10 1851 aged 25 years
    14 George W. son of Dr. George M. Chaytor who died April 12 1851 aged 8
    years
    25 Sallie daughter of Dr. George M. Chaytor who died April 24 1851 aged 10
    years 9 mos
Jun 10 Letitia Connel died June 8 1851 aged 18 years
    21 Hannah daughter of Joseph & Mary Ann Buckly died June 20 1851 aged 9
    mos
July 10 John William son of Daniel & Martha Bardsley died July 9, 1851 aged 11
    mos
    11 James son of David & Sebra Hanson died July 10 1851 aged 1 year 10 mos
Aug 12 Elizabeth Charlotte, daughter of Samuel & Elizabeth Sayres, who died
    Aug 10 1851 aged 7 mos
    14 Laititia Patton daughter of Joseph and Jane Davis died Aug 15 1851 aged
    5 years
Sept 17 Margaret J. M???? died Sept 16 1851 aged 20 years
Oct 3   Lewis Gilpin died Oct 2 1851 aged 8 years
    10 Wm. Postte died in Phila Oct 8 1851 aged 58 years
    31 Joseph Cass, died Oct 28 1851 aged 52 years
Nov 9 Jacob Derickson died Nov 7 1851 aged 71 years
20 Charles ???? son of John & Lydia David died Nov 19 1851 aged 2 years 6 mos
Dec 17 Tamor Boggs died Dec 15 1851 aged 32 years

New Castle County, Delaware Court Records
Docket Containing Records of Illegitimate Births 1759-1834.

Original docket in collections of the Historical Society of PA -   Cope Collection
A-74. Manuscript Guide Item 150.

29 Dec 1759 Susannah Holland of New Castle Hundred, single, saith she is with child and child is likely to be born a bastard and that William Smith of Wilmington afsd. atty at law is the father.

15 Nov 1764 21 Oct 1778 Hannah Cullen of New Castle Co., single saith that on 8 Sep in the year afsd. she was delivered of a female bastard child and that James McCalla of said hundred is the father.

18 Oct 1779 Margret Read, wife of Timothy Read, now a hired servant with Mr. Richard Dowdle at Christiana Bridge that he the said Timothy Read refused to contribute towards the support and maintenance of his said wife Margret who from sickness and other bodily infirmities is unable to support herself.

13 Nov 1799. Petition of Margaret Lackey of New Castle Co. that she hath not had fully allowance from the court of Chancery for her alimony against a certain James Lackey of New Castle Hundred.

22 Jan 1801 Elaner Griffin of Appoquinimink Hundred single, saith that she was delivered of a female bastard child and that William Foard of Kent Co. is the father.

23 April 1801. Charge of bastardy concerning a female bastard child born at Appoquinimink HD on 22 Sep 1799 of Eleanor Griffin single woman who saith the father is William Foard of Duck Creek Hundred, Kent Co., DE who makes no objection.

18 May 1801. Female bastard child on body of Prudence Gull, a single woman in Appoquinimink Hundred born 19 Nov 1800 William Shaddock of sd. hundred is the father.

8 June 1801 Male bastard child of St. Georges Hundred born last? of March 1801 of Nancey Taylor who saith Abraham Vicars of sd. Hundred farmer is the father who makes no object.

17 Oct 1801 Thomas McIntire of White Clay Hundred NC co. is ordered to pay unto Hannah Quandrill, single woman of said hd, 5 dollars for the lying in expenses of his female bastard child and $1.50 per monthly for 7 years.

2 Nov 1801 Elizabeth Roberts of St.Georges Hundred, single, saith on 26 May last past she was delivered of a female bastard child at the house of Mary Hanes? in the hundred afsd. and charged William Perrey as the father. who shall indemnify the state of DE.

19 Dec 1801 John Beaty of Mill Creek Hundred ordered to pay unto Mary Thompson of Mill Creek Hundred, single, $5 for the lying in expenses of her male bastard child whereof the said Mary Thompson hath declared that John Beaty is the father.

3 March 1802 Charlotte Armstrong of Christiana Hundred single on 14 Oct 1801 and having charged John Reece with being the father of a bastard child begotten on the body of said Charlotte Armstrong which child was born at the house of John Armstrong in Christiana Hundred on 4 Aug last past. John Reece is ordered to pay unto Charlotte Armstrong $6 for expenses and $2 for support and maintenance of the child for each month for 7 years.

25 March 1802 James Whitlock and John Wiley both of Pencader Hundred and Peter Miles of Cecil Co. MD, are to to idemnify the county from charges for the maintenance of the bastard child born of Poley Stewit? now in Whiteley Creek Hundred, single who says that James Whitelock is the father. 1.25 dollard monthly.

5 April 1803 William Bunker of Pencader Hundred to pay unto Rebecka Moore of hundred afsd. for the maintenance of a male bastard child begotten by him on the body of Rebecka Moore, to pay 6 dollars and monthly support of child from 10 aug 1801 for 7 years.

5 April 1802 Margaret Nicson, single charges Alexander Reynolds as father of male bastard child born at the house of Robert Nowan in Christiana Hundred on 14 March last past. Ordered to pay 5 dollard for maintenance and 1.50 monthly for 7 years from brith of child which was 14 March 1802.

10 Sep 1802. Female bastard child born St. Georges Hundred on the body of Sarah Vansant, single woman, delivered on 27 Nov 1798 at the house of Samuel Freman in Sd. hundred afsd. that the father is John Pearce of Cecil Co., farmer, ordered to pay 5 dollars and 1.5 per monthly from birth of child

24 Sep 1802. Hannah Bains of St. Georges Hundred, single, did on 18 Sep 1802 appeared. made known that she on 3 of present month at the house of John Cleaver in St. Georges Hundred was delivered of a male bastard child. and saith that William Vance of the Village of Port Penn, carpenter, is the father of said male bastard child. He is ordered to pay security of 160 dollars to indemnify the county of NC for maintenance of said child. and to pay the mother 5 dollars and 1.5 per month for 7 years to commence form the birth of said child which was on 3 Sep 1802.

21 Dec 1802 William Bunker of Pencader Hundred ordered to pay Mary Dushain of hundred afsd. to maintain male bastard child which he has begotten upon her the said Mary Dushain to pay her 6 dollars for expenses and monthly support commencing form 4 Aug 1802 12 shillings and 6 pence for 7 years.

13 June 1803 Mary Brooks of St. Georges Hundred single did on 11 June 1803 said that she on 17 May now last past at St. Georges Hundred was delivered of a male bastard child. That Adam Diehl, grazier, is the father. He is ordered to give security of 160 dollars to indemnify the co. and pay Mary Books 6 dollars and monthly 2 dollars

8 Sep 1803 Alexander McFarland charged as the father of a male bastard child begotton on the body of Mary Waggoner, born at the house of William Waggoner of Appoquinmink Hundred on 26 May last past. Pay to Mary W 5

dollars and 1.5 per month for 7 years for seven years fomr birth of child which was on 26 May 1803.

25 Nov 1803. Robert Morrison to pay Mary Rumsey 6 dollars and 2 monthly from birth of child whereof she is now pregnant until age of 7.

28 May 1804. Aaron Biggs to indemnify New Castle Co. male bastard child born of Sarah McDaniel of sd. co. and hundred of Appoquinimink, single, on 31 Dec 1803 at the house of Thomas Clark in Appoq. Hundred 160 security.

30 May 1804 to indemnify the co in keeping education and ... bastard child as Sarah Cather, single woman of hundred afsd. now goeth with whereof said James Huston is the father.

18 Dec 1804 male bastard child of Sarah Cather, delivered in Christiana Hundred, James Huston, weaver, [*see above*] the reputed father, to pay 6 dollars and 2. from time it was born for 7 years.

15 Feb 1806 Sarah Hains of Christiana Hundred single, charged Jacob Peirson as father of female bastard child born at the house of John Flinn in Christiana Hundred on 14 Jan last past. 6. dollars and 5 dollars per month from birth of child 14 Jan 1806.

3 July 1806. The examination of Thomas Graham, Negro man aged about 35 years who saith he was born in Prince Georges Co. Md

Hannah Johnson, single yellow woman, Christiana Hundred, on 23 Oct 1807 charged William Becket a blackman with being the father of a female bastard child born at the house of Jacob Shreve in hundred afsd. in July last past. 5 dollars and 1.25 monthly from July 1807 for 7 years. 23 Oct 1807.

Peggy Pierce, mulatto singe woman of Christiana Hundred, on 9 Nov 1807 charged Robert Anderson, a black man, with being father of a bastard child on her body, born at the house of James Pierce in borough of Wilmington on 12 Sep last. 4 dollars and 1. per month for 7 years.

16 July 1808 Samuel Jordan of Brandywine Hundred was ordered to give security of 150. to indemnify the co. of support and maintenance of a bastard child begotten on body of Peggy Washington, a free black woman, by Jeremiah Williams a black servant of Lawrence Jordan, born 4 March last.

30 July 1808 James Kelly of borough of Wilmington, laborer, to indemnify the co. from charges for maintenance of female bastard child begotton by said Kelly on body of Polly Campbell and born 6 July present.

30 Aug 1808 Thomas W. Kiltzhumer father of bastard female child begotten on body of Sarah Phillips, single. Ordered security of 160. to pay her 6. and 2 per month

12 Sep 1808 Female bastard child of Rebeca Dennis of borough of Wilm. delivered on 10 Aug last. John Trail the father .ordered to pay 160 as security.

9 Jan 1809 Mary Eaton of White Clay Creek Hundred, single, having charged Eaton Crawford with being the father of a male bastard child begotten on her body born at the house of Rebecca Reynolds in hundred afsd on 19 Dec last past. 6. and 2 monthly

4 April 1809 Sarah Woodward of Christiana Hundred, single, having charged
James Phillips on 9 Jan last with being the father of a bastard with which she
was then pregnant with and the child was born at the house of Mary
Hendrickson hundred of Christiana on 13 March last past. to pay Sarah 6. and
2 per month

17 May 1809. Father Samuel Campbell, farmer, Christiana Hundred., born on
body of Mary Tremble, born April last. She appeared 21 Dec last, male child.
born at the house of Joseph Tremble in Christiana Hundred. to pay her 5. and
2 per month.

8 June 1809 Father is Francis McGurgan begotten on Mary Fox, single, born 25
Nov last

15 June 1809. Michael Kain, male bastard child begotten by said Michael Kain on
body of Rhoda ---blann single

26 July 1809 Thomas Caldwell to indemnify the co. [of support of] bastard child
of Hannah Donehue delivered on 9 Sep last. Thomas Caldwell is the father.

28 June 1810. Mary Carson of borough of Wilmington, single, on 2 Oct last
charged Aquila Walraven as father of male bastard child begotten on her
body born at the house of John Sperry in borough of Wilmington on 29 May
1809.5 plus 2

5 July 1810 Mary Matthews of Christiana Hundred single on 3 July 1810 having
charged Thomas Morrison as being the father of a male bastard child
begotten on her body, born at the house of John Mulloy in sd. hundred on 15
March last past. 6. and 2

18 Dec 1811 Nathaniel Baldwin to appear at next court of General Sessions to
answer charge made by Mary Tremble of being the father of a bastard child
delivered 30 Nov last.

Rachel McConnell of Christiana Hundred, single, appears on 21 Jan 1812 and
charged James Hamilton, stage driver, as being the father of a bastard child,
delivered at the house of --- McConnell, her father, hundred afsd. on 27 Dec
last. 6. and 2

4 March 1812 Dinah Newlin of Christiana Hundred, single on 28 Feb 1812
charged Samuel Wilson as father of a male bastard child, born in Christiana
Hundred at the house of Eli Baldwin on 5 Feb last past. to pay 6 and 2

13 May 1812 Mary Tremble of Christiana Hundred, single, on 4 July 1811
charged Nathan Baldwin as father of bastard child of which she was then
pregnant with. He did give security for his appearance within one month after
the birth of the said child. and now on 18 Dec 1811 the said Nathaniel
Baldwin appears . She states she was delivered of a male bastard child on 30
Nov last at the house of Joseph Tremble, her father. 1. to pay 5. and 1.5.

26 Aug 1815. Isaac Walraven to appear within one month after Sarah Barns of
Christiana Hundred is delivered of a bastard child with which she is now
pregnant and which child she has charged to the said Isaac Walraven.

11 April 1817 William McCawtney ordered to appear to answer charges on 4 Nov

1816 to appear one month afer the birth of the child born to Jemima Griffin,

17 June 1817. Female bastard child begotten by Jacob Smith on body of Rebecca Phillips, born 30 June 1815. to pay 6 and 2.

21 June 1817. John Dawson for begetting a female bastard child on Jane Cully, born 21 June 1817. to pay 4 and 1.

25 Oct 1817. Female bastard child where of Margaret Smith of Brandywine Hundred was delivered on 22 Sep last whereof Joel Spencer is the father as she hath sworn. to pay 6 and 2.

21 July 1818. Elizabeth Evans single hath on 21 June last past delivered in Pencader Hundred a female bastard child which child and charged Ephraim Underwood is father. to pay 6 and 2

25 Jan 1819 Whereas Elizabeth Nicholson single of NC Co. on 1 July last past delivered a female bastard child. Eli Biddle of Red Lyon Hundred is father. to pay 5 and 1

27 Feb 1819 Kitty Shays charged Edward Duff and father. to pay 4 and 1.5

5 June 1819. Reuben Primrose father to pay Mary Pennywell 6 and 1 monthly from 11 May 1819 to 11 May 1826

18 Jan 1820 Phebe Seville of Christiana Hundred, single on 18 Jan last charged Eli Servix??? father of female bastard child on body of said Pheebe Seville born 1 March last. to pay to pay 6 and 2.

Proceedings and Records of the Presbyterian Church
At Christiana Bridge

In conformity to an Act of the Legislature of the State of Delaware, providing for the Incorporation of Religious Societies & legal notice having been previously given, the following Persons, Members of the Christiana Bridge Presbyterian Congregation, convened at the Meetinghouse, the 13th of March A.D. 1800, for the purpose of choosing five Trustees for said Congregation—

1. William Ruth
2. David Nivin
3. Thomas Moore
4. Jesse Devou
5. Samuel Ruth
6. Samuel Thomas
7. Doct. Smith
8. William Scott
9. Daniel Turner
10. Henry Boyd
11. Arthur Mason
12. George Pratt
13. John Hall
14. John Grooves
15. Robert Barr
16. Hugh McCrackin
17. Richard Hambly
18. Samuel Hannah
19. John Hannah
20. Robert Bryan
21. John Morrison
22. John McKinley
23. Nathaniel McCoy
24. William Shannon
25. Eaton Crawford
26. William Weir
27. John Brown
28. John Hannah Jr
29. Samuel Houston
30. John Crow
31. George Adams
32. James Couper
33. Samuel Moore
34. Nathan McCoy
35. Doct. Jas. Couper

Upon motion of Mr. Hambly, seconded by Mr. Ruth, the company proceeded to the choice of a Chairman and Secretary when it appeared that James Couper Sr was unanimously elected Chairman and Samuel Moore Secretary.

The Votes of the members present being then received and the Polls counted, the returns for Trustees appeared as follows;

For Samuel Moore 34, Jesse Devou 32, Benj. Patterson 26, Jas. Crawford 23, Thos. Moore 15, Wm. McMecham 14, Hugh McCrackin 14, Saml. Nivin 6, Geo. Pratt 6, Davd. Nivin 2, Robt. Smith 2, Saml. Ruth 1.

Whereupon the Chairman declared Samuel Moore, Jesse Devou, Benjamin Patterson, James Couper Jr, and Thomas Moore to be duly elected Trustees.

The Trustees being thus appointed, proceeded to the election of officers when

Samuel Moore was chosen Chairman, James Couper Jr Secretary, and Jesse Devou Treasurer. After which they proceeded to number and value the Pews which together with the names of the Persons who have rented the same are as follows;

No. of Pews By Whom Rented Yrly Rent Dos/cents
1 Mr. McClay, Thos. Moore, Doct. Smith 13/33
2 William Shannon 6/67
3 Gilbert Belcher 6/67
4 Richard Hambly 6/67
5 John Hall Senr 6/67
6 Joseph Janvier & Benjamin Ogle 6/0
7 Samuel Thomas & William Baily 6/0
8 Empty 5/33 and 9 Empty 4/0
10 Empty 5/0
11 Empty 5/67
12 Empty 5/67
13 John Morrison & Samuel Hannah 6/0
14 Robert Bryan 6/67
15 William Scott & Samuel Moore 6/67
16 James Couper 6/67
17 George Adams 6/67
18 Jacob Belvill 1/3 & Robt Barr 1/3 6/67
19 William Ruth and Samuel Ruth 6/67
20 James Caldwell 6/67
21 David Nivin 6/67
22 Jesse Devou & Arthur Mason 6/67
23 David Turner 6/67
24 Alexander Sterret 6/0
25 Mrs. Mann ½ 5/67
26 Jonathan Groves & John Groves 5/67
27 Empty 5/0 and 28 Empty 4/0
29 Lewis Rice & Michl. Nagle 5/0
30 Willm. Weir, John Dixon, & Robt. Montgomery 5/67
31 John McKinley 5/67
32 George Pratt & Nathan McCoy 6/0
33 Hugh McCrackin 6/67
34 Benjamin Patterson & Joseph Israel -----
35 Wm. McMecham, Nathl. Bines, & Saml. Barr 13/33

Gallery---seats 36-40 empty, valued at 2/67.

Talley-Foulk Burying Ground

This cemetery is located 60 yards west of the intersection of Foulk and Naamans
Road on the north side of Naamans adjacent to the Mobil Station. Entrance is
on Naaman's road at the drive of 2107. These records were presented to the
Delaware Genealogical Society in 1980 by Mrs. Viola Talley Hanby. By
June 1980 this cemetery is completely covered with underbrush and
overgrowth. A Few stones were visible on the ground. Otherwise is
completely "lost".

Smith, Aaron b. 1780 d. 5 Feb 1855 age 65yr 3mo 23da
Smith, Margaret daughter Priscilla Talley
Smith, Thomas, son of d. 15 Aug 1821 age 10mo
Aaron and Margaret b. June 1820

Talley, Samuel H d. 30 Dec 1802 age 76yr 8mo 4da
Talley, Mary, wife of Samuel d. 11 Aug 1842 age 71yr 8mo
Talley, Thomas d. 19 Aug 1836 age 77
Rebecca Lloyd, wife of Thomas Talley d. 28 Apr 1829 age 66
Talley, Jehu d. 7 May 1818 age 83
Talley, Jemina, wife of Jehu d. 17 Feb 1851 age 81
Talley, Thomas d. 31 Nov 1824 age 21
Talley, William d. 9 Mar___ age 16yr 6mo 14da
Foulk, Sarah, wife of John Foulk d. 9 Sept 1824 age 68yr 4mo 14da
Talley, Priscilla, wife of Harmon Talley d. 3 Mar 1802 age 27
Talley, Joseph d. 7 Sept 1815 age 51yr 5mo 5da
Talley, Margaret d. 20 Oct 1824 age 10yr

Caroline Sparks, Cemetery Chairman
Delaware Genealogical Society

Marriage License Bonds New Castle Co.
1801-1839
Collected by Gilbert Cope 1910. The records begin in 1744.

1801

Jan 9 John Peterson, Sarah Walraven
Jan 20 Levi Ferguson, no name
Jane 21 Ezekiel Starrate of New Castle Co., Hanna Patton
Jan 29 Jesse Weldin, Allice Henderson
Feb 24 Samuel Allen of New Castle Co., Hannah Jones
Feb 24 Ebenezer Eliason of New Castle Co., Ann Hershey of same
March 10 James Peirce, Mary Stapler
March 19 James Vail, no name
June 1 Lawrence Dill, Sarah M'Kinley
July 24 William Molton, Margaret Blee
July 31 Thomas F. Williams of New Castle Co., Esther Swann
Sep 3 Thomas M'Neel, Jane Barnet
Sep 4 Robert Whitley, Tamer Edwards
Sep 10 Samuel Shaw, Susanna Cloud
Oct 16 Solomon Gregg, Ann Vandever
Nov 10 John Cox of QA co, Md, Mary Stewart of St. Georges hundred Del.
Dec 8 David Sebo of New Castle Co., no name
Dec 24 Peter Bouchell of Cecil Co, Alice Cannon. Surety Isaac Cannon of Red
   Lion Hundred
No Day Thomas Maree, Abigail Israel.

1802

Jan 6 David Evans - Sarah Morton.
Jan 11 William Cann (mark) of New Castle Co, Sally M'Mullin
Jan 12 Laurence H. Miles of New Castle Co, Polly Williams
Jan 13 Hance Hanson of Pencader hundred, Susannah Alanander
March 17 James Coulter of New Castle Co, Jane Craig
March 18 Peter Ruth of New Castle Town, Margaret Ferguson
March 18 John Whitey of Pencader hundred (mark), Lidia Whitelock.
March 23 William Johnston of New Castle Co, Sarah Cavender
April 10 Samuel Cantwell of Pencader Hundred, Mary Jones of same
April 26 Charles Hartupe of New Castle Co, Rebecca Clarke
May 4 Robert Yocom of New Castle Co, Jane Richardson
May 6 John Wood of New Castle Co, Allice Wiley of same
May 8 Levi Clark of Red Lion Hundred, Lidia Mehes (?)
May 17 Joshua Dolton of New Castle Co, Jane Bell
May 18 David Witherspoon of New Castle Co, Susan Higgins

May 20 Amos Slack of Pencader Hundred, Martha Miller

May 26 Benjamin Andrews of Wilmington, Eliza Elberson
May 27 James M'Cowan (?) of Wilmington, Martha Byas.
May 29 Samuel Mathews of New Castle hundred, Johanna Jaquett
June 1 Nathan Bouldan of New Castle Co, Mary Ford
June 1 William A. Thompson, Sarah Clay
June 2 William Young of Wilmington, Sarah Drummond
June 2 Joseph Derickson of Christiana Hundred, Sarah Derickson
June 3 Benjamin Crips of Wilmington, Rebekah Beson, Surety, Mathew Crips.
June 9 George Young of New Castle Co, Eleanor Richardson
June 20 Robert Browning of St. Georges hundred, Maria M. Capelle of same
June 24 Joseph See of Pencader hundred, Elizabeth Hugg
Aug 4 Thomas Reilly of Philadelphia, Mary Miller of New Castle
Aug 5 John Brady of Delaware (mark), Margaret Brady, Surety, John Cranston
Aug 5 Thomas Pearson of Christiana hundred, Jane Calhoon of New Castle
    hundred
Sep 11 John E. Denny, Ann Ford
Sep 13 Robert Rogers, Martha Stuart
Sep 16 Robert Smith of New Castle hundred, Elizabeth Weldin
Sep 28 Thomas Magens of New Castle Co, Elenor Ruth
Oct 4 Samuel Watson, Mary Simpson
Oct 7 William Evertson, Maria Miller
Oct 30 Samuel Johnson of Christiana Hundred, Margaret Brown
Oct 16 John Edmunds of New Castle hundred, Ann Campbell
Oct 16 John King of New Castle hundred, Elizabeth Davy
Oct – William Hickey of New Castle Co, Mary Cummons of same
Oct -6 George Logan of South Carolina, Margaret Polk
Nov 3 Charles Anderson of Christiana hundred, Mary Walraven
Dec 9 Isaac Holmes of New Castle Co, Sarah McKnight
Dec 11 Caleb Cloud of Wilmington, Sarah Stidham of New Castle hundred
Dec 16 George Vandegrift of St Georges hundred, Sarah Pennington of same
Dec 23 John Anderson of Christiana Bridge, Sarah Gudgill, widow
Dec 24 Patrick Hill of Wilmington, Ann Davidson

1803
Jan 10 James Smith of Brandywine hundred, RebekahYoung
Jan 17 David Cavender, Mary Jones
Jan 19 Benjamin Groves of Pencader hundred, Elizabeth Allison
Jan 20 James Garretson of Pencader hundred, Hannah Willson
Jan 27 Samuel Holland of Brandywine hundred, Kathrine Almond
Jan 27 David Higgins of New Castle co, Sarah Britton
Jan 29 John Fitzsimons of Christiana hundred, Elizabeth Derickson

Jan 31 Nathan M'Coy, Jane Moody
Feb 2 Richard Talley of Christiana hundred, Sarah Cartmell
Feb 3 William M'Mullin, Ann Riley
Feb 8 John Belville (Belveal?) of New Castle co, Rachel Johnson
Feb 8 Samuel Shipley of Wilmington, Elizabeth Jefferis. Surety, John Dixon
Feb 9 John Hadden of Brandywine hundred, Isabella M'Kee
Feb 16 Archabald Rawlings of Christiana hundred, Lidia Derikson
Feb 22 Samuel Ogle of New Castle co, Deborah Woliston
March 1 James Bradford, Elizabeth G. Carty
March 2 William Eliason of St Georges hundred, Elizabeth Bunker of same
March 10 Christopher Vandergrift Jr. of St Georges hundred, Jane Ford of same
March 10 John Jones of New Castle co, Ann Bignall
March 21 Robert Porter of New Castle co, Jane Murphy
March 22 John Huslar, Catharine Evans
March 29 Patrick Call (mark), Betsy
April 2 George Lynam of New Castle co, Elizabeth Sterrett
April 9 William Armstrong of New Castle town, Ann Yeates (?)
April 12 Edward Collins of New Castle co, Ann M'Claningan
April 27 Alexander Vail of Pencader hundred, Deborah Smith
April 28 John Shakespear of New Castle co, Mary M'Kinley
May 25 Andrew Knox of Pencader hundred Sinia Price of same
May 26 Adolphus Husbands of Christiana hundred, Mary Ford
May 29 Robert Dining of New Garden township, Rebekah Husbands
June 8 William Dalzell, (No name)
June 25 William Bunker of Pencader hundred, Tamer Scott of same [This Wm.
    Bunker d. March 1803, so maybe date of marriage was 1800]
June 28 Nathaniel Covington of Appoqinimink hundred, Helene Hodson (?)
Jul 7 Adam Dihl of St. Georges hundred, Sarah Read
Jul 13 John M'Man, Jane M'Gee
Jul 19 Thomas Kelly of Pencader, Jane Kelly of same
Jul27 John Howard of New Castle co, Rebecca Price
Jul 30 Joseph Cox, Harriett Bennett
Aug 6 William Hazlett of New Castle town, Rebecca Crawford of same
Aug 11 Zenas Wells of New Castle Co. Sidney Harris
Sep 3 John Devin Stewart (mark) of Pencader Hd, Mary Ann Scott
Oct 11 John Lea, Mary Ferguson
Oct 15 William Fassitt, Mary Post
Nov 21 Henry M Ridgely, Sarah Banning
Nov 25 Benjamin Kersey, Katharine Keagy
Dec 20 Alban Roberts of New Castle Co. Lydia Price
Dec 22 James M'Nickle(?), Rebecca Bayes
Dec 24 Henry Colesberry, Sarah Brinley

1804

Jan 5 John M'Arthur of New Castle Co. Ann Wilson
Jan 5 Robert Blount of New Castle Co. Sarah Bonor
Jan 17 Joseph Justice, Jane Stroud
Jan 21 William Johnson of New Castle town, Elizabeth Andrews
Jan 29 Reuben Cerbe of St.George Hd, Nancy Wilkins
Feb 2 Barney M'Bride (mark), Rose Daniels
Feb 9 James Dawson of Appoquinimink Hd, Ann Roth of same
Feb 19 Jehu Chesterman, Deborah Perry (?)
Feb 19 Zacharias Roberts, Lydia Caulk
Feb 21 John Morrison, Elizabeth Madican
March 1s William M'Combes of Pencader, Elinor Nox
March 14 Thomas Booth of Pencader Hundred, Elizabeth Waite of same
March 31 Jonathan Kelly of New Castle Co. Rebecca Moore of same
April 30 John Morrison of New Castle Co. Margaret Poole
May 29 Alexander Reynolds, Elizabeth O'Flinn
June 9 Benjamin Parker, Sarah Passmore. Surety, Jacob Tanner
June 11 James Linch (mark), Eleanor Whitesides
June 19 David Morrison Jr. of New Castle Co. Ann Parker. Surety Charles
    Wallace.
June 23 Henry Morton of New Castle Hd., Lydia Stewart
June 23 James Sharkey of New Castle Co., Susan Conway
June 26 Nathan Bouldin of New Castle Co., Jenny Wann
July 25 James Price of New Castle Co. Anna Soper
Sep 18 Samuel Paulson, Lydia Foreman
Sep 20 John Waugh of New Castle Co. Mary Platt
Sep 22 James Williamson of Cecil Co, Elizabeth Smith
Oct 2 John Bereman, Isabella (blank)
Oct 7 Francis Sword, Maria Miller
Oct 10 James M'Cullough, Mary M'Cullough
Oct 31 James Springer of Maryland, Mary Reese
Nov 2 Anthony Creshen, Eliza Riggs
Nov 7 William Adair of Pencader Hd, Anna Underwood of same
Nov 17 William G. Lowe of Maryland, Sarah Graham
Nov 23 Benjamin Stanton of New Castle Co. Lydia Nutt of same
Nov 28 William Cowan, Martha Chambers
Dec 27 Daniel Holmes of New Castle Co. Mary Watson

1806 [sic]

Jan 13 Alexander H. Morton, Rebecca Harris
Feb 12 Kendal Derrickson, Rebecca Biddle
Feb 12 William Hugg, Ellen Harrison
Feb 19 Hugh Ferguson, Rebecca Downey

Feb 27 Matthew Driver, Charity Allford
March 6 Jesse Pryer of Appoquinimink Hd, Ann Reynolds
March 10 Joseph Kirkwood of New Castle Co. Margaret Gillespie of same
March 13 Andrew Barnaby of New Castle Co. Jane Rhroads of same
March 19 Kittle Sutton of New Castle Co. Hester Tindle of same
March 19 George Reynolds of New Castle Co. Sarah Woodland of same
March 27 George Vanzant, Margaret Sullivan
March 27 Amos Richardson of New Castle Co. Mary Shepherd
April 5 Robert Clement, Mary M'Knight
April 11 John B. Thomas of New Castle Co. Eliza Way
April 22 John Maree (mark), Margaret Ferguson
April 24 William Carrigan (mark), Nancy Cochran
May 2 Richard C. Dale of New Castle Co. Margaret Fitzgerald of same
May 6 Harlin Cloud, Ann Barclay. Surety, James Eves
May 29 James Stroud, Hannah Springer
June 13 "Old" Charles Graham, Elizabeth Jordan
June 14 William Veal (mark), Elizabeth Hart
June 18 James Willcox, Sarah Conwell
July 24 John Reece of Christiana Hd, Susannah Hogner
Aug 6 James Curlet, Nancy McKinley
Aug 26 George McClelland, Jane Erwin
Aug 29 David Lee of New Castle Co. Peggy Pendricks. Surety David Porter
Oct 4 Richard Highland of New Castle Co. Eleanor Bracken
Oct 7 Thomas Kirkland, Mary Harris
Oct 16 Bankson Taylor, Hetty M'Williams
Nov 20 John Newberry, Elizabeth Marshall
Nov 27 John Caldwell, Hannah M'callmont
Dec 8 John Ford, Eliza Weir
Dec 16 John Fisher, Elizabeth Shermizar
Dec 26 William McCartney, Ann Ferguson

1807
Jan 5 John File, Elizabeth Wells
Jan 8 George Peirce, Margaret Springer
Jan 9 Thomas Miles, Eleanor Shepherd
Jan 20 James David, Jean Rhoads
Jan 27 Evan Morris of Chester Co., Amelia Teressa Stone of the Village of
    Newport, Del. Surety William H Henry of the city of Phila.
Jan 26 Benjamin Watson, Ann Bunker
Jan 26 John Glenn, Mary Thompson
Jan 29 George Enos, Elizabeth Eaton
Feb 11 Robert M'Dowell, Esabella Morgan

Feb 12 Richard Jones, Mary Robinson. Surety, Holland Bowen
Feb 17 Benjamin Marley, Louisa Clark
Feb 18 William Bailey, Mary Riley
Feb 19 Charles Allen, Jane Ann Strong
Feb 24 Manlove Rowland, Rebecca Morgan
Feb 25 James Willcox, Sarah Fearis
Feb 25 Francis Todd, Frances Allen
March 3 Enos Howell, Rebecca Ford
March 6 Samuel H Black, (no name)
March 12 William Elliott, Isabella M'Kee
March 16 John Cargan, Nancy Masterson
March 17 Archibald Gordon of New Castle Co. Elizabeth Nail
March 17 John Hadden, Susan Alricks
March 17 James M'Callmont, Martha M'Mullen
March 19 Jacob Rogers, Ann Morton
March 19 James Simpson, Mary Tyson
March 21 Moses Jones of Redlion Hd, Mary Dawson
March 24 John Evans, Nancy Gillespie
March 25 Samuel Allen, Hannah Wollaston
March 27 Jacob Derrickson, Hannah Ford. Surety, Turvil Ford
April 1 Joseph Lewis (mark), Leah Pells
April 9 Samuel Carpenter, Mary Springer
April 14 John M'Clary, Elizabeth Armstrong
April 20 John Staunton, Margaret Porter
April 21 Lewis Jameson of Redlion Hd, Mary Clark
April 29 Samuel Stewart, Anna Faires
April 30 William Scott of Pencader, Catharine Ferris
May 5 William Scott of Pencader, Catharine Ferris
May 5 James Dickson, Catharine Pepper
June 11 John Janvier, Ann Jane Wiley. Surety, Geo: W. Janvier
June 15 John Lum, Hester Alman
June 18 John Magee, Martha Dorigan
June 24 Thomas Ross, Ann M'Guire
July 4 Benjamin Poulson, Eliza Fullam
July 20 Harman Bouldin, Sophia M'Intire. Surety Richard Boulden
Aug 19 Jonathan Bee of New Castle Co., Sinah Davis
Sep 1 Jesse Alexander, Mary Porter
Sep 7 Thomas Hawthorn, Sarah M'Coy
Sep 12 George Evans, Ann Wilson
Sep 29 Patrick Coulter, Martha Knox
Sep 29 Peter L. Ogle, Hetty See
Oct 8 Robert Smith of New Castle Co.(mark), Sarah M'Comb
Oct 21 Peter See, Susan Walker

Oct 22 Pennell Corbitt, Mary Clark

Nov 2 Joseph Tindall, Editha Civil

Nov 14 Basil Cuningham, Mary Robinson

Nov 12 Samuel A. Dushane, Amelia Hukens

Nov 12 Philip Heyl of Phila., Margaret A. Whan of New Castle Co.. Surety, Samuel Baker of Phila.

Nov 17 John Crow, Elizabeth Bradun

Nov 24 John Evans, Mary Wattson

Nov 25 John Parish, Margaret Dyer

Dec 5 William Stuart, Elizabeth Justice

Dec 10 Robert Thompson, Mary Sneath

Dec 1j6 Thomas Williams, Margaret Wattson

Dec 16 Thomas Fulton (mark), Margaret Allimas(?)

Dec 29 John Harper, Priscilla Bowman

Dec 30 John C. Petherbridge, Ann Cockshott

Dec 30 Isaac Scott, Mary Bird

1808

Jan 4 Andrew Topless, Jane Ryan

Jan 5 William Dowell, Eleanor Price

Jan 7 Daniel Holmes of Christiana Bridge, Elizabeth Crouch

Jan 11 William Gilleland, Margaret Noble

Jan 11 Patrick M'Cannon, Eleanor Jones

Jan 18 Joseph W. Cochran, Frances S. Lewis

Jan 19 Sisby Griffin of New Castle Co. Imees Grubb

Feb 9 William Pusey, Sarah Davis (or Davey)

Feb 10 Thomas Wardell, Sarah Quail

Feb 17 John Lewden, Mary Harriss

Feb 18 John C. Vanzant, Eleanor Kenney

Feb 29 Robert M'Farlin, Sarah Hayes

Feb 29 Christian Griffenberg, Nancy Hayes

March 2 Elijah M'Cluer Sarah Willson

March 7 Richard Boulden, Dorcas Bouldin

March 8 Frederick Wilson, Sarah Stewart

March 9 Lewis Turner, Sarah Stoops

March 14 Benjamin Bouldin, Hannah Shields

March 17 James A. Price, Mary Parmer

March 21 Justis Wilson, Sarah Reece

March 31 William Green, Eliza Swallow

March 31 James Crawford, Rebecca Hezlett

April 4 Thomas Booth, Catharine Stoops

April 5 John Macmullan, Anna Maria Alexander

April 7 Nathaniel Wilcox, Tabitha Alexander
April 14 Robert Cochran, Rebecca Ryland
April 16 John Gray, Sarah M'Cay
May 24 John Stockton, Sarah Hyatt
June 8 Francis Naghel, Ann West. Surety, Thomas Shoemaker.
June 23 Adam Diet, Sarah Marshbank
July 11 Daniel Dingee, Elizabeth Bateman
July 14 David Wilson, Ann Jefferis. Surety, David Roberts
July 25 William Taylor of White Clay Creek Hd, Mary Taylor
July 26 Robert Gordon, Rebecca Read. Surety, Caleb P. Bennett
July 27 John Harp, Mary Adams. Surety, Ralph Dawson
July 28 James R. Garrish, Loran Peterson
Aug 6 Jesse Devon, Margaret Ford
Aug 18 Benjamin Walmsley, Catharine Jamison
Sep 1 James Welsh, Agness Hannah
Sep 17 Pierce Maree of New Castle co, Eliza Frazin [should be Frazer]
Oct 28 Archibald M'Mellan, Mary Sterratt
Nov 10 Israel Davis, Sarah Wiliman
Nov 10 Henry Egnor, Elizabeth Nicholson
Nov 19 Benjamin Merritt, Martha Kerr
Nov 22 Dennis Dougherty, Margaret Baldwin
Nov 24 Richard Clayton of New Castle co, Mary Lawrenson of same
Nov 26 John M'Lean, Mary Swallow
Dec 5 Richard Jones, Catharine Clark
Dec 14 William Wilson, Deborah Twaddle
Dec 21 Ephraim Sterling, Sarah Stanton
Dec 29 Kittle Sutton, Rebecca Tindall
Dec 27 James Allen, Lydia M'Donough
Dec 29 Joseph Richardson, Sarah Evans

1809
Jan 7 Samuel M'Donnough, Eliza Thomas
Jan 9 Harman Cox, Elizabeth Lamb
Jan 10 William J. Crouch, Martha A. Heath
Jan 10 Enos Slack of Pencader, Esther Chapman
Jan 13 Calvin Tubbs of Philadelphia, Mary Ferral of Delaware
Jan 31 William Downes, Ann Wilson
Feb 7 John Barber of New Castle co, Rebecca Bailey of White Clay Creek
    hundred
Feb 16 William Jaquett of New Castle co, Elizabeth Paulson
Feb 16 John Cavender, Jane Moody
Feb 16 John D. Eves, Mary Crow
Feb 21 James S. Naudain of New Castle co, Ann Mountain

Feb 23 Wingate Prettyman, Elizabeth Biddle
Feb 23 Jeremiah Taylor, Mary Griffin, Surety, Isaac Taylor
March 13 Owen Zebley, Mary Webster
March 16 John Morrison, Margaret Armstrong
March 27 William M'Millin, Mary Pennington
March 30 Elijah Cantwell, Sarah Boys
April 1 Tobias Pritchard of New Castle co, Mary Israel
April 6 David Stewart, [he was of Port Penn, St. Georges hundred, N.C. co.],
    Mary Kenedy
April 15 Thomas Vail of New Castle co, Mary Smith
April 24 Peter Springer of New Castle co, Margaret Phillips of White Clay Creek
    hundred
April 26 Thomas Turner, Mary Holland
May 11 William Anderson of New Castle hundred, Mary Jaquett
May 16 William W. Ward of New Castle co, Maria Reading
May 16 John Colgan, Mary M'Dowell
Aug 8 Kendell Blizard, Sarah Willson
Aug 9 Isaac Penny of New Castle co, Elizabeth See of Pencader
Aug 19 Benjamin Mendenhall, Rebecca Seal
Aug 31 David Sample, Elizabeth Walker
Sep 4 Robert M'Murphy, Mary Springer
Sep 12 Zachariah Deputy, Elizabeth Deputy
Sep 25 James Foster, Mary Allman
Sep 30 Thomas Hickman of New Castle co, Rachel Cox of same
Oct 6 William Crim, Mary Castalow
Nov 2 William Johnson, Margaret Martin
Nov 2 James Vandegrift of New Castle co, Nancy Button of same
Nov 4 Alexander Davis, Sarah Jefferson
Nov 7 John Stanton, Maria Bolden
Nov 15 Nicholas Shepherd, Eleanor Wilson
Nov 21 John Alrichs, Mary Lord
Nov 27 James Doran, Ann Pearce
Nov 29 Abraham Cannon, Elizabeth Colley
Nov 29 George Jackson, Mary Femister
Nov 30 Barzillai Jefferis, Esther Stoops
Dec 1 Joseph Drummond, Hannah Marsh
Dec 7 Joseph Durell, Ann M'Nelly
Dec 11 John Mony, Mary Hugg

1810
Jan 9 John Wiley, Elizabeth M'Kinsey
Jan 23 James Taylor, Ann Murphy, Surety, Isaac Flinn

Feb 3 Walter Nedery, Mary Wiley
Feb 7 John Miskimin, Elizabeth Houston
Feb 7 Elijah Boldin, Rebecca Hukill
Feb 14 Samuel Chestnut of New Castle co, Aseneath John
Feb 14 John Wilson, Ann Scott
Feb 21 John Johns, Catharine Sellers
Feb 27 Joseph Hudson, Henrietta Pennington
March 1 William B. Weaver, Elizabeth Sheward
March 8 William Baldwin, Molly Donnell
March 12 Paul Rosin, Lydia Ratliff
March 13 Joseph P. Ryland, Hannah Vandegrift
March 13 Isaac Cunningham, Rachel Stanton
March 15 John Drummond, Hester Rezoe
March 20 Thomas M'Kinsey, Sarah Harris
March 21 John M. Lotz, Susan Stewart
March 28 James Henry of St. Georges hundred, Agnes Brittain of same
April 11 Isaac Brannon of New Castle co, Margaret Todd
April 19 George Read Jr., Louisa Doury (?)
April 24 Edward Jones (mark), Susanna Delcart
April 25 James Foard, Elizabeth Howell
May 2 Charles H. Cobb of New Castle co., Catharine Worth
May 3 George H. Wood, Martha Eaton
May 7 George H. Wilcutts, Elizabeth Sorden (or Jorden)
May 9 Samuel Pennington, Hannah M'Connaughey
May 9 Isaac Stidham of New Castle hundred, Ingeber Lafever
May 22 Francis M'Guigan (mark), Mary Fox
May 23 George Stroup of New Castle co, Hannah Cord of same
May 24 John Swift, Sarah Turner
May 24 John Gibbins, Hester Giffin
June 7 Peter Ball, Mary Warnick
June 11 Jacob M'Collister (mark) of New Castle co, Rebecca Warrich of same
June 13 John Robinson, Margaret Aulmond
June 21 Miller Barns (mark), Catherine Holleson
Jul 7 Lewis Nicholas (mark), Margaret Brown
Jul 12 James Glasgow, Ann Ross
Aug 6 John Wroth, Lydia Rothwell
Aug 22 Jacob Egner, Sylvia Evans
Aug 23 Jacob Ratcliff (mark), Catherine Jordan
Aug 25 William Grimes (mark) of New Castle co, Susan Dalton
Sep 13 Isaac Sherkey (mark), Sarah Gest
Sep 19 Thomas Culbertson, Mary Carruthers
Sep 19 Philip Cavender of New Castle co, Mary Mann of same
Sep 21 William Hill Gent, Elizabeth Foot spinster

Sep 25 George Hart of St. Georges hundred, Peirce Holden
Sep 27 Amos Sanders of New Castle co, Ann Barton
Oct 24 Oliver Mitchell (mark), Abbey Cole
Nov 7 Alexander Huston, Catherine Rubecamp
Nov 8 Zachariah Helman, Louesa Taylor
Dec 5 William Groves, Frances Morrison
Dec 18 Abraham Sevil (Signed Abel Sivil), Elizabeth M'Cormic
Dec 25 Jesse Adams (mark), Rachel Carvill
Dec 22 Bartholomew Etherington, Susan Walmsley
Dec 31 Justa Justis, Ann Bracken

1811
Jan 30 George Nebeker, Susannah Meredith
Feb 18 Elias Gardinier, Charlotte M'Beath
March 9 George Barr, Rebecca Ball
March 13 James Twedy, Mary Smith
March 20 John Kensey (or Hensey), Elizabeth Johns
March 23 John Cunningham, Betsey Stanton
March 27 Joseph Jaquett, Jain Phillips
March 29 Charles Gwinn, Eliza Phillips
April 1 William Dever, Mary Ring (or King?)
April 23 William Wilkinson, Mary Rhodes
May 15 John Ward, Ann Otley
Jul 16 William Scott, Jane Adair
Jul 16 Jeremiah Lewden, Cave K. Williams
Jul 20 Thomas Middleton, Joanna Mason
Jul 29 John Deakyne, Ann Ward
Sep 7 William Blackiston, Rachel Simans
Sep 12 Evard Everson of Pencader (mark), Katharine Watson
Sep 16 John Mullin, Ann Stuart
Sep 17 William Gregg, Mary Ring
Oct 5 Stephen Boddy, Ann Brown
Oct 8 Robert M'Mellin of White Clay Creek hundred, Elizabeth Robinson
Oct 21 Thomas Robinson, Susan Van Dyke
Oct 24 William Chandler, Sarah Stuart., Surety, Stephen Boddy
Oct 31 William Stephenson, Catharine Vandegrift
Nov 30(?) Gilbreath Mathewson, Margaret Kidd (?)
Nov 20 John Dougherty, Nancy Holland
Nov 21 James Belville, Rebecca Eanos
Nov 26 William Dickinson, Margaret Hanson
Dec 17 David Wasson, Eleanor Butler
Dec 21 Aaron Brackin, Margaret Sharp

Dec 26 Allen Willis, Catharine Moody
Dec 26 James Russel, Cenath Watters (Walters?)
Dec 26 Thomas Gray, Lydia Woodcock

1812
Jan 2 Doctor David Stewart, Susan Johns
Jan 6 Thomas Caldwell, Hannah Donohoe
Jan 19 George Jones, Rebecca Rodman
Jan 28 Andrew Quinley, Ann Morton
Feb 5 William Robinson, Injeber Stidham. Surety, Ashton Richardson
Feb 21 Jeremiah Williams, Margaret Harris
Feb 26 James Penington, Henrietta Mary M'Gill
March 1 William B. Cochran, Mary Middleton
March 10 David Burnes, Mary Kincaed
March 12 Stacy Bowin of White Clay Creek hundred, Eleanor Montgomery of
 same
March 12 Richard Hall, Nancy Paul
March 13 James Worth, Mary Thatcher
March 17 Elisha Boldin, Sarah Couden
March 18 James Jones, Sarah Rogers
March 22 Jonathan Kelly, Ann Wilson
March 24 George W. Price, Elizabeth Vandegrift
March 26 Nathaniel Jaquett, Nancy Shannon
April 1 Henry Stalcup, Elizabeth Sparks
April 4 James Johnston, Jane M'Clellen
April 6 William Pearce, Elizabeth Price
April 7 Thomas Calhoun, Sarah Cary
April 11 Nathan Jones, Margaret Wattson
April 15 Benjamin Sanders, Eleanor Clark
April 16 Robert Money (mark), Letitia Jeans
April 23 John P. Penton, Mary Weaver
May 4 Richard Cochran, Eliza Evans
May 13 James Battersby, Jain M'Finley
May 18 Jacob Caulk, Mary Pontsell
May 25 John Swinfin, Hannah Quandrile (?)
May 25 Zachariah Smith, Margaret M'Kinsey
June 5 George White, Rebecca Gunn
June 12 John Leech, Maria Phillips
June 18 David Jarman, Margaret Starling
June 20 James Strong, Jane M'Calley
June 24 Wingate Prettyman, Nancy Price
June 24 Amos Faris, Catherine Stewart
July 9 John Dolton, Rebecca Vandegrift

July 23 Robert C. Ludlow, Catharine Wethered
Aug 1 Lodia Jefferson, Synthia Howell
Aug 27 Isaac Thomas, Mary Meteer
Aug 28 John Holmes (mark), Rachel Leivis
Sep 3 William Dawson, Mary Stoop
Sep 26 Henry Rowen, Margaret Lackey
Oct 7 Charles M'Namee, Alice Porter
Oct 13 Andrew Ford, Sarah Higgins
Oct 20 George Gunn, Rebecca Brinton
Oct 21 Selden Towner, Nancy Carson
Oct 29 Joseph Alston (mark), Jeny M'Clure
Oct 29 Stephen Townsend, Mary Rogers
Nov 2 Thomas Painter, Susanna Israel
Nov 2 Orrin Beckley, Prudence Jefferis
Nov 4 Moses Martin, Sarah Perkins
Nov 5 John Collings, Lydia Cannon
Nov 9 James Bateman, Susan Marim
Nov 10 Daniel Newman, Eliza Vanderford
Nov 17 William Lindsey, Mary Sergeant
Nov 18 Edward Parker (mark), Phebe Dushane
Nov 19 Barnet Israel, Margaret Allen
Nov 29 Henry Batten, Elizabeth Foster
Nov 24 Benjamin Brown, Elizabeth Sterrett, Surety, Thos. Witherspoon of
    Wilmington
Dec 3 William Florbit, Rhoda Davis
Dec 5 George Rhoads, Sarah Lindle
Dec 16 John Johnson (mark), Sarah Mullen
Dec 16 Elisha English, Mary Sanders

1813
Jan 7 Moses Garland, Nancy Rogers
Jan 11 John Williams, Esther Adams
Jan 14 George Moffett, Martha Bayard (?)
Jan 20 John Green, Rachel Rothwell
Jan 21 John Miller, Margaret Scott
Feb 8 Charles Justice, Rebecca Justice
Feb 18 James Henry, Ann Jefferson
Feb 22 Levi Adams, Dorcas Bishop
March 2 William L. Bouldin, Anne Patterson
March 17 William Vandegrift, of St. Georges hundred, Mary Walraven
March 20 Ezekiel Roe, of Appoquinimink hundred, Mary Donohoe
March 27 William Crosson, Margaret Kennedy

April 3 Thomas Ward, Sarah M'Guire
April 8 Andrew Allison, of New Castle Co, Ann Curlett
April 27 Adam Deihl, Elizabeth Danel
May 15 Robert Banner, Martha Smith
June 1 Robert Huggins, Mary Finley, both of Mill Creek Hundred
June 2 Robert Caswell, Bersheba Cleland
June 9 Thomas Lollar (mark), Margery Abercrombie
Jul 1 John Cloward, Mary Mellon
Sep 4 Nathan Bouldan, Mary Dunlap
Sep 14 James Garretson (mark), Charlotte Palmer
Sep 8 Jacob Vanhorn (mark), Catharine Wright
Sep 16 Joseph Marich, Margaret Stone
Sep 29 Joseph Lindle, Sarah Batton
Nov 17 Jacob Blackshare, Mary Litman
Oct 28 William Scott, Amelia Stewart
Nov 8 Ferdinand Bauduy, Victorine Dupont, Surety, Peter Bauduy
Nov 27 Jacob Rothwell, Deborah Brown
Nov 27 William Wright, Sydia Ann Tilton
Dec 2 John Hansen of New Castle Co, Mary Bryan of same.
Dec 8 Seneca Siney, Sarah Hill
Dec 9 James Vandegrift, Ann Hackett
Dec 9 John Biddle, Harriett Biddle
Dec 11 David Lewis (mark), Sarah M'Kee
Dec 14 Samuel Walker, Mary Keagey
Dec 25 William Rush, Hannah Webb, ("to be married Dec. 28, 1813.")
Dec 29 Jacob Whiteman, Jane Mullan
Dec 29 John Calander (Callender), Nancy Glackin
Dec 29 John Hart, Jane Little
Dec 30 Nehemiah Delaplain, Lavinia Springer

1814
Jan 1 James M'Vay, Eliza Kiblee
Jan 3 Charles Springer, Harriet Stewart
Jan 8 Joseph Hossinger, Martha Wollaston
Jan 8 William Bannard, Eliza Bailey
Jan 13 Leonard Sparks, Sarah Caldwell
Jan 17 John Bennett, Hannah King
Jan 17 Thomas Wallace, Margaret Gunn
Jan 17 Eaton Crawford, Eleanor Coates
Jan 17 Robert H. Barr, Eliza Peirce
Jan 17 John Ford, Ann Ward
Jan 18 Thomas Newton, Mary Smaltz
Jan 18 John Evans, Mary Pearce

Jan 19 Robert Glasgow, Nancy Black
Jan 24 John Shirvan, Margaret Ford
Feb 8 Lazarus Martin, Julian Pearce
Feb 10 Ephraim Sears Junr, Sarah Jackson, [*Writing very faint*]
Feb 24 Silas Parvin, (Name not given)
Feb 24 Frederick Houck, Maria Gilbert
Feb 26 John C. Hull, Jane Thompson
Feb 26 Benjamin Read, Ann Price
Feb 26 Samuel Toppin, Ann Bole
Feb 28 John Miller, Rebecca Stevenson
March 1 Jacob B. Vandever, Rebecca Vandever
March 5 Jesse Brannon, Ann Anderson
March 10 William Pogue, (Name not given.)
March 3 Ebenezer Greenough, Abaigael Israel
March 14 Samuel Howell, Elizabeth Little?
March 15 Levi Bunker, Eliza Simpson
March 20 William Cray, Eliza Barnett
March 22 Thomas Bradley, Sarah Diet
March 22 John Davidson, Jane Hutchison
March 31 John Gill, Edith Robinson
April 1 Albert Bryan, Martha Smith
April 1 Joseph Grimes, Ann Adams
April 7 Abraham Bennett, Hester Sharp
April 7 John Lawler, Ellen M'Dowell
April 15 Benjamin Jefferson (mark), Ann Hilman
April 18 Stephen Townsend, Ann Simpson
April 18 James Hamilton (mark), Elizabeth Shirley
April 20 Benjamin Simmons, Sarah Ford
May 10 Stephen Davis, Sarah Chapman
May 19 Alexander Bowers, Sarah Pettit
May 31 John Allis (mark), Mary Munro
June 27 Isaac Casho, Ann Ash
June 29 Samuel Fisher, Mary Burns
Jul 5 John Galloway of New Castle Co., Ann Silvers of same.
Jul 16 Richard Laurendson, Mary Clayton
Jul 26 Nathan Brooks, Hannah Wilson
Jul 20 John Ellwood, Nancy Elsbury
Jul 23 Robert Holmes, Elizabeth Elsbury
Aug 4 Thomas King, Jane Herring
Aug 15 Jeremiah M'Danal, Rebecca Anderson
Aug 16 Joseph Thompson, Mary Thomas
Aug 19 Jesse Rogers (mark), Ann Rhodes

Aug 25 Arthur M'Cormic, Sarah Cloud
Aug 31 Isaac Cummins, Matilda Newson
Sep 1 Charles T. Vanhekle, Rebecca Pennington
Sep 8 Richard Clayton, Mary Grubb
Sep 16 James Hickman, Martha Rothwell
Sep 17 James Rich, Mary Merrit
Sep 18 James Ratliff, Mary Rosin
Sep 29 John Larkin, Margaret Bradley
Oct 6 George Hodgson, Mary Anderson
Oct 13 Charles Deputy, Rachel Hayes
Oct 27 William M'Grath, Ann Dougherty
Oct 27 Elizah Massey, Rachel Nebaker
Nov 1 John Bates, Elizabeth Newel
Nov 3 Peter Snyder, Margaret Kerr
Nov 3 Robert Keddy, Ann Gay
Nov 7 Samuel Crosson, Hannah Ford
Nov 8 French Rambo, Sarah Ware
Nov 15 William Work, Mariah Fobes
Nov 21 Joseph Chamberlin, Eliza Thompson
Nov 22 William Sergeant, Rebecca Femister
Dec 1 Abraham Sevil, Mary Davis
Dec 7 Lewis McCormick, Ann Sevil
Dec 16 Richard Simmons, Mary Turner
Dec 19 Joseph Hallowell, Mary Simmons
Dec 19 William Grave, Martha Mendenhall
Dec 19 Benjamin Wells Jr., Rebecca Long
Dec 21 Richard Craddock, Ann Springer
Dec 21 William Eliason, Sarah Douglas
Dec 22 James Brown, Mary Simpson
Dec 22 William Nicholson (mark), Millicent Thomas
Dec 22 James Smith, Mary Yates
No Day John Patterson, Elizabeth Jefferis

1815
Jan 23 James Russel (mark), Elizabeth Evans
Jan 27 James Crossan, Abigail Sharp
Feb 21 John Frist, Susan Stidham
Feb 22 John P. Morris, Mary Martin
March 6 James Murray, Ruthy Knight
March 8 Henry Brackin, Mary Burchard
March 9 Samuel Yeals (mark), Martha Robinson
March 21 Thomas Williams, Susan Deputy
April 5 John Griffith, Deborah Kimble

April 5 John Forman, Ann Brynberg
April 6 John Stroud, Elizabeth Walker
April 28 Eli Garrison, Mary Red (Rea?)
May 4 John Gray, Esther Hemphill
May 10 Joseph Burn, Rebecca Talley
May 22 Samuel McBride, Elizabeth Hunter
June 15 Moses Baxter, Lydia Burrill
June 24 John Bouldin, Margaret Faris
July 1 William Waeks (Wakes?) (mark), Margaret Burns
July 4 Henry Lindon (mark), Eliza Atkinson
July 18 Ashbury S. Pennington, Jane Eves
July 22 Robert Bradley, Sarah Baker
July 29 John Hilman, Hetty Sergeant
Aug 8 John Duncan, Hannah Wells
Sep 14 John Dunn, Sarah Askew

1815
Oct 4 Matthew Smith, Rachel Weaver
Oct 4 Joseph Barr, Sarah Forrester
Oct 4 Phillip Jones, Mary Gillespie
Oct 4 Amos Wheeler, Margaret Stevenson
Oct 9 Henry Reed, Letitia Yeates
Oct 14 Isaiah Bowen, Lydia Hannah
Oct 18 William Kerby, Araminta Cooch
Oct 19 Daniel Bratton, Mary Bollin
Oct 30 Joseph R. Forman, Eliza Hay
Oct 31 Josiah L. Foard, Lydia S. Caulk
Nov 2 Joshua Deputy, Nancy Richards
Nov 6 Robert Walker, Hannah Weldin
Nov 7 Samuel Chesnut, Jane Ellesbery
Nov 7 Edward Lewis, Elizabeth Carroll
Nov 8 James Price, Mary Morris
Nov 9 John Shockley, Elizabeth Veach
Nov 15 George Rowland, Elizabeth Green
Nov 29 James P. W. Kollock, Elizabeth Loffland
Dec 2 James Emery, Elizabeth Robinson
Dec 4 John Pink, Nancy Edgar
Dec 4 Samuel Smith, Mrs. Rachel Mercer
Dec 6 Joseph Kid (mark), Mary Jones
Dec 7 Jesse Hastings (mark), Nancy Downing
Dec 12 Stratton Virden, Abigail Maree
Dec 15 Isaac Moody, Elizabeth Chestnut

Dec 27 John Imley, Mary Ann Smith
Dec 27 James Rosseun (Rezaw), Catharine Baley

1816
Jan 1 Cornelius Dushane, Ann McMurphey
Jan 2 John H. Cannon, Lydia Vanhickle
Jan 2 John Bryan, Mary Clark
Jan 6 Joseph Russel, Sarah Moore
Jan 10 Hyland B. Pennington, Elizabeth Rothwell
Jan 13 Joseph Wollaston, Elizabeth Douden (Doughten?)
Jan 13 Edward Walton, Margaret Culson (?)
Jan 17 William Clungeon, Mary Burns
Jan 30 John Martin, Esther McGinn(?)
Feb 7 Isaac Jefferson, Sarah Groves
Feb 7 James Lafferty, Mary Ann Baheum
Feb 13 Joseph Hill, Ann Gomer (?)
Feb 13 John M'Cormick, Mary Jamison
Feb 14 Joseph Hickman, Mary Hickman
Feb 19 John Springer, Ann Elliott
Feb 22 Daniel Collins, Kitty Stidham
Feb 28 Robert R. Hall, Elizabeth T. Pearce
Feb 29 William Adams, Rebecca Allison
March 7 Samuel McDaniel, Eliza Delaplain
March 7 John Yates, Willemina Johnston
March 7 John Gunn, Mary Wilkinson
March 7 John McCrone, Hannah Farmer
March 8 James Hanson, Ann Hook
March 13 Almarin Woodruff, Rebecca Martain
March 16 Robert A. M'Guffin, Mary Stewart
March 19 Jesse Bryan, Eliza Allfree
March 20 William McIntire of New Castle Co., Catharine Reece of same.
March 21 John Hanbey, Sarah Abbot
March 22 Justa Justis, Catharine Phillips
March 23 Israel Israel, Susan McGloughlin
March 30 William Whittam, Ann Henson
April 1 Edward C. Johnson, Ann Dutton
April 8 Andrew Thompson, Rebecca Wilson
April 11 William Belew (Bulue?), Ann Bratton
April 11 Samuel McClary, Susan Springer
April 12 Joseph Rankin, Sarah Crawford
April 15 Elias Ball, Betsy Lockard
April 27 James Davis, Ann Morton
April 27 William Kinkead, Amelia Kaats

April 30 Benjamin Chandler, Rebecca Hindman
May 2 Jacob Derickson, Isabella Ruther
May 2 Joseph Roop, Maria Wood
Mar 8 Leonard McVay, Susan Adair(?)
Mar 11 Alexander Hall, Elizabeth Cuddy
May 17 Manlove Rowland, Unity Rath
May 23 Daniel Stidham, Mary Coverdill
May 28 Seneca Sinex, Margaret Gest
May 28 Curtis Grubb, Susanna Peirce. Surety, Joseph B. Grubb
May 28 George E. Mitchell, Mary Hooper
May 29 James Parrott, Lydia Gray
May 30 Joseph Bennett, Ann Fell
June 15 Joseph Brown, Ann Johnson
June 25 John Guthrie, Ann Blackburn
July 2 James Mellon (mark), Phebe Meredy
July 10 Robert C. Ritchie, Sarah H. Thomas
July 13 William Pritchard, Mary McManus
July 16 Silas Peirce, Susanna Bradshaw
July 20 William C. Foulke, Sarah Sibbets
July 27 William Ryan, Margaret Stuart (Stewart)
July 27 William M'Connaughey, Mary Griffith
Aug 17 John A. Dilworth, Ann Jefferies [*in pencil* "He was of St. George Hd., New Castle - his 2nd wife"]
Aug 26 Thomas M'Kennan, Isabella Ocheltree
Aug 27 Daniel Thomas, Jane Ferris
Sep 11 James Anthony Biderman [signed Ante. Biderman], Evalina Gabriel Dupont
Sep 11 Caleb Hall, Kitty Williams
Sep 17 George G. Faries, Sarah Alrichs
Oct 2 Solomon Hersey, Hannah B. Springer
Oct 4 Ezekiel Fols, Martha S. Humphries
Oct 9 Owen Lloyd (mark), Delila(?) Peirce
Oct 14 Robert Moore, Dorcas Bradley
Oct 16 Thomas C. Alrichs, Mary Ann Taylor
Oct 16 David Tweedy, Ellen King
Oct 21 William Corrie, Rebecca Cann
Oct 23 George Henderson, Susanna Lisle
Oct 23 Joshua Massey (mark), Sarah Phillips
Oct 24 James L. Devon, Ruth Wade
Nov 10 Charles P. Lisle, Eliza Bennett
Nov 12 Jared N. Downing, Abigail Femister
Nov 13 John Moore, Mary W. Temple

Nov 14 Richard Vansant, Eliza Streats (?)
Nov 16 David Bryan, Hannah Hanson
Nov 23 Timothy Pierce, Eliza McConnel
Nov 23 Robert W. Bradley, Nancy Oliver
Nov 28 Francis Moore, Mary Mahannah
Nov 28 Jeremiah Ford, Eliza Flinn
Nov 28 James Spencer, Elizabeth Stephenson
Dec 2 Robert Miller, Ann Vance
Dec 3 Nathan Bouldan, Elizabeth Thomas
Dec 4 Richard Westley, Ann Young
— 5 Samuel Creppin (mark), Margaret Powel
Dec 26 John Quinn, Jane Lindsey
Dec 27 Henry Whiteman, Ann Kinsey

1817
Jan 8 Samuel Redman, Sarah Wiltbank
Jan 10 Allain Corlay, Sophia Enos (?)
Jan 14 John Janvier, Susan Biddle
Jan 15 William Dickinson, Eliza Baker
Jan 22 Isaac Woods, Rebecca Hill
Jan 29 John Bell, Susanna Lee
Jan 30 Enoch Hugg, Margaret Walker
Jan 30 Samuel R. Conlyn, Sarah Stidham
Feb 12 William Lister, Susan Biddle
Feb 15 John Ritchie, Martha Foster
Feb 20 Peter Hanson, Christian Flintham
March 6 John Aldred, Mary Talley
March 11 Thomas Mullin (mark), Elizabeth Roberts
March 13 David Burchard, Lydia Carty
March 22 Thomas Little, Mary Little
March 24 John Allman (signed Almon), Mary Ann Sheppard
March 26 Levi Talley, Ann Boggs
March 31 Daniel L. Cahill, Prudy King
March 31 Charles Rumsey, Ann Harker
April 3 Robert Eggleston, Etta Lyons
April 3 James Smith, Maria Anger
April 8 Bennett Lewis, Mary Jane Smith
April 11 Charles King (mark), Biddey Fox
April 11 Nathan Dilworth, Lydia Cross
April 22 Robert Johnson, Ann Clark
May 1 Matthew Newkirk, Jane R. Stroud
May 3 William H. Murphey, Susan E. Wolfe
May 3 Andrew O'Daniel, Rebecca Dushane

May 6 George Walker, Miss Mary Jones
May 9 James B. Kanady, Eliza Thompson
May 12 James Bartley, Honour Davis
May 17 Moses Bradford, Phebe George
Mary 17 Richard McClary, Mary Pennington
May 20 James Denney, Amy Staats
May 21 Charles Hickman, Margaret Fulton
May 21 John Sammon (mark), Keziah Batton
May 21 John A. Weldin of Brandywine hundred, Eliza Martin
May 24 William Christy, Hannah Otley
May 28 Benjamin David, Ann McCracken
May 29 Thomas McCalmont, Sarah Hickman
May 29 William Batten, Mary McCoombs
May 29 Benjamin Thomas, Elizabeth Moffet
June 2 John Bradford, Margaret Weldin
June 5 Hugh Welsh, Ellen Weir
June 9 Samuel Wilson, Jane Welsh
June 16 Jacob Biddle, Elizabeth Biddle
June 19 William Bates, Elizabeth Durand
June 19 William Guthrie, Maria Magens
July 5 Joseph K. Robinett, Sarah Yeates
July 9, William Hutson (mark), Mary Ann Garretson
July 12 Adam Peirce, Tirzah Peirce
July 15 Thomas McConnell, Hannah Green
July 28 George Collins, Henrietta Deakyne
Aug 21 John Gordon, Sarah McClure
Aug 25 Samuel Grubb, Elizabeth Cloud
Aug 28 James Drummond, Mary Evans
Aug 28 Charles Rea, Ann Brown
Sep 2 Mathew Macklem, Catharine Jacobs
Sep 3 Charles Anderson, Sarah Derrickson
Sep 4 Samuel Daniel, Mary Kitchen
Sep 8 Isaac Wiltbank, Elizabeth Brannon
Sep 9 Enoch Coles, Margaret Henderson
Sep 10 John Hopper, Eliza Ogle
Sep 16 Thomas Jaquett, Kitty Wallace
Sep 17 Thomas Walker, Achsah Reed
Sep 18 John Kanady, Rachel Simpson
Sep 18 Jesse Moore, Eliza Wiley
Sep 25 Daniel McIntire, Sarah Houston
Oct 1 Barge Vanderslice, Maria Herring
Oct 4 William Palmer, Elizabeth Chesnut

Oct 9 Abraham Schrader, Ann Caldwell
Oct 9 Robert McMellen, Hannah Todd
Oct 11 John Tebow, Agnes S. Mullin
Oct 18 A. Cardon de Sandran, Mary Honaria Pogy
Oct 22 James Moody, Sylvia Watson
Oct 23 William Redding, Milicent Spencer
Oct 24 Thomas S. Bowers, Mary Coleman
Oct 27 Richard Lockwood, Mary Wilson
Oct 29 James Delaplain, Mary Hendrickson
Oct 29 Isaac Janvier, Matilda Shaw
Oct 30 Jesse Ash, Charlotte Carswell
Nov 6 Peter Staats, Jane Naudain
Nov 14 Isaac Walraven, Jane McNamee
Nov 15 Adam Grubb, Mary Hemphill
Nov 26 Jacob Haddock, Susan Brindly
Dec 2 James Boon, Catharine Sordin
Dec 9 James Stalcup, Creasy Morton
Dec 11 Andrew Walker, Eliza Logan
Dec 16 Azariah Foster, Charity Batten
Dec 17 William Anderson, Jane Bracken
Dec 17 Andrew Bradley, Mary Moore
Dec 17 Murthy Gargan, Rose McCallister
Dec 24 Samuel Burnham, Martha Burgess
Dec 24 Lewis May, Elizabeth Davis

1818
Jan 12 John Jamison, Sarah Bratton
Jan 15 Thomas Knox, (mark), Sarah Nivin
Jan 19 John Sheppard (mark), Sarah Baker
Jan 20 Amos Eastburn, Sarah Chambers
Jan 21 John Stidham, Sarah Bates
Jan 29 Benjamin Lobb, Mary Heald
Jan 29 John Kennard, Rebecca Bouldin
Jan 31 William Tussey, Eleanor Dixon
Feb 2 John Barton, Sinah Barr
Feb 3 James Gibson, Sarah Evins
Feb 9 William Forwood of Maryland, Sarah Forwood, Surety Wm. Forwood of
    Del.
Feb 16 John C. Melvin, Eliza Wier
Feb 16 David Stevenson, Mary Preston
Feb 17 John Farley (mark), Catharine Griffin
March 4 Abel Holland, Louisa Lincoln
Blank 7 James M'Kean, Sarah Robinson

March 9 John M'Cullough, Eliza Stirey
March 10 James Lindsey, Mary Wollaston
March 12 Isaac Hanson, Eleanor Hugg
March 12 William Ozier, Elizabeth Drummond
March 14 William Simmons, Elizabeth M. Pepper
March 16 Nathan W. Thomas, Martha Nivin
March 16 Samuel M'Intire, Elener Veil
March 17 Abraham Vandegrift, Mary Bowman
March 18 Andrew Gun (mark), Polly Vert
March 21 Luke Townsend, Louisa Devon (?)
March 23 William Rankin, Lea Stilby
March 24 George Grubb, Margaret Hanby (Hanbey)
March 26 John Ball, Margaret Kelly
March 30 Adam Diehl, Junr., Elizabeth Smith
April 2 Oliver Draper (mark), Elizabeth Alexander
April 16 James Richey, of New Castle Hundred, Mary Crippen
April 21 Alexander Wilson, Ann Rice
April 25 Jacob Peirce, Lydia Weldon
April 25 Edward Walker, Sarah Johnson
May 5 William Rice, Mary Smith
May 18 Roger Duckworth, Elizabeth Smith
May 26 Samuel Faris, Mary Holmes
June 2 Joseph Reece, Mary Holland
June 3 George Turner, Olivia M'Intire
June 3 Jacob Blackshear (mark), Margaret Price
June 4 Abraham Kelly, Ann F. Waley
June 9 Thomas M' Daniel (M'Donal), Mary M'Lane
June 11 Michael Wall, Rachel Conaway
June 19 Jacob Caulk, Julia Zellefro
June 24 Moses Morrison, Mary Black
Jul 8 Patrick Higgins, Mary Giffin
Jul 8 David Campbell, Elizabeth Talley
Jul 8 Adam Moffit Jr., Jane Smith
Jul 10 Joseph Hendrickson, Mary White
Jul 25 William Harper, Catherine Plenharty (?)
Aug 10 John Mendenhall, Eliza Woodward
Aug 17 Nathan Quillen, Mary Brown
Aug 29 James M'Ayale, Margaret Miller
Sep 3 Alexander Allison (mark), Sarah Smith
Sep 10 Alexander Cummins, Sarah Bartley
Sep 19 Savory Toy, Reuhama M'Kerson
Sep 24 Levi Roberts, Ann Parmer

Oct 1 Edward Hughes (mark), Ann Rhodes
Oct 3 John Toples, Mary M'Quay
Oct 13 Patrick M"Guire (mark), Elizabeth O'Brine
Oct 14 Abram Ray, Jane Moore
Oct 21 Thomas F. Pim, Harriet C. Sellars
Oct 22 John M'Mahan, Martha Kirl
Oct 24 Thomas Vail, Margaret M'Intire
Oct 31 Henry Hukil, Hannah Ozier
Nov 7 A. R. Palmer, Rachel Bines
Nov 12 Robert Gredd, Jane M'Clelland
Nov 12 Patrick O'Neil, Mary Dushane
Nov 19 John Aspril, Ann Vandegrift
Nov 25 Samuel Paul, Nancy Rigs
Dec 1 Andrew M'Intire, Elizabeth Hosenger
Dec 10 Henry Finegan, Jane Mathews
Dec 19 Simon Kerns of Mill Creek Hundred, Elizabeth Ocheltree of same
Dec 12 William Evans, Sarah Mountain
Dec 16 William Senix (mark), Margaret Badger
Dec 16 Peter Johnston, Eleanor M'Coy
Dec 23 James Brison (mark), Sarah Jones
Dec 23 John Guyer, Ruth Simmons

1819
Jan 5 Daniel Dewees, Mary Turner
Jan 5 Edward Croft, Alice Frazer
Jan 14 Thomas Montgomery, Susanna Trippet
Feb 3 Woodgate Smith, Lydia Cavender
Feb 13 Joseph French (mark), Mary Benderman
Feb 17 John Boys, Mary Stidham
Feb 22 Robert P. Robinson, Lydia Brynberg
Feb 28 Robinson David, Elizabeth Kinkead
March 3 Hicklen Gould (Goulil?), Elizabeth M'Cullough
March 4 Daniel Skinner, (mark), Lare Gore
March 6 Thomas Smith, Phebe Hartshorne
March 6 Samuel Smith, Tacy Stilly
March 11 Robert Ritchie, Maria Pearce
March 17 Benjamin Pearce, Mary Ware
March 27 Dickinson Webster, 2d, Mary Daily
March 27 Levi Clark, Sarah Miles
March 29 Obadiah Wade, Edith Price
April 1 Samuel Loyd, Mary Clayton
April 7 Alexander Ore, Elizabeth Little
May 13 John H. Metts, (no name)

June 1 James Booth Jun., Hannah W. Rogers
June 7 Garrett Lewis, Elizabeth James
June 19 Abel Jeanes, Priscilla Bracken
June 23 Thomas Seal, Maria R. Justis
June 30 Jacob Bolton, Maria Feris
July 12 Archibald Dick, Maria Rakes
July 17 Solomon Maxwell, Marion Middleton
July 22 Henry Fink, Eliza Davis
Aug 6 John Sharp, Sarah Miller
Aug 7 John Durnin, Catharine McCaskar(?)
Aug 12 Brinkly Lucas, Mary Mann
Aug 19 Charles Layton, Elizabeth Newlin
Sep 3 Fredus Pennington, Elizabeth Vanhikle
Sep 9 John T. Cochran, Margaret B. Penington
Sep 13 John Douglas (mark), Lydia Eliason
Sep 15 William Silver, Jur., Sally R. Weir
Sep 16 Azariah Rowles, Sarah Hendrickson
Oct 4 Levi Bates, Lydia Randall
Oct 6 William Stewart, Martha Stanton
Oct 6 Thomas Freese, Mary Ann Miller
Oct 6 James Giffin, Mary Foote
Oct 14 Benjamin Tyson, Mary Kelly
Oct 14 John Barr, Ann Quinn
Oct 20 Joseph Oliver, Hannah McBride
Oct 30 James Galagher, Ann Gallagher
Oct 30 Jonathan Bee, Sarah Sutton
Nov 3 George Quin, Hannah King
Nov 5 Owen King (mark), Eleanor McCafford
Nov 5 Francis Petitmanche (signed Francouse Pettitnche), Julia Bland
Nov 8 Silas Crippen, Maria Townsend
Nov 8 Samuel Meeteer, Ann Chamberlain
Nov 9 Moses William (Moyse Gillome Francourse), Christiana Oura Chrin
Nov 10 Francis A. Thornton, Sally Ann Heap
Nov 10 Samuel L. Brown, Phebe Craig
Nov 11 John Foulk Talley, Hannah Paulson
Nov 13 Edward Haman, Rebecca Smith
Nov 17 George Griffin, Anna Maria Allmond
Nov 17 William Thompson, Sarah Bradley
Nov 20 James Clark (mark), Sarah Shippy
Nov 29 Isaac Thomas, Margaret Cavender
Nov 29 James McMullin, Hannah Beetle
Dec 1 David Johnson, Ann Hammonod

Dec 3 William Armstrong, Jane Todd
Dec 13 George Winslow, Elizabeth C. Welsh
Dec 15 Charles Kennedy, Elizabeth Veineman
Dec 16 Thomas Powel, Catherine Wright
Dec 9 William MeCluer, Rebecca Lee
Dec 23 Charles McCarran (M'arn), Mary Fox
Dec 27 Charles McCullough, Mary Coulter
Dec 27 Levi Miller, Mary Rozell
Dec 28 John Flinn, Eliza Carey

1820
James Kibbler (mark), Mary Marshall
Jan 8 Jesse Adams (mark), Nancy Mabery, widow
Jan 8 Wistar G. Dixon, Sarah Morrison
Jan 12 Samuel Boldin, Sarah Caulk
Jan 12, Joseph Lindsey, Sarah Bracken
Feb 2 Thomas T. Tasker, Elizabeth Hickman
Feb 8 Eli Sinex, Mary Mchaffy
Feb 11 Lewis Foulk (no name)
Feb 14 James Watson, Margaret McAllister
Feb 19 Joseph Springer, Sarah Evans
Feb 23 William Davis (mark), Eliza Boulden
Feb 29 Daniel Buffum, Mary Ann Landers (Sanders?)
March 6 John Holland, Mary Boulden
March 7 Robert Porter, Susan E. Fromberger
March 9 Nathan Holland, Hannah Lincoln
March 13 Samuel Medill, Rosanna M'Neal
March 14 Frederick Hilyard, Mary Veach
March 21 Jacob Robinson, Eleanor Garner
March 22 Eli Evans, Ann Poulson
March 27 Joseph Diehl, Sarah Bennett
April 1 William Miller, Elizabeth Walker
April 8 William Wilson, Jane Galbraith
April 22 John MacNeill, Elizabeth Graham
April 24 Edmund P. Kennedy, Ann P. Harden
April 24 John Hamilton, Rachel Moore
May 8 Joseph Mahon, Hannah Baily
May 22 Joseph Rozell (mark), Margaret Clark
May 30 Lewis Thomas, Jane Guthrie
June 6 William Whaley (mark), Martha Bryan
June 8 Henry M'Cluer, Maria Pike
Tul 27 John Austison, Margaret Blackiston

Jul 21 William Bratten, Isabella Carr
Jul 13 John Dodd, Ann Bowman
June 7 John Biggs, Diana Bird
Jul 6 William B. Smith (mark), Susan Meredith
Jul 3 Ephraim Underwood, Sarah Hackett
Jul 31 Nathaniel Wolf, Lydia Hall
Aug 1 John Wiser, Sarah Davis
Aug 8 Alexander M'Caully, Mary Oliver
Aug 19 William Way (mark), Mary Stanton
Aug 26 Robert Curry, Jr., Elizabeth Baylor
Sep 2 Peter Quigley, Mary Melloy (Meeloy?)
Sep 6 John Rumford, Sally Moody
Sep 12 Robert Eakin, Elizabeth Huxley
Sep 17 Thomas Moore (mark), Mary Ann Sparks
Oct 5 Henry Grimes, Elizabeth Turner
Oct 7 Robert M'Evoy, Margaret Lafferty
Oct 16 Edward Bodle, Phebe Turner
Nov 7 Patrick M'Adams, Catharine Fitzpatrick
Nov 22 John Lynam, Sarah Long
Nov 25 Jacob Welch (mark). Mary Ann Seville
Nov 26 Patrick Donelly (mark), Ann Kain
Nov 29 John Burgess, Mary Daily
Dec 7 Abel Tyson, Rebecca Walker
Dec 12 John Colesberry, Eliza Turner
Dec 16 Nathan B. Moore, Eliza Boulden
Dec 16 Joseph Finley (Findley), Delia Reecs
Dec 19 Noah Morris Jr., Mary Tatler
Dec 20 Thomas Meeter, Margaret Simpson
Dec 29 Samuel Sappington, Jannett Keith

1821
Jan 9 Morton Morton, Rachel Brothers
Jan 23 Jonathan Jones, Francina White
Jan 31 Patrick Coyne, (no name)
Jan 31 William Currens, Elizabeth Jump
Feb 6 David Justis, Maria Springer
Feb 7 Thomas Sinex, Elizabeth Foulk
Feb 8 Henry Brackin, Susan Yarnall
Feb 8 Hugh Johnson, Margaret McCall
Feb 13 Caleb Foster, Margaret Hughes
Feb 13 David Green, Hanna H. Mitchell
Feb 19 Samuel Rambo, Margaret Chapman

Feb 19 James Bird, Elizabeth K. Clarke
Feb 20 Hance Shad, Elizabeth Evans
Feb 21 Isaac H. Vandegrift, Martha Vandegrift
Feb 22 Elias Johnson, Lydia Fredd
Feb 27 James Smith, Sarah Reynolds
March 1 Robert Greenly, Rebecca Pitts
March 1 Richard W. Mason, Rachel Ryland
March 3 Blair Kincaid, Mary Lancaster
March 3 William Smith, Rebecca C. Bird
March 5 Samuel L. Eccles, Rebecca Vandegrift
March 7 Archibald A. Enos, Jane McCombs
March 13 William Peterson Provost, Sarah Penington
March 14 Stephen Foulk, Priscilla Cloud
March 14 Thomas Bird (mark), Sarah Pierce
March 14 John Foulk, Elizabeth Story
March 15 Charles Farra, Ann Carey
March 17 James Hughes, Hannah McMellen
March 17 Thomas Elliott, Sarah D. Edinborough
March 20 Purnal Jefferson, Margaret Walraven
March 23 Josiah Caruthers (mark), Eliza Albertson
April 2 Robert Shipley, Hester Canby
April 3 Henry Witsil, Hannah Lowden
April 4 John M. Woods, Catharine Jamison
April 10 John A. Craig, Elizabeth Custilow
April 10 Joseph Hanson, Eliza Flintham
April 20 Henry M. Hayes, Eliza Brooks
April 26 David Roe (mark), Elizabeth Hutton
May 1 Samuel Bingham, Ann Hudson(?)
May 9 Bennet Gay, Rosalie Coudere
May 17 Benjamin Willis, Sarah Richisson
May 25 Robert McBride, Mary Ann Robertson
May 25 Henry Gagan (mark), Mary Brady
May 28 William Burrows, Susan Ayres
May 28 Thomas Price, Eliza Ann Price
May 29 Alexander Henry, Eliza Boyd
July 13 William Watson, Sarah Pryor
July 17 Christopher Countiss, Sarah Hudson
Aug 8 William W. Ford, Cornelia Stoops
Aug 8 William Lowry, Mary Hollinger
Aug 10 Nicholas Quinn, Eliza Carnahan(?)
Aug 13 Benjamin Dougherty, Rebecca Evans
Sep 8 James Davis (mark), Jane Mullen
Sep 15 George Platt, Ann H. Gemmill

Sep 19 Thomas W. Couden, Eliza Redman
Oct 2 James Davis, Sophia Louisa Nutter
Oct 4 John G. Whilldin of Philadelphia, Miss Jane Janvier of the town of New Castle
Oct 4 Daniel Thompson, Letitia Steward
Oct 5 John Hatcher (mark), Mary Hendrickson
Oct 6 William Kelley, Catharine Morrison
Oct 12 Abel Hyde, Sarah Anderson
Oct 17 Benjamin Hyland, Ann Boulden
Oct 30 Samuel Holland, Ann Casho
Nov 2 Francis D. Wait, Eliza G.Newell
Nov 8 Benjamin Groves, Mary H. Francis
Nov 13 Henry Clark, Ann Buckanan
Nov 17 Richard Posthill, Mary Ann Robinson
Nov 24 James Carnahan, Sarah Spencer
Nov 28 Elisha Huxley, Elizabeth Derrickson
Dec 10 William Pippen, Hannah Aspril
Dec 13 David T. Jones, Hannah Giffin
Dec 15 James Milby (mark), Hester Gordon
Dec 20 Samuel Adams (mark), Ann Witsill
Dec 24 Cyrus Abbett, Sarah Y. Pierce
Dec 25 James Clarnan, Mary Crossan
Dec 26 Alexander Patterson (mark), Isabella Adair

1822
Jan 19 Lewis McPherson, Margaret Jane Kidd
Jan 23 Andrew Thompson, Sarah Silver
Jan 30 Francis Hyatt, Ann Witsil
Jan 30 John Crouch, Mary Morton
Feb 4 Townsend Meredith, Mary Fisher
Feb 14 William Mifflin, Sabiner Biddle
Feb 19 John McWhorter, Mary Segars
Feb 26 Samuel Riley, Elizabeth Stewart
March 9 Hamilton Warren, Darcus McBride
March 22 Elijah Start, (no name)
March 22 John Wright, Ann Hendrickson
March 25 Edward Collings, (no name)
March 26 Charles Foster, Sarah Streets
March 28 David P. Best, Ann Hall
April 2 Aaron Daniel, Mira B. Skillington
April 3 George Harriss, Janet Barmaid
April 12 John Tumblin (mark), Vica Cordary

April 15 William Dyer, Hannah Wiltbank
April 15 John Bensill, Eliza Lowens
April 15 Moses Hickman, Catharine Cavinder
April 15 James Galloway, Elizabeth Brown
April 15 John M Ocheltree, Hannah King
May 7 Isaac Francis, Eliza Groves
May 16 John Donnaldson Jr., Catharine Maria Black
May 16 Andrew M'Guyre, Jemimah Mountain
May 22 David Chambers(?), (no name)
May 28 Adam Morton, Sarah Ward
No day (George Watson)?, Lydia Killman
June 6 Lewis R. Springer, Mary Bowman
June 17 George Rice (mark), Mary Boys
Aug 5 John M. Clayton, Sally Ann Fisher
Aug 6 Alexander Cavender, Hester Drummond
Aug 29 John Ford, Ann Williams
Sep 12 Joseph Smith, Mary Lonnon
Sep 14 Isaiah Stanton, Maria Brannen
Sep 19 William C Mount, Ann Austin
Oct 16 Thomas Jefferis, Nancy Saunders
Oct 22 Thomas Armstrong, Anna Ogle
Nov 2 Robert Guthrie, Elizabeth M'Murray
Nov 4 Archibald Barton, Ann Furgeson
Nov 4 John Addison, Mary Craven *(nee Aspril), widow of Thomas Craven of St. Geo. Hd.* [italicized portion added in different handwriting]
Nov 9 Abraham Eliason, Nancy Israel
Nov 9 William J Christie, Elizabeth Nicholson
Nov 13 Francis Dickinson, Eliza Irwin
Nov 20 Andrew Alston, Sarah Archer
Nov 25 Andrew Barnaby, Mary B. Penton
Nov 28 Samuel Rothwell, Ann M'Craching
Dec 4 James Clark, Martha Cummins
Dec 5 John M'Intire, Matilda Williams
Dec 5 Nicholas Coleman, Susannah Allcorne
Dec 14, James Laird (Lard), Sarah England
Dec 16 Levi Hanson, Elizabeth Turner
Dec 17 James (or Isaac) Moody, Mary Wood

1823
Jan 15 William Richison, Catharine Hilles
Jan 28 Alexander Anderson, Mary Floyd
Jan 29 Leonard Vandegrift, Elizabeth Vandegrift
ᵇ 13 Jonathan O. Wiltbank, Elizabeth Spencer

Feb 17 George C Rumsey, Mary W. Buchanan
Feb 25 David Burchard, Elizabeth Burges
March 10 William Rochester, Eliza Peacock
March 11 Levi Hutton, Sarah Man
March 12 John Cannon, Rachel Campbell
March 19 Joseph Walraven, Martha Richard(?)
April 17 William Dean, Ann Evans
May 5 Christian Shuster, Mahala Evans
May 12 Eli Foster, Hannah C. Tweedy
May 15 James H Briscoe, Catharine S. Gemmell
May 21 John D Dilworth, Eliza F Gordon
May 22 George P Allcorn, Elizabeth Montgomery
May 24 John Davis, Ann Price
June 10 Thomas Challenger, Sarah Price
June 19 Charles E. Stuart, Luthena S. M'Dowell
June 19 Jonas Stidham, Sarah Eves
July 12 John Higlee, Rebecca Tribute(?)
July 23 John C. Thomson, (no name)
July 30 Daniel Dawson, Martha Mitchell
Aug 12 Robert Orr, Jane Lochard
Aug 21 Clement Tucker (mark), Catharine Starling(?)
Aug 23 Ceaser Bell (mark), Ann Passway
Aug 26 Robert Bakum, Elenor B D Glassock
Aug 28 Samuel Ringgold, Mary H. Smith
Aug 30 John Sebo, Rebecca Hartley
Sep 10 James Daily (mark), Rebecca Morton
Sep 20 Thomas Harvey, Rhoda Foster
Oct 11 Joseph Titus, Jane Ralston
Oct 21 Samuel Battersley, Jane M'Intire
Oct 29 William Curlitt, Elizabeth Loper
Nov 26 James Watson, Margaret Smith
Dec 2 Wessell Alrich, Mary Ann Bowers
Dec 8 Joshua M'Clay, Mary Ann Abbott
Dec 22 Levi Hopper, Elizabeth Warrick
Dec 24 Adam M'Gilton, Dorcas Morton
Dec 26 John B. Pierson (mark), Jane Boyle
Dec 30 Joseph J. Flinn, Ann Stidham (not signed by anyone)

1824
Jan 4 John Finney, Ellin Grimes
Jan 6 Thomas J. C. Ringgold, Sarah Isreal
Jan 6 John Glenn, Catharine Faris

Jan 7 Joseph Ameline, Amelia Gilmore
Jan 8 Edward B. White, Sally Ann Plungin
Jan 12 Joseph Ashe, Ann M Bennett
Jan 13 James Shaffer, Jane Byers
Jan 19 Simes Mills (mark), Mary Rechie
Feb 4 Joseph L. Stidham, Elizabeth Reynolds
Feb 5 William Eliason, Ann Williams
Feb 10 William Lloyd, Ann Gray
March 4 John (or David) King, Catharine Owens
March 6 John W. Adams, Mary Ann Davis
March 17 James Patton, Fransina B Griffith
March 21 John Moody, Susan Titler
March 22 Isaiah Grimes (mark), Sarah Jemmison
March 29 Thomas Prettyman, Margarit Faris
April 1 Thomas H. Tatlow, Eliza Jane Barr
April 5 William Ford, Eliza Hamilton
April 12 Joseph Hossinger, Charlotte Kerr
April 15 Joseph Sinex, Ann Thomas
April 20 Augustus H. Pennington, Mary Ann Coombe
April 20 John Hudson, Ann Glenn
May 6 Michael King, Barbary Kellberry
May 8 Ephraim Knoles (mark), Margaret Murry
May 8 Francis A. Whitaker, Leah Evans
May 18 Abraham Warrick (mark), Eliza Stewart
May 28 Andrew Donnan, Susan Aiken
June 2 Andrew Armstrong, Margaret Beach
June 8 Alexander S. Boulden, Ann Porter
June 9 Pears Dunniham, Ann Hewes
June 10 Peter Torbert (mark), Eliza Stockley
June 18 Aaron Britain, Lettice Ashton
June 19 Silas Polke, Elizabeth M'Cracken
June 24 John Peterson Bodett (mark), Ann Traverse
July 3 Edward Beeson, Mary Hexham(?)
July 21 Matthew Kean, Elizabeth L. Robison
Aug 1 Richard B. Gilpin, (no name)
Aug 9 Samuel Riley (mark), Hannah PettiJohn
Aug 16 John Hays, Mary Banton
Aug 16 James Dick, John Sammon
Aug 18 George Gore (mark), S. A. Rothwell
Aug 19 Abraham Pierce, Ann Chatman
Sep 1 Joseph Bartley, Mary Hutton
Sep 15 John Morton (mark), Eliza Rothwell
Sep 21 Vanslych Clute (mark), Amelia M'Creeching (M'Cracken)

Sep 30 Henry Melvin, Sally Ann Howell
Oct 5 William Vanzant (mark), Maria Dick
Oct 5 Charles Irene Dupont, Dorcas M. Van Dyke
Oct 8 Jacob Peirson, Susanna Goodwin
Oct 18 James C. Thompson, Sarah Ann Thompson
Oct 30 James Huston, Rebecca Simmons
Nov 1 John Van Burkalow, Patience Hickman
Nov 9 William H. Foster, Mary E. Downs
Dec 9 Samuel Hayes, Ann B. Warrington
Dec 28 Aaron Klair, Hannah R. Stidham

1825
Jan 9 John Bayly, Tabitha N. Smith
Jan 9 Thomas M'Nutley (mark), Mary Lauper
Jan 25 Levi Miller, Esther Ann Martin
Jan 27 William Legg, Sarah Elder
Jan 28 Henry Cassidy, Mary M'Canna
Jan 31 James Milby (mark), Catherine Owins
Feb 1 John Crumpton, Ann Graham
Feb 3 William Jones, Elizabeth Green
Feb 19 James Jefferis, Jr., Sarah Ann Moore
Feb 21 Thomas L. Biddle, Sarah Stewart
March 1 John L. Bennett, Jane Griffith
March 1 William Spencer, Sophia Moebous (?)
March 2 William Buck, Sarah Fitzsimmons
March 3 Archibald Taylor, Mary Little
March 7 Alexander M'Calla, (or M'Cullough), Rebecca Griffith
March 10 Samuel M'Intire, Sarah Watson
March 12 James Clark, Ann Hutton
March 13 Abraham Hawkins, Eliza Rice
March 16 John A. Love, Abigail Jane Andress
March 23 Thomas M. D. Penington, Henrietta Barr
March 23 Nelson Naudain, Helen Grose
March 30 Cormick Branard (?), Biddy Carl
March 31 Stewart Barnes, Elizabeth M'Coy
April 1 Nehemiah Spencer, Sarah Lackey
April 1 Joseph Cleaver, Catharine Biddle
April 2 Robert Karr, Margaret Gurrie
April 11 William B. M'Intire, Mary Gilbert
April 12 John Roberts, Mary Ann Greatrake
April 15 John Whitby, Lydia Wilson
April 18 Abraham Vandegrift, Sarah Janvier

April 19 Samuel Galbreath, Eliza M'Clintock
April 21 John Green (mark), Sarah Read
May 3 Samuel Black, Martha Andrews
May 10 William Stewart, Rebecca E. Thomas
May 14 John H. Moore, (no name)
May 26 Levi Johns, Lydia Holton
May 28 H. W. Peterson, Hannah Ann Jones
June 8 James Barcus, Mary Cummean
June 9 Jonathan Williams, Margaret Holland
June 16 Nicholas Lewis, Elizabeth Morton
June 19 William C. Brooks, Sarah M. Roberts
June 23 William Lloyd, Martha Reece
Jul 5 Edward Kelly, Nancy Trasey
Jul 18 John M'Anestry, Ann Foley
Aug 16 James H. Miles, Margaret Stewart
Aug 25 William W. Brooks, Sarah Williams
Sep 10 William M'Dowell, Hannah Coulter
Oct 5 Joseph Thompson, Eliza Warren
Oct 13 Hugh Hammond, (mark), Margaret Yokum
Oct 22 William Polk, Margaret B. Cochran
Oct 22 William C. Thomas, Sarah Ann Davis
Oct 26 Henry Rowen, Mary Ann M'Coy
Oct 29 Washington Russell, Mary Thompson
Nov 1 Robert Ferguson, Elizabeth Collins (no year mentioned)
Nov 4 Benjamin Whitely, Elizabeth M. Robinson
Nov 7 James M'Dowell, Rebecca Whiteside
Nov 16 Christian Egbert, Elizabeth Austen
Nov 17 Ezekiel Gordon, Ann Ogden
Nov 17 James H. M'Cracken, Elizabeth Ireland
Nov 21 John Lyle, Jane Lewis
Nov 23 Samuel A Dushane, Mary Prichard
Nov 24 William Reynolds, Ann Weir
Dec 12 William Morrison, Elizabeth Scott
Dec 15 Alexander Laws (mark), Susan Howell
Dec 21 August Eckard, Augusta Kolba
Dec 24 Isaac Morris, Eliza D. Venn
Dec 26 John R. Comegys (mark), Annabella Williams
Dec 28 Isaac Cunningham, Temperance Norton

1826
Jan 4 Thomas Craven, Letitia Robinson
Jan 11 James Kincaid, Susan Hewlet
Jan 11 William Taylor, Sarah Boulden

Jan 17 Jeremiah Williams, Sarah Ann Price
Jan 21 John Steel, Margaret Huggins
Jan 23 Jeremiah Sutton, Amelia Kendrick
Jan 30 John Hannon, Sarah Timpson
Feb 15 John Farr, Mary Jane M'Cullough
Feb 15 Benjamin Stanton, Ann Stanton
Feb 16 Robert M'Coy, Mary Rowan
March 2 Elias Cox, Eliza Winchester
March 10 John Thomson, Elizabeth M'Beath
March 11 John Morrison, Martha Holland
March 30 George Janvier, Catharine M. Paynter
March 13 Benjamin F. Sluyter, Sarah G. Newland
March 14 James Buck, Mary Thompson
March 15 David Medill, Jane Ferguson
March 15 William Cohee (mark), Harriet M'Gee
March 15 James W. Wilson, Eliza M'Cowen
March 15 William M Gemmill, M.D., Margaret Ann Sutton
March 16 John Blackburn, Barbara Lebur
March 24 Thomas Charlton, Mary Kearns
March 27 David Cooper, Sarah Ann Biddle
April 1 Barnard M'Gayan (mark), Catharine M'Grand
April 18 Thomas A. Walraven, Ann Whitfield
April 19 Augustine F. Biddle, Sophia Bratton
April 20 Abraham Short, Nancy Clark
April 20 Abraham Martin, Margaret Ogden
April 25 John Price, Jane Underwood
April 26 William Darrach, Margaretta Monroe
April 29 John Jones, Lydia Craven
May 3 Nathan Hendrickson, Sarah Ann Saunders
May 3 Lawrence Sheridan, Ellenah Lettin
May 6 Barney Murphy (mark), Eliza Eliason
May 18 Spencer Holton, Mary Ann Eliason
May 13 John Atwell (mark), Mary Farice
May 17 George E. Thompson, Elizabeth Prettyman
May 22 John H. M'Farlan, Ann Hyatt
May 23 William Meeteer, Mary Jones
May 31 James M'Dowell, Ann B. M'Carton
June 8 William Wingate, Frances Whitley
June 13 James H Benson, Louisa Rumford
June 14 Eli Biddle, Ann Eliza Vandegrift
June 21 Hugh M'Goovin(?), Ann Lavery
June 22 Daniel Lafferty, Hannah Sharkey

June 29 Abraham Boyd (mark), Mahali Jackson
June 29 George Morton, Elizabeth Hampshier
July 3 Liston Huston (mark), Sarah Ann Sherer
July 6 Samuel Morton, Hannah Ferguson
July 11 Samuel Hughes, Mary Taylor
July 15 Robert Evans, Ann M'Mullen
July 15 Daniel Sweetland, Mary Burns
July 17 James Sims, Ann Hall
July 18 Henry Grimes, Elizabeth Speck
July 19 John C. Clark, Elizabeth Reybold
July 21 John Stotsenburg, Maraet Caswell
July 24 Martin West (mark), Judah Farrell
Aug 1 Martin Dunn (mark), Fanny Brannan
Aug 20 Aaron Baker, Elinor Newlin
Sep 4 James Houston, Hellen Wilson
Sep 7 Robert M'Farland, Deborah Hudson
Sep 11 Thomas Steel, Mary Huggins
Sep 27 John H. Cannon, Ruth Ann Vandegrift
Oct 2 Henson Glandin (mark), Sarah Evans
Oct 2 Samuel Hyatt, Sarah Derrickson
Oct 11 Hugh M. Koontz, Matilda H. Handy
Oct 11 Louis Paul Dautremont, Hannah M'Gee
Oct 18 Peter W. Miles, Elizabeth Saxton
Oct 31 William Bryson, Charlotte Coverdale
Nov 3 Joseph Gilbert, Jane Laws
Nov 7 Caleb Starr, Mary A Hamilton
Nov 8 John Rame(?), Elenor Rogers
Nov 10 Robert Flintham, Sarah Veasey
Nov 14 Samuel W. Woodland, Martha N. Thomas
Nov 14 James Culbert, Martha Morrison
Nov 14 Joseph Kenyon, Sarah Pierce
Dec 1 Robert M'Cracken, Mary Buchanan
Dec 15 George Griffin, Mary Hunt
Dec 19 Nathan Cornish (mark), Sarah Gunn
Dec 19 Charles Cornish (mark), Elizabeth Pue
Dec 23 John M'Cormick, Bridget Kerigen
Dec 25 John Barton, Mariah Miller
Dec 12 Job D. Kerns, Eliza Ann Moore

1827
Jan 8 Elisha Cole, Lydia Cann
Jan 9 William Magens, Sarah Ann Solomon
Jan 11 Peter Cleaver, Ann Jefferis

Jan(?) 15(?) Alexander Mitchell, Sarah Wills
Jan 16 Thomas Clark Junior, Ann Reybold
Jan 28 James Moon, Marther Ann Quinby
Jan 31 Charles Pusey, Ann R. Stidham
Feb 1 Jesse Gregg, Hannah Simmons
Feb 3 George W. Bowman, Mary G Moore
Feb 3 James Hodgson, Elizabeth Gillespie
Feb 8 George H Read, Elizabeth Hickman
Feb 12 Bartholomew M'Kanna, Mary M'Cann
Feb 23 George Pine, Sarah Stilley
Feb 23 Thomas Lauller (mark), Mary Pearce
March 4 William Hutton, Elizabeth Guthrie
March 5 John M. Woods, Elizabeth V Frazer
March 6 James A. Thompson, Margaret Stroup
March 8 James Shaffer, Sarah Reece
March 10 Samuel Tibbitt, Elizabeth Kean
March 29 James S. Robinson, Jerusha Baker
April 7 Joseph Hibberd, Elizabeth Gray
April 11 John Ginn, Catharine G. Bradford
April 14 James Woolson, Elizabeth Foster
April 17 Jefferson Cole (mark), Sally Ann Derrickson
April 25 Anthony C Lain, Ann Merrick
April 26 Samuel Miller, Elizabeth Smyth
April 28 David Reed, Hester Ann Pennington
May 1 Robert Whitesides, Mary Evens
May 1 George W. Karsner, Eliza Sebo
May 2 Edward Bullen, Mary Emmens
May 3 Isaac Johnson Phillips (signed Isaac Phillips), Maria Fulton
May 10 William Pettit, Mary Spencer
May 11 Jesse Taylor, Sarah Ann Noblit
May 17 Aquilla Thomas, Phebe Seeds
May 21 Thomas Rankin, Sarah Crawford
May 23 John M Turner, Mary Garland
May 26 James Ritchyson (mark), Ann Hicks
May 28 William B Armstrong, Mary Tyson
May 31 Hiram Ditterline, Sarah Luff
May 31 Alexander M. Biddle, Mary Crow
May 31 Francis Desaugue, Ann P Lockerman
June 2 George Biggs, Ann Noland
June 7 James Meredith, Ann Morton
June 11 Peter B. Porter, Rachel Eliza Vance
June 12 Thomas M'Mullen, Caroline H. Ryland

June 19 Michael Byrnes (mark), Aderline Ramo
June 20 Robert Harner (mark), Jane Harner
June 23 Gassaway Watkins, Hester M'Donough
June 18 James L Miles, Harriet Black
June 27 James T Harden, Catherine Roberson
June 27 Amos H. Slaymaker, Harriet S Ostlere
June 30 Samuel W. Black, Lydia Mann
June 30 John Lamdin, Dorcas Cannon
June 30 Isaac J Rush, Mary Walmsley
July 7 Samuel Simpson, Hannah Maria S. Ogle
July 14 Charles Stanly Jr., Mary Harvey
July 18 John Barr, Isabella M'Kee
Aug 1 Solomon Huff, Pheoby Ann Mason
Aug 7 John S Thompson, Mary Butler
Aug 9 John Russell (mark), Nancy Baker
Aug 11 Samuel Jefferson, Ann Ball
Aug 18 Samuel Thompson (mark), Sarah Thomas
Sep 3 Robert Ocheltree, Rebecca Ann Vandegrift
Sep 8 Joseph Kurns (mark), Catharine Stradley
Sep 12 Thomas M'Neal, Hannah Davis
Sep 13 James Spare, Catharine Milby
Sep 17 Jonathan Jones, Jane Cavender
Sep 22 Isaac Cleaver, Priscilla Murphy
Sep 26 Phillip M'Dowell, Hester Ann Morris
Sep 26 Samuel Fisher, Melinda Mitchell
Oct 1 Jacob Morton, Isabila Bratton
Oct 3 James R. Anderson (Randerson), Sophia Rishstine
Oct 3 Obadiah Clark, Susan Hukill
Oct 8 Amer L Talley, Mary Rutter
Oct 15 Benjamin S Roach, Sophia Biddle
Oct 18 Fergus Hutton, Eliza Ann Biddle
Oct 24 John A. Monges, Sidney Ann Gordon
Oct 25 William Baldwin, Jane Y Matthews
Oct 27 Edward G. Janvier, Ann Cleaver
Oct 27 Samuel Aldridge, Catharine Beatty
Nov 6 John Goodin Jr., Margaret Colesberry
Nov 6 John Woolson, Mary Robertson
Nov 9 James F Robinson, Mary D Moore
Nov 14 John Hickey, Elizabeth Price
Nov 19 Jacob Boys (mark), Mary Ellis
Nov 22 John Simmons, Margaret Talley
Nov 24 John Williams (mark), Elizabeth Green
Nov 12 James Welsh (mark), Ann Holland

Nov 29 John Menkins (?), Elizabeth Jester
Nov 29 William Rothwell, Lydia Rebecca Price
Dec 1 John Gilbert, Rebecca Cannady
Dec 13 Irwin W. Peirce, Christiana Long
Dec 17 Amos Warrick, Mary Ogle
Dec 17 Richard Topham, Mary Jane Smith
Dec 19 David Hendrickson, Margaret Jones
Dec 20 Aaron Peirce, Margaret White
Dec 20 Thomas Hannah, Lius(?), M'Daniel
Dec 20 William Alexander, Margaret P Wilson
Dec 24 John W Price, Sally Jackson

1828
Jan 7 William Chesnut, Ann Eliza Rice

1829
Jan 5 William Merrycroft (mark), Jane Boyl
Jan 26 William Burgess, Eliza Ann Burchard
Jan 31 Samuel Burnham, Elizabeth Parker
Feb 7 John R. Hogg, Ann Boulden
Feb 11 Sylvester Townsend, Sarah Selby
Feb 18 Isaac Parsons, Mary Wood
Feb 19 William Hanes, Jane Starr
Feb 28 William Cleaver, Jr, Mary Stilley
March 2 Samuel Thomas, Milicent Jones
March 9 Edward R. Evans, Sally Ann Rice
March 14 George Vansant, Sarah Ann Houston
March 18 Daker T. Jester, Mary Jane Hershey
March 20 Dennis Dougherty, Martha Kirkwood
April 24 William Woodcock Jr., Eliza Ann King
April 28 George Vernon, Mary Pusey
April 29 William P. Smith, Priscilla B. Worrell
May 6 Phocion P. Lewis, Ann Murphy
May 15 Elihu Jefferson, Ann Jones (or James)
May 23 James Newell, (mark), Sarah Ann Sullivan
May 25 Stephen Sanders, Sarah Thomas
May 26 Alexander D. Anderson, Eliza Dickinson
May 26 Manlove Killingsworth, Ann Cloward
May 27 William Baldwin, Ann Kimble
June 3 James Watts, Rebecca Beetle
June 12 Thomas Simmons, Maria Price
June 16 William D. Eves, Mary Gelespie

June 24 Thomas Hanley (mark), Ann M'Carton
June 30 William M'Whorter, Marian Campbell
Jul 13 John Wood, Rebecca E. Corse
Jul 13 James N. Sutton, Eliza Jane Janvier
Aug 6 Joshua N. Danforth, Jane J. Whilldin
Aug 12 Daniel Cann, Sarah Stanton
Aug 27 Benjamin Dougherty, Margaret Weir
Sep 10 Ephraim Sterling (mark), Rebecca Jackson
Oct 6 Robert Russell (mark), Ellen Ford
Oct 14 Isaac H. Davis, Elenor Stokely
Oct 15 William Johnson, Sarah Ann Cunningham
Oct 19 Albert Gallatin Lewis, Catharine Ann Lum
Oct 31 Alexander Macintosh Macpherson, Susan Dauphin
Nov 5 Josiah Foard, Harriet E. Thompson
Nov 6 Joseph Draper, Martha S. Inskip
Nov 23 Stillman Ames, Catherine Ann Gamble
Nov 26 John L. Robeson, Mary G. Janvier
Nov 18 Thomas Laws (mark) Mary Howell
Dec 2 John B. Suter, Elizabeth Keyser
Dec 5 Andrew K. Nielson, Ann Greenwood
Dec 18 John Millett, Augusta Calverly
Dec 21 John Eagle (mark), Sally Ann Biddle
Dec 24 John Goodwin, Lusetta Ann Hall
Dec 28 Abraham Cannon, Jr., Mary Dalton

1830
Jan 9 Thomas Williams, Eliza Parsons
Jan 14 Ignatius Garcia De Soter, Amelia Elvira Buchey
Jan 18 Stephen Heveren, Harriett M'Coy
Jan 22 Francis A. Price, Louisa Jane Lowper
Jan 23 John M'Caulley Junr., Mary Ann Scott
Jan 25 John Boyd Jr., of St. Georges hundred, Elizabeth Smith
Jan 27 John Moore of Brandywine hundred, Ann Magee
Feb 3 Edward R. Ryland, Mary Douglas
Feb 10 John Besse, Sarah Golden
Feb 13 Eli Davis, Margaret Steel
Feb 15 John Currinder, Elizabeth Ogle
Feb 16 Samuel B. Foard, Alice R. Cochran
Feb 22 John Houston, Henrietta Ann Hook
March 1 Hugh Fleeman, Sarah Jane MacMullan
March 3 William Hawthorn, Matilda Morrison
March 8 Boulden Biddle, Elizabeth Egnor
March 10 Thomas S. Merritt, Sarah G Noxon

March 30 Lewis Titter (Titler?), Susanna Eagle
March 13 William Ruth, Phebe Sanders
March 13 Joshua E Driver, Mary Jemima Merritt
March 15 Robert Adair, Jane W. Thomas
March 15 Thomas Caulk, Mary Ann Homestead
March 15 Jacob Currinder, Mary Fulton
March 23 Jarad Hawthorn, Anna Rowan
March 23 Joseph West, Rebecca Mallster
March 23 George Johnson, Lydia Gooden
March 27 John H. Bolton, Rachel Sutton
March 31 Jonathan Jones, Ann Derraham
April 3 Elias A. Naudain, Piercy Ryan
April 6 James Price, Lucinda Dunlap
April 10 Charles Wilson, Eliza J. Ford
April 13 Edward Williams, Maria Johnson
April 19 Isaac G Colesberry, Mary Reynolds
April 19 Robert D Carson, Susanna M Waugh
April 21 James Bolton, Francina Underwood
May 1 Thomas A Biddle, Margaret Ann Smith
May 25 Isaac Titter, Sarah Ann Eagle
June 1 Samuel Higgins, Harriett Witherspoon
June 17 Benjamin Morton, Mary Clifton
June 19 William Grimes (mark), Mary Battle
June 21 Charles Springer, Hannah Mendenhall
June 22 Levi Ryan, Elizabeth Lydia Carty
July 6 Josiah Murch, Harriett Caroline Waugh
July 14 Junifer Taylor (mark), Susan Harris
July 22 John Hollingsworth (mark), Mary Merrick
July 29 Jesse Hull, Leah Bartlett
July 31 Aaron Schellinger, Mary Miels
Aug 23 William Perry, Susan Graydon
Aug 31 Lemuel Wotters, Sarah Lusby
Sep 2 Levi Ferguson, Rebecca Cannon
Sep 7 Obadiah Clark, Mary Price
Sep 9 Ebenezer Boyd, Mary Frazer
Sep 14 David Townsend (mark), Catharine Townsend
Sep 18 John Veach (?), Mary Morton
Oct 1 Robert M'Dowell, Rachel Coleman
Oct 7 Newton Pyle, Mary Sturges
Oct 11 Andrew Morton, Deborah Reynolds
Oct 12 John H Cannon, Lydia Vandegrift
Oct 21 Thomas Hawkins, Jane L M'Call

Oct 25 John Kirkpatrick, Catharine Enos
Nov 11 James Biggs, Martha Fols
Nov 11 Jacob Oldham (mark), Nancy Gurley
Nov 13 Charles C Bigger, Mary Draper
Nov 18 Kensey Barr, Caroline Turner
Nov 22 Charles Klair, Sophia Springer
Nov 27 R. H. K. Whitely, Esther Dodson
Dec 2 Hamilton Walker, Mary Ann Steanaker
Dec 7 Hiram H. Lodge, Margaret Webster
Dec 11 John M'Cracken, Rachel Eliason
Dec 28 James Merritt, Charity Smith

1831
Jan 3 Hiram Hall, Rachel Maree
Jan 12 H. W. Peterson, Harriett M. Douglass
Jan 27 Thomas Denney (mark), Sarah Melville
Jan 27 John W Kane, Ann Simpers
Feb 7 Henry Kirby, Mary Ann Price
Feb 9 Joseph Strulenger, Mary Clark
Feb 15 Andrew Kerr, Hannah Gillespie
Feb 16 James Brackinridge, Mary Eddie
Feb 19 James West, Rachel Ann Davis
Feb 28 David S Craven, Rebecca Jane Vandegrift
March 3 Joseph G Sickler, Ann Sharp
March 12 Robert Chandler, Elizabeth Wilson
March 15 John Mason, Mary Cordery
March 16 William Hamilton, Anna Maria Peters
March 16 George S Parsons, Therisa Ogle
March 21 Samuel P. Fowler, Rebecca Ann Titter
April 6 James Ryland, Mary Riddle
April 14 John R Tweedy, Susanna Boulden
April 21 Thomas F Dale, Margaret K Stewart
April 28 John Anderson, Mary Ann Peirce
May 5 Thomas Williams, Miss Sarah Donaldson Reynolds
May 10 Nicholas Manly, Sarah W. Hyland
May 12 John Smith, Eliza Newlin
May 19 Thomas Corbit, Catharine Springer
May 24 William Johnson, Marietta Lockerman
May 26 Robert R Robinson, Sarah Norris
June 8 Hugh Steele, Rebecca Welsh
June 11 Henry Jones (mark), Elizabeth Wright
June 13 William Garthwait, Sarah Thorn
June 16 John D Bird, Lucinda Moody

July 20 David Caldwell, Sarah Ann Heller
July 20 William Weswall, Ann Jane Harp
July 28 Charles Boulden, Eliza Ann Taylor
Aug 11 James Davenport, Sarah Sylvester
Sep 19 Joel Spencer, Margaret Gibson
Sep 26 Adam Dayett, Eliza Hendrickson
Sep 29 John Kirk (mark), Sarah Ann Cleves
Oct 6 Thomas M'Clune, Martha Russell
Nov 16 Peter Riley (mark), Hannah Mary Titter
Nov 25 John W. Evans, Margaret Ann Evans
Nov 29 Clement Palmer (mark), Elizabeth Anderson
Dec 8 Isaac Woods, Lydia Bennett
Dec 13 David Ford, Hannah Faris
Dec 15 Thomas Hamilton, Elizabeth Enos
Dec 16 John Kincaid, Eliza Huggins
Dec 19 John B. M'Cay, Lydia Lodge
Dec 21 Alexander W Reynolds, Sarah F Denny
Dec 22 Mahlon Foster, Harriett Sterling

1832
Jan 3 Andrew Biddle, Sarah Biddle
Jan 4 William M'Cracken, Mary Ann M'Manus
Jan 5 Eli Smith, Elizabeth Merrett
Jan 11 Joseph Cochran, Margaret Little
Jan 12 Andrew Harman, Martha Ann Smith
Jan 24 John Bordley, Catharine Gemmill
Jan 26 William Ellis, Mary Vansant
Feb 2 Edward Thomas, Jane M Burnham
Feb 8 Jonathan Groves, Elizabeth Rebecca Vandegrift
Feb 13 Joel Evans, Deborah Hull
Feb 18 Amer Perkins, Kerenhappuck Sharpley
Feb 23 Isaac D. Gardner, Margerit O'Neal
March 14 Edward Worrell, Louisa Rodney
March 18 William Morrow, Mary N. Carlisle
March 19 George Harbert, Sarah Pennington
March 21 Samuel Biddle, Jane Tatman
March 24 Peter Hanson, Susan Flintam
March 31 Thomas C Price, Martha Jane Pennington
April 12 Cyrus Pyle of Wilmington, Julia Ann Pearson of same
May 2 William Stoops, Emeline Casper
May 8 Edward Bringhurst of the city of Wilmington, Sarah Shipley of the said
    city

\May 11 Abraham S Crawford, Keziah Jane Stewart
May 15 Ira Sweat, Mary Eliason
May 17 Benjamin R Blackiston, Susannah Bennett
May 22 William W Morris, Mary A Ritchie
May 30 Samuel Yapp, Delilah Ferrell
May 31 Isaiah Taylor, Catharine Boyd
May 31 John Hinson, Rebecca Barclay
June 9 William Roberts, Nancy Stileman, both of Wilmington
June 11 Henry F Reynolds, Hester R Young
June 20 John M Clark, Elizabeth Banks
June 21 George Powell, Ann Jane Duncan
June 30 Peter Gouché   (Pierre Goujet), Margaret LeConte
July 19 Amos L Holmes, Mary Barclay
July 21 James Couper Junr, Mary Black
July 23 William P. Wasson, Ann Graham
Aug 25 Abraham Gooding, Hetty Clark
Aug 27 George Cooper, Margaret D Ford
Sep 1 George H Smith, Harriett Alricks
Sep 3 William T Saville, Mary Elizabeth Moody
Sep 26 Luther Mahoney (mark), Martha Smith
Sep 26 Martin Miller, Ann Justison
Oct 2 Benjamin B Davis, Rebecca Broadway
Oct 2 Isaac Nunviller, Sarah Ann Davis
Oct 4 James Bowen, Prudence Nevil
Oct 4 Absalom Jamison (mark), Jane Murch
Oct 8 David M'Whorter, Margaret Ann Burchard
Oct 11 John Anderson, Carraline Clungun
Oct 11 John Hill, Mary Ann Vanemin
Oct 13 Samuel Allen, Rachel M'Dowell
Oct 13 Curtis Bowman, Sarah Ann Burgess
Oct 27 William Groves, Mary Jane Mercer
Oct 30 Charles T Reynolds of Brandywine hundred, Isabella C Bennett
Oct 30 Thomas Roach, Ellen B. Willis
Oct 31 John M'Cracken, Catharine Bowman
Nov 5 John Voshell, Ann Craw
Nov 7 Phillip Cavender (mark), Martha Ann Ryland
Nov 15 Robert Ferguson, Sarah Camelon
Nov 22 Charles G Oslere, Louisa Grubb
Nov 29 Thomas Curns (mark), Hannah Patten
Dec 4 Lorenzo Thomas, Elizabeth B. Colesberry
Dec 18 James Jack, Helen Lindsey
Dec 18 Jacob Boggs, Margaret Smith
Dec 20 George Racine, (Jean Geo. Racine), Sarah Rollin

Dec 22 Nathaniel Dixon (mark), Alice Beetle
Dec 26 Luis Patterson (mark), Fanny Young
Dec 26 William M'Namee, Eliza C. Wright
Dec 31 Joseph Ferguson, Catharine Rumer

1833
Jan 12 C. W. M'Cracken, Elizabeth R. White
Jan 17 Nicholas Quinn, Ellen Whitelock
Jan 29 John P. Cann, (mark), Prudy Fisher
Feb 9 William W. Ford, Ann Stoops
Feb 11 Peter Bouchell, Maria Ann Hyatt
Feb 16 James R. Brown, Eliza A. Mc Clarey
Feb 18 Joseph Springer, Sabilla Ann Springer
Feb 20 Lorenzo D. Hammond (mark), Mary Jane Vandegrift
Feb 26 David Morrison, Rachell Cann
Feb 26 Jonathan Drennen, Ann Holland
March 4 Samuel Wright, Ann M'Caslem
March 6 Henry Hukill, Lear Morford
March 7 Andrew M'Intire, Sarah L. Moore
March 11 Joseph Walraven, Sarah Murch
March 16 Andrew Eliason, Lydia Ann Cann
March 18 John S. Carnahan, Sarah Barnard
March 25 Samuel Hale Higgins, Margaret Stevenson
March 26 John Frazer, Injuber Stidham
March 26 John P. Cochran, Eliza Polk
April 1 John Gordon, Mary Ann Cann
April 3 Alexander Murdaugh, Jane M'Coy
April 11 John O'Neal (mark), Mary Floyd
May 1 Collins Stevenson, Eliza Duncan
May 9 William H. Boulden, Elizabeth M'Cracken
May 9 Alexander D. Shortt, Ann I. (J.?) Naudain
May 13 Edward Stapleford, Mary Lewis
May 20 Anthony M. Higgins, Sarah C. Corbit
May 22 Elias Cole, Ann Hendrickson
May 23 William M. Henry, Jane Hutton
May 30 William Anderson, Sophia Parson
June 24 John H. Cannon, Mary Jefferson
Jul 4 Christian Egbert, Rachel Hayes
Jul 18 George W. Johnson, Jane M. Holliger
Jul 22 William Watton of East Fallowfield, Chester County, Amelia Saciste
Aug 15 Thomas J. Gillespie, Mary C. Eves
Aug 29 William Faris, Catharine M. David

Aug 31 William Reed, Lucina Matthews

Sep 5 John Goldsberry (mark), Margaret Anderson

Sep 18 William Batten, Eleanor M'Namee

Oct 2 Isaac Moody, Sarah Ann Hayes

Oct 10 William Coverdill Cummins (mark), Margaret Lenderman (of Christopher)

Oct 16 Samuel Wright, Elizabeth Wollaston

Oct 17 Lemuel M'Donnol (mark), Bridget Donohoe

Oct 17 Dr Richard D Moore, Elizabeth A Stockton. Surety, Thomas Stockton, U.S.A.

Blank Leonard Vandegrift

Oct 19 Mary Ann Townsand, License also filed, endorsed, Married Oct, 22d 1833 by Henry L Davis, minister of the Gospel.

Nov 18 William Hawthorn, Elizabeth Greenawatt [or Grunawalt]

Nov 22 John Kirkpatrick, Elizabeth Reed

Dec 5 Benjamin Hudson, Ann White

Dec 5 Charles C. De Goey (De Goy), Mary Ann Kline

Dec 6 Joseph E Palmer, Elizabeth Raymond

Dec 7 James H Burnham, Eliza Mahannah

Dec 26 Daniel Broomall of Ashton Township, Delaware County, Mary Zebley of Brandywine Hundred

1834

Jan 28 Martin M'Kue (mark), Mary O'Donnan

Feb 3 James Wilson, Eliza Hammon

Feb 3 Ebenezer Marvin, Jane Ogle

Feb 4 Emory Sudler, Elizabeth Worrell

Feb 11 William Patterson Bradley, Eliza Caldwell

Feb 13 Morton Righter of Wilmington, Sarah Hyndman of the same place

Feb 21 George Cox, Mary Ann Avines

Feb 26 John A Assay, Lydia T. Ford

March 10 George S Templeman, Mary Eliza Lawrenson

March 11 William Purse, Mary M'Coy

March 18 Solomon Morgan (mark), Dorcas Lambdin

March 19 Owen Wyett, Mary Tolbert

March 26 Samuel L Eccles, Margaret C Hall

March 28 John Williams, Margaret Sinnex

April 10 Frisby Bowlen (mark), Sarah Russel

April 10 James Lewden (mark), Rachel Culberson

April 12 William W Palmer, Elizabeth Jones

April 28 Phinias H. Jones, Mary Cunningham

May 3 Jeremiah Castlow (mark), Susan Fowler

May 20 Alfred Patterson, Mary Caroline Whiteley

May 21 Josiah Ridgway, Matilda Biddle
May 21 Spencer Hukill Rebecca M'Dowell
May 27 William M Fowler, Eliza Stroup
May 31 William M'Mullin, Margaret Jane M'Cay
June 2 David Sutton, Sarah Ann Faris
June 5 Edward Warner, Williamina Young
June 17 Abraham G. Shortt, Mary S M'Intire
June 25 Robert M'Coy, Jane Sample
June 28 Jonathan Holedger, Clarinda Fitham
July 18 Ephraim Knowles, Rachel Green
July 23 Abel Franklin Grant of Brandywine Hundred, Phoebe Ann Jefferis of said
    hundred
Aug 6 Perrigan Purse, Mary Webster
Aug 28 James Kendrick, Eliza Hill
Sep 6 James King (mark), Ellen Loller
Sep 15 Richard James Ford, Susan Jefferson
Sep 15 Thomas Smith, Jane M'Crone
Sep 15 Curtis Dempsey, Hetty Jarvis
Sep 15 Edward Armstrong, Mary W. Boulden
Sep 22 James N Sutton, Abigail B Barbour
Sep 24 Nicholas Patterson, Elizabeth Haughey
Sep 24 David S Casperson, Sarah Shaw
Sep 2 William M. Myers, Ingeber Bowman
Oct 8 Thomas M'Whorter, Mary M'Caulley
Oct 14 Thomas R Reid, Euphemia R Newbold
Oct 14 Joseph Richardson (mark), Rebecca Longfellow
Nov 13 William Hanbey, Ann M'Coy
Nov 20 James M'Coy, Elizabeth Morrison
Dec 4 James Lyle Vining, Margaret Robinson
Dec 31 John MaGee, Eliza Jane Moore

1835
Jan 5 William Hukill, Jane Vail
Jan 7 Joseph Crawford, Susan Ellis
Jan 28 William Slack of Pencader hundred, Mary Ann Fisher
Feb 2 Richard Moore, Ann Eliza Swift
Feb 7 David Cooper, Rosalinda Biddle
Feb 9 James B Rogers, Sarah A Rogers
Feb 9 John Ash of New Castle County, Susan Rowan
Feb 10 Richard Jackson, Mary Ann Alrich
March 10 John Alrichs, Sarah Ann M'Farlan
March 18 William H. Deshaine, Ann Rebecca Thompson

March 19 Samuel Williams, Lydia Truett
March 21 Jacob G. Morton, Rebecca Armstrong
March 23 Henry P Bennett, Ellen J Scott
March 28 James Jamison, Mary Elizabeth Bowers
April 2 Nathaniel Young, Elizabeth Maxwell
April 10 John Whitley, Eliza Biddle
April 11 William Pugh, Ellen Reynolds
April 21 John Ward, Catharine Reiley alias Catherine Slaughter
April 25 Joshua Eliason, Catharine Boyes
April 25 Edward Gordon, Sally M Pusey
April 29 Robert Adair, Sarah Ann Faris
May 10 Eluthere Irene Martin, Maria Jane Rankin
May 14 Lewis V. Crips of Wilmington, Eliza C Somers
May 18 Samuel E. Thompson, Anna Maria Meeteer
May 21 Joseph S. Keen of Wilmington, Eliza Ann Stewart
May 23 Richard J Boulden, Mary Boulden
June 1 Benjamin A. Janvier, Margaret R Barr
June 2 Thomas Massey Jr., Eliza Jane Anderson
June 3 John Aaron, Mary Ann Leister
June 4 James Jones, Mary Ann Baldwin
June 8 James M'Michael of Mill Creek hundred, Ann Greenwalt
June 9 William Hope, Henrietta Rackliff
June 13 Daniel Kerbaugh, Elizabeth Griffith
June 17 Jacob Wortz, Mary Jane Boyes
June 20 James F. Smith, Martha Ann M'Dowell
July 1 John Drennen, Mary Lindsey
July 4 William K. Crips of Wilmington, Amelia Morrow of same place
July 7 Mark Harper, Hannah Chandler
July 14 Archibald Flemings, Sarah M'Kay
July 21 Samuel Foster of Christiana hundred, Isabella King of same place
July 23 Robert Miller (mark), Jane Eliza Burk
Aug 5 James Webb (mark), Sarah Ann Murch
Aug 19 Alfred Francis, Julia Garesche
Sep 3 Henry D Gilpin Esquire of the City of Philadelphia, Eliza Johnson of
    Louisiana, surety Joshua Gilpin Esq of Christiana hundred
Sep 10 James Maxwell, Elizabeth Barns
Sep 12 Peter Kelso (mark), Mary Johnson
Sep 16 Andrew Gibson, Jane H Rambo
Sep 16 Henry Hicken (mark), Hester Barnes
Sep 16 Spencer D. Eves of Wilmington, Elizabeth Porter. Surety, Richard B.
    Gilpin
Sep 28 Charles M'Dade, Hannah Giberson
Sep 30 John Harp of Wilmington, Elizabeth Elders

Oct 7 Thomas J. Ogle, Isabella M'Coy
Oct 8 William Daughters, Laian Holliger
Oct 14 John Hasson of Christiana hundred (mark), Sarah Travers of same hundred
Oct 20 William Forrest of Christiana hundred, Margaret Parvis of same
Oct 31 James M'Guire of Wilmington, Ellen Talley
Oct 24 Alfred C Rowland, Ann J Mansfield
Oct 27 John Jeandell, Jane Moncton
Oct 28 James P Stayton, Sarah Foster
Nov 9 Jacob K Higgins of Wilmington, Martha Jaquett Murray
Nov 19 Nathan Boulden, Mary Ford
Nov 30 Abraham Comegys (mark), Elizabeth Thomas
Dec 1 Jacob Barr of Wilmington, Rebecca Zebly of same city
Dec 1 James Shortt, Rebecca Ann Barr
Dec 10 James Gagen (or Philip Gagen?), Betsey M'Guire of Christiana hundred
Dec 10 James R Wiley, Susannah Fryer
Dec 14 Peter Bowman, Mary A Clark
Dec 22 Jesse Allen of Pencader hundred, Caroline Rusham of same hundred
Dec 22 Benjamin Staggers, Mary Clark
Dec 28 James Hollingsworth of Wilmington, Sarah Ann M'Minn of same city
Dec 28 Samuel H Clendenen, Maria Goudy
Dec 31 Hugh Peoples of Wilmington, Elizabeth Nixon of Christiana hundred

1836
Jan [blank] James Landragin, Biddy Ann Hollahan
Jan 4 George Sturges, Mercy Moore
Jan 13 George F. M'Cullmont of Pennsylvania, Mary Anna M'Callmont
Jan 13 Elijah Smith, Ann Rosan
Jan 23 John D Cannon, Mary Jane Reyhow
Jan 25 George Derrickson, Ann B. Zelifer
Feb 1 Augustus J. Nowland, Mary Jane Stiden
Feb 12 Richard Lewis Hays (mark), Mary Ann Davis
Feb 16 David Reed, Margaret Ann Tweedy
Feb 20 Marcillus Price, Mary Ann Richeson
Feb 24 John Matthews, Susan L Steward
Feb 28 James Clayton Luff, Dianah M'Gee
No date Penrose Stidham, Mary Sergeant. Returned Feb 1 1836 by A. Macbeth
    Esq.
March 1 David Price, Jane Tweed
March 1 Timothy P. Denney, Ann Jane Merrett
March 7 John Reynolds, Mary G. Bowman
March 9 William Bennett, Mary Robinson
March 9 Ebenezer Eliason, Sarah Ann Walker

March 10 Jaques Koelig, Susan Belicks
April 11 Robert Heberton, Arabella Lockerman
March 12 Adam Carpenter, Ann Phillips
March 17 Thomas M Ogle, Tabitha N. Stroup
March 26 John W. Murdock, Amelia Sutton
April 2 James Bradway, Rhoda Mason
April 14 William Dodd, Elizabeth Ann Jones
April 16 Thomas M Robinson, Eliza Ann Curlett
April 21 Charles Marshall (mark), Elizabeth Campbell
April 27 Robinson Dunn, Susan Walmsley
May 4 William D Herdman, Eliza Jones
May 5 Lewis B Hedrick, Hannah Quillan
May 7 Hugh White, Mary Lynch
May 7 Thomas Gordon, Sarah Jane Folcom
May 7 John Kennedy, Sarah Oliver
May 18 Andrew Fisher, Ann Maria Clendenin
June 1 David W. Gammill, Elizabeth B. Hamilton
June 15 Stephen Pluck of White Clay Creek hundred, Mary Elizabeth M'Mullin
     of same place
June 20 James Hurton of Wilmington, Mary Hicker of same place
June 21 Ignatius Gillet of Christiana hundred (Ignatz Gillet), Hannah King
June 23 Louis Gateau of Wilmington, Elizabeth Maxwell, widow of same city
July 9 William T. M'Kee of Brandywine hundred, Ellen Mansell of same
July 14 James Servetus Mason of Philadelphia, Ann Jane Graham. Surety
     William Graham of Christiana hd.
July 21 Joshua Benson (negro), Mary Ann Gooding (negress)
July 22 Cornelius M. Carey of Wilmington, Amelia Martin of Appoquinimink
     hundred
July 22 George S. Hagany of Wilmington, Sarah Ann Lowe of same city
Aug 8 Henry Sharpe (mark), Susan Neals, both of New Castle County
Aug 19 John Conner or Connell (mark), Rachel Ann Gray
Aug 25 Samuel W Stewart, of Wilmington, Mary Ann Short (daughter of Abm
     Short of sd county
Sep 5 Philip Johnson of Wilmington, merchant, Louisa Kendrick of said city.
Sep 13 Philip M'Grade of New Castle County, Sarah M'Kenna of said county
Sep 15 James Smith of Brandywine hundred, Cecilia Brennen of same hundred
Sep 17 Samuel Fleming of Mill Creek hundred, Ann Graham
Sep 22 Henry Smith of Christiana Hundred, Elizabeth Mercer of Wilmington
Sep 26 Alexander Bratten of Brandywine hundred, Mary Ann Hulmes of same
     hundred
Sep 27 Sarah Webley of Wilmington
Sep 29 Ezekiel Blackiston of Christiana hundred, Sarah Webley of Wilmington.
Sep 29 William Franks of Philadelphia, Elizabeth Arbuckle of Feltonville, Bristol

twp, PA. Surety William Y. Love of Brandywine hundred
Oct 3 William Breck of New Castle County, Gabriella Josephine Dupont of same
Oct 8 Robert Mitchell, Mary Aiken of Christiana hundred
Oct 8 William Grubb Talley of Brandywine hundred, Margaret Bell of same
    hundred
Nov 24 Hezekiah Biddle, Margaret Jetton

1839 June 30 Nathaniel Bailey (mark), Mary Pennington.

(Taken from original papers: completed 2/17/1893. *[comment by Gilbert Cope.]*

Pidgeon Run Presbyterian Cemetery

.ocated near Red Lion, Delaware on Rt. 71 at Fritz's Garage – up hill behind garage through field or behind Garwood Estates in Bear Delaware. On Garwood Rd. there is a walk path to the cemetery between houses # 21 & 22.

$arratt, Susanna, dau of Robert Age 3 years. d. 12 Sept 1865

$utler, Thomas, Co. 1 1st Del. Inf. No dates

$ole, Lodiwick, son of Thomas & Catherine Bole No dates

$ole, Thomas No dates

$ole, Catherine, wife of Thomas No Dates

$owl, George, "My Brother" b. 11 Apr 1810 d. 24 Jan 1877

$ryan, Catherine, wife ____, record in Tatnall file — no stone Age 80 d. 4 Jun 1736

$ryan, John Age 62 d. 19 Mar 1841

$ryan, Robert, record in Tatnall file, no stone Age 65 d. 9 Oct 17__

.avender, Alexander Age 65 d. 28 Nov 1826

.avender, Margaret Age 60 d. 23 Dec 1820

.lark, Hannah b. 20 May 1816 d. 30 Jun 1887

.ouper, James, Table stone "A native of town of Leith in Scotland, a sincere and devoted husband" Age 85 d. 14 Mar 1819

.ouper, Jane Age 70 d. 24 Feb 1807

.akin, Samuel, the Rev., late minister of the Gospel in the Presbyterian Church of Pencader New Castle Co., b. at the family residence near the place where his body now rests in the year 1745; he married Mary Purviance, dau of Samuel Esq. of Philadelphia. Age 38 d. 29 Aug 1783

.rwin, Rachel Age 46 d. 15 Mar 1792

aris, Amos, husband of Catherine, Tatnall file, stone broken Age 39 d. 15 Sept 1820

aris, Henry M., son of Jacob and Susan Age 1 year, 3 mo., 22 days d. 1 Mar 1826

aris, Jacob Age 75 d. 1 Sept 1818

aris, Jacob Jr., Age 6 year 9 mos d. 21 Nov 1831

aris, James H., son of Jacob & Susan Age 6 mos, 14 days d. 4 Jul 1827

aris, Kezia, wife of Jacob Feris Age 50 d. 2 Jun 1801

aris, Kazia, dau of Jacob and Kezia Age 18 d. 19 Sept 1802

ritz, Josephine, wife of Wm. V. and dau of Enoch & Sarah Loll b. 11 Jun 1845 d. 2 Sept 1867

$arretson, Rebecca, b. 23 Sept 1811 d. 20 Feb 1900 m. (1) John M. Porter (2) Robert Grimes Footstone — RHG

$lenn, Catherine, wife of John Glenn and & late widow of Amos Feris Age 41 d. 8 Mar 1824

$rimes, Geo., W., son of Robt & Rebecca b. 1847 d. 1906

Hamilton, Thomas Age 58 d. 21 Dec 1831

Hukill, Spencer, "Our Father" Age 74 d. 21 Aug 1875

McClay, Frances, wife of Wm. Age 51 years d. 6 Nov 1802

McClay, John, son of Wm. and Frances - In Tatnall file, no stone Age 34 d. 27 Jan 1816

McClay, John Age 59 years d. 9 Feb 1774

McClay, Robert, son of Wm. & Frances Age 18 d. 5 Feb 1805

McClay, William Age 62 d. 10 Aug 1794

Porter, Mary, wife of Thomas, in Tatnall File, no stone b. 12 Jun 1837 d. 3 Oct 1888

Porter, Robert Age 53 d. 28 Nov 1832

Porter, Thomas G. son, of John & Rebecca b. 25 Apr 1836 d. 13 Feb 1908

Rhodes, Ann, wife of Wm. Rhodes b. 24 Dec 1805 d. 28 Sept 1841

Rhodes, Elizabeth, in Tatnall file, no stone b. 10 Mar 1786 d. 11 Aug 1876

Rhodes, Robert, in Tatnall file, no stone b. 21 Sept 1790 d. 25 May 1852

Rhodes, William, son of Thomas and Jane, no stone b. 23 Feb 1797 d. 16 Nov 1841

Sharrard, Bertha, dau of Samuel C. and Josephine b. 22 Jul 1889 d. 12 Apr 1890

Smith, James, Co. I 6th U.S. (in Tatnall file—no stone 1980)

Steele, Lousia and James, enfant children of Henry & Ann

The following Stewart family was not found at all in May 1980 but all listed from the Tatnall File of the 1930's. These may not be accurate:

Stewart, Ann (Faris) wife_____ age 47 d. 6 Sept 1822

Stewart, James, son of Samuel & Ann age 6yr 6mo d. 28 July 1815

Stewart, Jane A., wife of James Jr. age 26 d. 16 Apr 1796

Stewart, Samuel age 47 d. 30 Jan 1824

Toppin, John Alexander, son of John and Mary Ann, b. 29 Jan 1854 d. 4 Oct 1854

Toppin, Sarah E., dau of Amanda age 13yr; 2mo;16da d. 18 May 1858
 Toppin

Toppin, Sarah E., dau of John & b. 20 Aug 1851 d. 5 March 1866
 Mary Ann (can't read-1980)

Whann, Jane, wife of Wm. age 42 years d. 26 Feb 1798

Whann, Samuel age 25;7mo; 5da d. 7 Sept 1806

Whann, William age 6yr-6-9 d. 26 Mar 1803

Wiley, Clara b. 11 June 1856 d. 23 Aug 1881

Wiley, John age 63 year d. 9 Sept 1886

Wiley, Mary Ann b. 1 Sept 1835 d. 22 Apr 1901

Wright, Charles H. age 49 d. 4 May 1900

Wright, Emley C. age 31 d. 29 Sept 1884

Wright, Roddy Orlando age 4 year d. 29 Sept 1884

INDEX

Heritage Books by F. Edward Wright:

18th Century Records of the German Lutheran Church at Philadelphia, Pennsylvania
(St. Michael's and Zion): Volume 1, Baptisms, 1745–1769
Robert L. Hess and F. Edward Wright

18th Century Records of the German Lutheran Church at Philadelphia, Pennsylvania
(St. Michael's and Zion): Volume 2, Baptisms, 1770–1786
Translated by Robert L. Hess, Ph.D. Edited by F. Edward Wright

18th Century Records of the German Lutheran Church of Philadelphia, Pennsylvania
(St. Michael's and Zion): Volume 3, Baptisms, 1787–1800
Translated by Robert L. Hess, Ph.D. Edited by F. Edward Wright

18th Century Records of the German Lutheran Church at Philadelphia, Pennsylvania
(St. Michael's and Zion): Volume 4, Marriages and Confirmations
Robert L. Hess and F. Edward Wright

18th Century Records of the German Lutheran Church at Philadelphia, Pennsylvania
(St. Michael's and Zion): Volume 5, Burials
Robert L. Hess and F. Edward Wright

Abstracts of Bucks County, Pennsylvania, Wills, 1685–1785

Abstracts of Cumberland County, Pennsylvania, Wills, 1750–1785

Abstracts of Cumberland County, Pennsylvania, Wills, 1785–1825

Abstracts of Philadelphia County, Pennsylvania, Wills:
Volumes: 1682–1726; 1726–1747; 1748–1763; 1763–1784; 1777–1790;
1790–1802; 1802–1809; 1810–1815; 1815–1819; and 1820–1825

Abstracts of South Central Pennsylvania, Newspapers, Volume 1, 1785–1790

Abstracts of South Central Pennsylvania, Newspapers, Volume 3, 1796–1800

Abstracts of the Newspapers of Georgetown and the Federal City, 1789–99

Abstracts of York County, Pennsylvania, Wills, 1749–1819

Adams County [Pennsylvania] Church Records of the 18th Century

Baltimore Directory of 1807

Berks County, Pennsylvania, Church Records of the 18th Century, Volumes 1–4

Bible Records of Washington County, Maryland

Bucks County, Pennsylvania, Church Records of the 17th and 18th Centuries,
Volume 1: German Church Records

Bucks County, Pennsylvania, Church Records of the 17th and 18th Centuries,
Volume 2: Quaker Records: Falls and Middletown Monthly Meetings
Anna Miller Watring and F. Edward Wright

Bucks County, Pennsylvania, Church Records of the 17th and 18th Centuries,
Volume 4

Caroline County, Maryland, Marriages, Births and Deaths, 1850–1880

Citizens of the Eastern Shore of Maryland, 1659–1750

Colonial Families of Cape May County, New Jersey, Revised 2nd Edition

Colonial Families of Delaware:
Volumes: Volume 1; Volume 2: Kent and Sussex Counties;
Volume 3 (2nd Edition): Kent and Sussex Counties;
Volume 4: Sussex County; Volume 5: New Castle; Volume 6: Kent County

Colonial Families of New Jersey, Volume 1: Middlesex and Somerset Counties

Colonial Families of Northern Neck, Virginia, Volume 1 and Volume 2
Holly G. Wright and F. Edward Wright

Colonial Families of the Eastern Shore of Maryland: Volumes 1 and 2
Robert W. Barnes and F. Edward Wright

Colonial Families of the Eastern Shore of Maryland: Volume 4
Christos Christou and F. Edward Wright

Colonial Families of the Eastern Shore of Maryland:
Volumes 5, 6, 7, 8, 9, 11, 12, 13, 14, 16, and 19
Henry C. Peden, Jr. and F. Edward Wright

Colonial Families of the Eastern Shore of Maryland: Volumes 15 and 17
Ralph A. Riggin and F. Edward Wright

Colonial Families of the Eastern Shore of Maryland: Volumes 10, 18, 20, and 22
Vernon L. Skinner, Jr. and F. Edward Wright

Colonial Families of the United States of America, Volume II
Holly G. Wright and F. Edward Wright

Cumberland County, Pennsylvania, Church Records of the 18th Century

Delaware Newspaper Abstracts, Volume 1: 1786–1795

Early Charles County, Maryland, Settlers, 1658–1745
Marlene Strawser Bates, F. Edward Wright

Early Church Records of Alexandria City and Fairfax County, Virginia
F. Edward Wright and Wesley E. Pippenger

Early Church Records of Bergen County, New Jersey, 1740–1800

Early Church Records of Dauphin County, Pennsylvania

Early Church Records of Lebanon County, Pennsylvania

Early Church Records of New Castle County, Delaware, Volume 1: 1701–1800

Early Church Records of Rockingham County, Virginia

Early Church Records of Somerset County, New Jersey, Volume 1

Early Lists of Frederick County, Maryland, 1765–1775

Early Records of the First Reformed Church of Philadelphia, Volume 1, 1748–1780

Early Records of the First Reformed Church of Philadelphia, Volume 2, 1781–1800

Frederick County, Maryland, Militia in the War of 1812
Sallie A. Mallick and F. Edward Wright

Henrico County, Virginia, Marriage References and Family Relationships, 1654–1800

Inhabitants of Baltimore County, Maryland, 1692–1763

Judgment Records of Dorchester, Queen Anne's, and Talbot Counties [Maryland]

Kent County, Delaware, Marriage References and Family Relationships

King George County, Virginia, Marriage References
and Family Relationships, 1721–1800
Anne M. Watring and F. Edward Wright

Lancaster County Church Records of the 18th Century, Volumes 1–4

Lancaster County, Pennsylvania, Church Records of the 18th Century, Volume 1
F. Edward Wright and Robert L. Hess

Lancaster County, Pennsylvania, Church Records of the 18th Century, Volume 3

Lancaster County, Pennsylvania, Church Records of the 18th Century, Volume 5

Lancaster County, Pennsylvania, Church Records of the 18th Century: Volume 6
Robert L. Hess and F. Edward Wright

Lancaster County, Virginia, Marriage References and Family Relationships, 1650–1800

Land Records of Sussex County, Delaware, 1769–1782

Land Records of Sussex County, Delaware, 1782–1789: Deed Book N No. 13
Elaine Hastings Mason and F. Edward Wright

Marriage Licenses of Washington, District of Columbia, 1811–1830

*Marriage References and Family Relationships of Charles City,
Prince George, and Dinwiddie Counties, Virginia, 1634–1800*

Marriages and Deaths from Eastern Shore Newspapers, 1790–1835

*Marriages and Deaths from the Newspapers of Allegany
and Washington Counties, Maryland, 1820–1830*

Marriages and Deaths from the York Recorder, *1821–1830*

*Marriages and Deaths in the Newspapers of Frederick
and Montgomery Counties, Maryland, 1820–1830*

*Marriages and Deaths in the Newspapers of
Lancaster County, Pennsylvania, 1821–1830*

*Marriages and Deaths in the Newspapers of
Lancaster County, Pennsylvania, 1831–1840*

Marriages and Deaths of Cumberland County, [Pennsylvania], 1821–1830

Marriages, Births, Deaths and Removals of New Castle County, Delaware, 1801–1850

*Maryland Calendar of Wills:
Volume 9: 1744–1749; Volume 10: 1748–1753; Volume 11: 1753–1760;
Volume 12: 1759–1764; Volume 13: 1764–1767; Volume 14: 1767–1772;
Volume 15: 1772–1774; and Volume 16: 1774–1777*

*Maryland Eastern Shore Newspaper Abstracts
Volume 1: 1790–1805; Volume 2: 1806–1812;
Volume 3: 1813–1818; Volume 4: 1819–1824;
Volume 5: Northern Counties, 1825–1829*
F. Edward Wright and Irma Harper;
*Volume 6: Southern Counties, 1825–1829;
Volume 7: Northern Counties, 1830–1834*
Irma Harper and F. Edward Wright;
Volume 8: Southern Counties, 1830–1834

*Maryland Eastern Shore Vital Records:
Book 1: 1648–1725, Second Edition; Book 2: 1726–1750; Book 3: 1751–1775;
Book 4: 1776–1800; and Book 5: 1801–1825*

*Maryland Militia in the War of 1812:
Volume 1: Eastern Shore; Volume 2: Baltimore City and County;
Volume 3: Cecil and Harford Counties; Volume 4: Anne Arundel and Calvert Counties;
Volume 5: St. Mary's and Charles Counties; Volume 6: Prince George's County;
and Volume 7: Montgomery County*

Maryland Militia in the Revolutionary War
S. Eugene Clements and F. Edward Wright